Also by Sue Washington

"Peace of Mind – Pathways to successful Living" (2009)
Mnemodynamics Unlimited

"Hypnotherapy" from **"Medical Marriage"** (1997) Findhorn Press

The Mnemodynamic Practitioner Manual: An Aid to Every Therapist

Sue Washington, MSc, MA, BA, Cert.Ed.,

**UKCP Registered Psychotherapist
and Mnemodynamic therapist**

Mnemodynamics Unlimited
United Kingdom

**Mnemodynamics Unlimited, Mnemodynamic House
145 Chapel Lane, Longton, Preston, PR4 5NA**

Copyright

Cover designed by John Quigley

Includes biographical references and index

ISBN 978-0-9559263-1-0

Printed and bound by Lightning Source

www.suewashington.com

With the deepest love to my husband, Don Hatherley, who is my partner in all I do. He is my rock, and, as the most marvellous bonus, makes me laugh too. He is everything I have ever wanted in my life and more besides …

Acknowledgements

A book doesn't magically appear on the shelves one day. The final product is a result of many efforts by many people, some directly involved, some indirectly. I want to acknowledge those who helped bring this all-consuming project of mine to life. My heartfelt appreciation is extended to all of them.

Thank you to the practitioners who have been kind enough to endorse this book. They learned from my training over the years and make a real difference to the planet. Of these, Vicki Rebecca is extra special to me. She was the first person who came to me having learned Mnemodynamic Therapy from a trainee of mine. I helped her as a supervisor and was delighted to watch her 'flying' with her clientele.

I share my professional life with friends and colleagues who unselfishly lent their time and expertise to my work by brainstorming at the planning stages or by reviewing my work with a critical eye. Dr Hugh Quigley and Dr Paul Birley helped with that and gave me valuable feedback that had a marked influence on me. Thanks also go to Dr Fran Renwick, who named this model from the Greek goddess of memory, Mnemozyne.

I want to gratefully acknowledge the many people who have shared with me their painful life stories and mostly have blossomed leaving the past behind and moving on. I have changed their names to protect them.

I am grateful to the late Ivan Sokolov (1953-2009) and his wife Jacqui Pearson who have allowed me to reprint the material they wrote originally for "The Parent Network". Thank you.

Thanks to John Quigley who designed the cover of this book and also has been invaluable in terms of technical support. My son Ben Chieffo did the diagrams and flow charts for me – thank you. Thanks also to Tony Clarke for his stimulating artwork. My assistant Anne-Millne-Riley has also been there for me with feedback as has Sue Senior with autobiographical details and anything else I asked of her. Thanks to Matthew Senior too. My sister Angela Washington has proof-read for me, my brother George Washington took my picture on the back cover; thank you both. It feels good to have family to turn to.

Last, but not least of all, thanks to my husband Don who has read for me, looked after me and inspired me also.

The Mnemodynamic Organisation Licensing Agreement

Mnemodynamics Unlimited™ is set up for the purpose of exerting quality control over any training programmes, services and materials claiming to represent the model of Mnemodynamic Therapy©. This book is licensed and released by Mnemodynamics Unlimited. Any training you attend should be licensed and have an Organisational Certificate and be advertised by Organisation approved centres. When you purchase Mnemodynamic Therapy© products and Mnemodynamic Institute seminars, ask to see this certificate of legitimisation. This is your guarantee of quality.

It is often the case for many students and practitioners who are introduced to Mnemodynamic therapy™ and begin to learn the techniques embedded in the model to be cautious and concerned with the possible uses and misuses.

As a protection for you and those around you Mnemodynamics Unlimited™ now requires participants on the Mnemodynamic Register to sign a licensing agreement which guarantees that those certified in this technology will use it with the highest integrity. It is also a way to ensure that all the trainings you attend are of the highest quality and that your trainers are updated and fully conversant with the evolution of the field of Mnemodynamic Therapy™.

Your trainers come highly recommended. Their skill bases and experience are huge, and they are in tune with any new Mnemodynamic Therapy™ training developments.

For a list of other trainers and registered therapists plus recommendations please see www.mnemodynamics.org .

Sue Washington – founder of Mnemodynamic therapy.

Welcome to your Mnemodynamic Therapy©
Practitioner Manual

Please be aware that the manual is NOT your Mnemodynamic training. The altered state we mis-call hypnosis needs to be used by an experienced operator and with care and respect for the client.

Hypnopsychotherapeutic techniques are embedded in the integrated model of Mnemodynamic Therapy©.

This manual is produced by Mnemodynamics Unlimited and contains some background information on Mnemodynamic therapy© that you may find helpful. It contains some of the exercises and examples that are used during the Mnemodynamic training. It also contains examples and case histories to show you what is possible.

The manual is for your use. Please enjoy it.

You can find additional resources which will help you to enhance your practice and use of Mnemodynamics online at www.mnemodynamics.org. These resources include DVDs and downloadable videos of actual Mnemodynamic sessions and details of introductory and advanced Mnemodynamic training courses.

There you will also be able to subscribe to the Mnemodynamic Therapy mailing list so that you can be kept up to date on Mnemodynamic developments, training course and practitioner meetings in your area.

Endorsements by Mnemodynamic practitioners

"The Mnemodynamic Training Manual" is a comprehensive, information - packed manual detailing Mnemodynamics, the process and its relevant sources. I found the manual very useful to read through thoroughly after the weekend classes, and continue to use it regularly as reference tool to work through as and when necessary.

The Mnemodynamic Master classes run by Sue Washington have been a true source of inspiration for me therapeutically, and as a practitioner-based training resource. After two Master classes I find that I gained clarity and insight about the mechanics and derivation of the technique, and am also able to navigate my way through the Mnemodynamic process smoothly with absolute confidence and effective outcome for my clients.

Elfreda Affleck DHP, NLP Practitioner, MNRHP
Mnemodynamic Practitioner

I was taught Mnemodynamics years ago and began using it immediately. In the early days I stayed true to the given 'script' with very good results. Later I attended a Master Class and learned how to 'personalise' the technique to each individual, improving results and aiding healing.

Clients arrive with their problems, but once a relationship is established it is usually found that there is an underlying cause to the presenting problem. Mnemodynamics is very good for establishing this. I use the technique regularly – especially with clients who have revealed that they were bullied or who have had earlier trauma.

Some of my clients have previously seen other therapists and have commented that the effects didn't last. Underlying emotions surrounding the problem had not been dealt with, therefore the problem reoccurred. Using Mnemodynamics these issues are dealt with and the client is left feeling positive and with a new perspective. The change is immediate. Mnemodynamic therapy helps to shorten the therapeutic time without compromising client care.

Jacqueline B Collins DHP, MNRHP, Lic.NLP Master Practitioner.
Mnemodynamic Practitioner

My use of Mnemodynamics has been invaluable within my practice and I use the technique 99% of the time. I find the technique useful with phobias through to habits and from depression to pain relief. Mnemodynamics also works well with other disciplines. Even when the client has been undergoing counselling previously for months, they have achieved the changes desired and empowerment after only 5-6 sessions.

I have UK ex-patriot clients who live in Cyprus as well as local Cypriots. Mnemodynamics is a wonderfully simple technique and the language barrier can be overcome. Barriers have gone which may not have been possible otherwise and I have increased my client base. I would highly recommend that all psychotherapists train in this method.

Lorna Firth DHP Lic. NLP Practitioner
Mnemodynamic Practitioner

One client comes to mind most clearly when thinking about the usefulness of Mnemodynamic therapy. She had been seeing a therapist for a number of years, especially regarding her relationship with her mother. She came to me in an attempt to come to terms with those issues, as well as to explore herself in more depth. Mnemodynamic therapy helped her to finally be able to lift her old burdens. She also then felt able to "lift the lid" on so many things which had been haunting her for a long time including addressing her problem with her alcohol consumption. Mnemodynamics helped me to help her healing process.

Ellen Goldman Cert Counselling, PGDHP
Mnemodynamic Practitioner, **UKCP registered psychotherapist.**

As a Hypno-Psychotherapist I was trained in the use of Mnemodynamics and have been actively using this technique since 2003. Because of the effectiveness and speed at which this technique enables clients to get past the presenting problem to the underlying cause of their issue and then start the healing process, not only has Mnemodynamics become a major tool in my toolkit as a therapist, it has also become one of the few techniques I use with every client.

Debbie Holden MBA, PGDHP, Cert. Sup., Lic. Trainer NLP,
Mnemodynamic Practitioner, **UKCP registered psychotherapist.**

The Mnemodynamic technique is available via practitioners in many places throughout the UK. Working this way you can benefit on a one-to-one basis with your practitioner, ridding and releasing accumulated stress and tension in the mind and body. During the sessions you will accumulate empathy and understanding. The benefits will stay with you for life.

Margaret Jones Dip. Counselling.

The aspect of Mnemodynamic Therapy that I have found extremely useful is the emphasis on feelings. Feelings that overwhelmed us as children can be brought into the present where they are no longer so destructive. To help our clients understand that they are now adults and in charge of their lives is so empowering and sets the stage for much positive change. As therapists we often take our working philosophy from many sources. It is good to have a book that looks at the spread of ideas that have grounded psychological thinking, distilling what is important and that can be applied to the Mnemodynamic method.

Sue Martin PhD, MSc, CQSW, PGDHP.
Mnemodynamic Practitioner, **UKCP registered psychotherapist.**

I find Mnemodynamic Therapy particularly helpful in working with issues of unknown origin, or with those clients experiencing a block in therapeutic processing – allowing for new insights and reparative release.

Lorraine Mawhinney MA, PGDHP
Mnemodynamic Practitioner, **UKCP registered psychotherapist**

Wow.... When one, as a therapist, discovers the Mnemodynamic therapeutic approach, it transforms the way you work. The effects can be powerful and life changing and the fact that it has been used within various therapeutic disciplines demonstrates its importance. I have also found the practitioner manual a useful aid and often refer to it. Becoming a Mnemodynamic practitioner represented an important advancement in my effectiveness as a therapist. Thank you.

Anne Millne-Riley BA(hons), DHP
Mnemodynamic Practitioner

I trained with and have worked with Mnemodynamic therapy from every aspect: as client, therapist, assistant trainer and trainer. I find it the most thorough, elegant & effective therapy to use for any childhood, and indeed any emotional issues whatever the symptom. I have used it with clients for eleven years now with honestly quite amazing results - it cuts through to that level where healing occurs in a few sessions leaving your client a new person – it is wonderful to see. Sue's "Mnemodynamic Practitioner Manual" is informative and clear. I thoroughly recommend it.

Vicki Rebecca, LLB (Hons), PGDHP, Cert. Sup., Lic. NLP practitioner, Mnemodynamic Practitioner, **UKCP registered psychotherapist.**

I'm so glad I have your Mnemodynamic Practitioner Manual. It has proved to be a valuable resource and I love the way it is written, so easy to follow and find the information I need quickly.

Sue Senior PGDHP, Mnemodynamic Practitioner, **UKCP registered psychotherapist.**

Since using Mnemodynamics with most of my clients I have found improvement in their condition much more effective and successful than before. I am fortunate to have a very detailed Mnemodynamic Practitioner Manual to refer to if I come across any problems.

My clients are always amazed with the results and agree that the method is very successful, enabling them to cope with their lives again.

Judith Sharpe RN, PGDHP, MNRHP Mnemodynamic Practitioner

Much of my work is in a secondary school. At first I imagined the technique may be of limited use with young people but I have been using it pretty regularly after I had a very positive response in the initial trials.

At this time of year we encounter many pupils who begin to have self-doubt as the examinations approach. Some get overwhelmed with exam stress and the technique is used along with other approaches to help pupils deal with the emotion which they cannot explain and seems to 'come from nowhere'. I have encountered a pattern which has been repeated in a number of cases where a young person, now aged 15 or 16 has 'gone back' to a time when a comment or a feeling in a particular situation has been recalled from younger days with intense clarity.

Following the use of Mnemodynamic Therapy pupils often say that they feel 'lighter', 'calmer', and 'more in control'. This seems to give them more confidence in their abilities to cope with perceived stressors like exams.

I have also used the technique successfully with pupils who have general anxiety, low self-esteem and those who have self-harmed

Mo Whittam BEd., PGDHP
Mnemodynamic Practitioner

One of the pitfalls of childhood is that one doesn't have to understand something to feel it. By the time the mind is able to comprehend what has happened, the wounds of the heart are already too deep.

- Carlos Ruiz Zafón

CONTENTS

Copyright	iv
Acknowledgement	vii
The Mnemodynamic Organisation Licensing Agreement	viii
Welcome!	ix
Endorsements by practitioners	x
Contents	xvii
Preface – Mr Shine	xxvii
Attitudes behind the Mnemodynamic therapy model	xxx
Definition	xxx
The name Mnemodynamic therapy	xxxi
Therapeutic Methods and Theoretical Underpinning	xxxii
Assumptions of the model for a successful session	xxxii

PART 1

Chapter 1:

Model of the Mind - How problems arise	1
Frozen in time	1
Why this symptom?	3
How Problems Arise – the "Full-Cup" Theory	4
Explanation of the diagram	4
"The Dynamic Model" – How the Mind Works	7
Explanation of the "Dynamic Model" diagram	8
The Mind according to Sigmund Freud	9
Association and the mind	10
Preconscious	10
Parts of the Mind: basic strong drive – The ID	10
The EGO or Consciousness	11
Cesspits?	11

SUPER-EGO 12

To store or not to store? 13

Denial 14

Hypnosis 16

Mind domination 17

The Organ of Choice 17

Freud and Conflict 18

Assumptions of the Mnemodynamic Model 19

Chapter 2:

The Therapeutic Sessions 21

The First Session 21

1. LISTEN and find out positive details about your client 21

2. THE FIVE MINUTE CONTRACT, consent, setting

  the scene and distance 22

3. DISTANCING the client by space and language 22

4. THE ALTERED STATE 23

5. THE SCENARIO 24

  Leading the Client? 25

6. ANCHORING 25

  Child Abuse 27

  Normalising "That's what 10 year olds do" 28

  Intention 28

  Cognitive Connections 29

  Bullying and intimidation 29

  Put the old head on younger shoulders 30

  Mental Instability 30

7. RE-FEELING 30

  What if the client says "I can't"? 31

  What if the client gets upset: is 'flooded' with

a feeling or feelings?	32
To take away a positive feeling?	32
8. Your most creative part of the process	32
Dissociation	32
8 (i) Validation	33
8 (ii) Normalise	33
Association v Dissociation	33
8 (iii) "Trapped"	34
8. (iv) "Dirty"	35
8. (v) "Problem Ownership"	35
8. (vi) Listening for "Sad", "Upset"	36
8. (vii) "Shock",	37
8. (viii) "Confusion", "Bewilderment"	37
8. (ix) "Lonely", "Alone", "Unsupported", "Unloved", "Unlovable", "Rejected"	37
8. (x) Intention	38
8. (xi) "Drained"	38
8. (xii) "Manipulated"	39
8. (xiii) "Insecure"	39
8. (xiv) "Guilty" or "Responsible"	39
8. (xv) Acknowledgement	40
9. Re-resourcing	40
10. Checking out	41
Representational Systems	41
Predicate Words	42
11. Is the process finished? Options in closing the altered state session	45
Multiple Incidents	47
12. Bottoming - after altered state work	47

Chapter 3:

    Session 2 - Opening the second session   49

    Percentage improvement: a measure for both you and

     the client   49

    Cultural differences   50

    Client perception   51

Chapter 4:

    Specific Conditions   53

    Mnemodynamic Therapy for smoking   53

    Mnemodynamic Therapy and physical symptoms   54

    "Turned Eye" getting rid of physiological constant

        strabismus   56

    Irritable Bowel Syndrome (IBS)   58

    Weight loss and loss of libido   59

Chapter 5:

    Variations on a theme   61

    Content Free   61

    Listening to client disclosure as a narrative   61

    "Sergeant Pepper's Lonely Hearts Club Band"   62

    "Hypnotic Time Distortion   62

    Perfect?   64

    Someone who can't visualise   64

PART 2:

Concepts

Some concepts that will be used in your Mnemodynamic Session 67

Good Enough   67

The Learning Stair   72

Needs behind Behaviour   72

Problem Ownership   75

PART 3:

**Diagrammatic representation of the Mnemodynamic process
for your note-taking: Theoretical Mnemodynamic Sessions**

Case 1: John Smith aged 46   83

Case 2: Chrissie Evans aged 50   85

PART 4:

Appendices

Appendix 1   **Feelings**   87

Feeling good about ourselves   89

We never grow up   89

Accepting the way others feel   90

Manipulation of emotions   91

Labels and expressing feelings   93

Self-Esteem   94

Some ways to develop your own self-esteem   95

The child within us   100

Appendix 2   **Labels**   103

Say what you want   106

Different people, different experiences   107

The development of self-esteem   108

Praise versus Encouragement   114

Defences   118

Appendix 3 **Whose Problem**   119

    Needs behind behaviour   121

    Acceptable and unacceptable behaviour   121

    Who owns a problem   121

    We are not our behaviour   121

    Behaviour and needs   123

    The same needs   124

    Acceptable and Unacceptable behaviour   124

    Problem ownership   120

    A matter of priority   128

    More problem ownership   129

Appendix 4 **Being a helper**   131

    It's enough to listen   133

    Being there for someone   133

    The essential ingredients for a helping relationship 135

    Communication   139

    Using the child as a guide   140

Appendix 5 **Introduction to Listening**   143

    Silence is not enough   145

    Open ended questions   145

    Learning from our successes and mistakes   146

    What might get in the way of listening   146

    Taking listening a step further   147

    Trusting   148

    Asking questions   149

    Emotional flooding   151

    Learning from past experience   152

    Fear of failure   153

    What might stop us listening?   153

	Go easy on yourself	154
Appendix 6	**Reflective Listening Part 1**	157
	What happens when we get upset	159
	Reflective listening	159
	The value of expressing feelings	160
	More on reflective listening	161
	Key phrases	162
	How reflective listening helps the speaker	164
	Repressing our feelings	166
	Reflecting emotions	168
	Giving feedback	171
Appendix 7	**Reflective Listening Part 2**	175
	When not to reflectively listen	177
	Listening to yourself	177
	Communication barriers	178
	Unhelpful responses	178
	More about reflective listening	178
	More about when not to reflectively listen	180
	Too close for comfort	181
	More about Listening to yourself	182
	More about communication barriers	184
	What do we do instead of listening?	185
	Stock responses	187
	Being there	189
Appendix 8	**Needs and Wants**	191
	Defining ourselves	193
	Valuing our own needs	194
	Ways to meet needs	195
	Behaving submissively	196

Behaving aggressively 198

Learning by watching others 200

Behaving assertively 201

The difference between NEEDS and WANTS ... 202

Appendix 9   **Sharing Feelings** 205

Getting closer to people 207

But who am I? 209

The risks of self-disclosure 210

Saying what you think 211

Saying what you feel 212

Saying what you would like 214

Openness, honesty and truth 215

Not telling the truth 216

Ways we block self-disclosure 218

Appendix 10   **Challenging** 223

Challenging unacceptable behaviour:

the 4 part I-message 225

The aims of challenging 225

Expressing yourself congruently 226

Behaving congruently 227

More on challenging 228

Examples of challenging 230

When I messages don't work 232

The hypnotic effect of language 234

Appendix 11   **Being Firm and Gentle** ... 239

Styles of parenting 241

The authoritarian approach 242

The permissive approach 244

A new way 245

	Behaving assertively	245
	When I-Messages don't work	245
	Saving energy with the "Soft No"	248
	Sticking to agreements	249
Appendix 12	History regarding the Muses	251
Appendix 13	The case of Janie	255
Appendix 14	Quotes from Freud	259
Appendix 15	Transcript of Freud's paper	263
	"On the psychical mechanism of hysterical	
	phenomena"	
Appendix 16	Winnicott: background information	279
Appendix 17	Notes from a Mnemodynamic Practitioner	283
Appendix 18	Outline 'script' for Mnemodynamic Therapy	291
Bibliography		299
Index		303

Preface

This was written by a Mnemodynamic Register member …. It moved me to tears. I am glad to say he got rid of his Mr Shine and now helps others to do the same …

Mr Shine

When I was young I had an English teacher called Mr Shine.

Mr Shine was very big.

Mr Shine was very loud.

Mr Shine was very powerful.

Mr Shine never had any trouble.

Mr Shine was somebody that you just didn't cross.

Mr Shine was a god and you just didn't know what he was capable of; you just knew that he could destroy you.

So imagine the scene; the class of thirteen year olds sit in absolute silence, their heads down, the only sound the sounds of their fountain pens on the paper of their exercise books as they set about the task of writing the essay that Mr Shine had set earlier.

Mr Shine sits at the front of the class behind his desk and I stand facing him as he reads and marks my essay from last week… in silence.

"What does gullible mean boy?" asked Mr Shine. The class quietly listens; to every word. I'm sure that even the sound of the pens stops. You really could have heard the sound of a pin drop.

I am terrified; my mind has gone completely blank, but I instinctively know that I stand next to destruction.

I stay silent.

"It means easily taken in boy." He pauses. Maybe it's over.
"What does easily taken in mean boy?" he asks.
My mind remains blank but I know that I have to speak.

"It means gullible sir" I offer meekly.

Mr Shine is incandescent with rage. "Don't you try to make a fool of me boy! I'll teach you what happens when you try to do that to me!"

I cringe, the class cringes, and each and every child thanks God that it isn't them.

I am destroyed. I want to run away but I am rooted to the spot. Such is the power of repression that I can remember no more of Mr Shine's extended diatribe.

I am humiliated. I am ashamed.

In a few moments Mr Shine taught me something about myself that stayed with me for the next thirty years.

He taught me that I can't write an essay to save my life. He taught me always to remain silent when I worked in groups. He taught me to hesitate. He taught me never to speak unless I was certain. And it didn't seem to matter how well I did subsequently, or how many distinctions I got, because both Mr Shine and I knew the truth. He taught me that I was stupid.

Thank you Mr Shine.

Of course, now and with the wisdom of years, I realise that Mr Shine was the stupid one. Now I realise that Mr Shine was the one that should've stayed silent, not me. Now I know that Mr Shine was a bad and a lazy teacher who relied on his ability to intimidate to motivate rather than any ability to nurture, to inspire or to engage imagination. Forgive me lest I offend your ears, but Mr Shine was a tosser.

But then I was only thirteen and I didn't know any better; because the teacher god had spoken; so it must've been true.

It took me a long time to find my Mr Shine; and make friends with him; and let him go.

Now I don't blame Mr Shine; because he had a Mr Shine too.

Most of us have a Mr Shine or a Mrs Shine, maybe more than one.

Sometimes they teach us; sometimes they parent us; sometimes they marry us; sometimes they bully us; sometimes they don't exist, they're just a thought or a way of thinking or an experience. Sometimes Mr Shine stands right in front of us and glares in our face; more often he hides away quietly making sure that we follow his rules. You might have met him 35 years ago or yesterday. Mr Shine can take many forms but he always teaches us something that limits or dis-empowers us.

I think of a child learning to walk. Does she turn her back on the challenge or give up after a few falls? Does she contemplate failure? No, she persists and she considers only success. And can you imagine that feeling of elation that she has when she takes those first independent steps of her new life?

Confidence is not something that we have to achieve; it is something that we are born with.

But Mr Shine takes it away.

Do what do I do? I help people find their Mr Shines … and let them go.

Bob Dixon, DHP (Mnemodynamic therapist)

Attitudes behind the Mnemodynamic Therapy model:

Firstly, that all personal and social behaviour is learned.

Second, that at any given time, current behaviour - however socially unacceptable or inappropriate - is a response to current situations and an attempt to satisfy valid human needs, based on past experience and present circumstances.

(Here it is important to remember that we don't necessarily have to understand the underlying need. Just acknowledging that it exists will help us bring about changes in the behaviour).

Thirdly, that all people, children as well as adults are equal in terms of human worth and dignity. Children are equally valid as human beings, equally loveable and capable of love and have an equal need to develop a strong sense of their own worth as adults.

(N. B. This does not mean that they are the same!)

Fourthly, change is always possible providing one is open to finding ways to change

Definition

Mnemodynamic therapy is a set of existing techniques further refined to help the client remove and come to terms with their life issues both past and present. It integrates the best of CBT and NLP with Freudian analysis adding the benefit of the speed of hypnotherapy. A state of great improvement with equilibrium is usually reached in 6 sessions.

The model was designed to help people deal with simple or complex and traumatic past events in what we consider to be the most fluent collection of methods, or model, yet put together. Examples Written in the text refer to children very often. You will need to "chunk up" to make relevant for yourself.

xxx

The Name Mnemodynamic Therapy

We are aware that Mnemodynamic Therapy is a new name to some of you. The name is important. It was chosen by Dr Fran Renwick to embrace the breadth of this brilliantly working model, which this volume will explain to you enough for you to be able to use as a qualified therapist. For the rest, it will explain how people can be released from simple or complex and traumatic past events in what we consider is the most fluent collection of methods yet put together.

Mnemodynamic therapy takes its name from the Greek goddess Mnemosyne (pronounced knee-mo [like hoe] zzy-knee), the goddess of memory. She was the mother and Zeus the father of the Muses - nine sister Goddesses, each of who was regarded as the protectress of a different art or science. Mnemosyne was worshipped in later times in conjunction with her daughters. When represented pictorially, her attitude is calm and thoughtful, and her hands are folded in her raiment, thus representing symbolically the inward and abstracted nature of memory.

There is much written in psychology about memory – how reliable is it? We will come to this later.

Of Mnemosyne's famous and talented daughters it was only in later times that different functions were assigned to separate Muses, and distinction made in the manner of representing them. (Please see appendix 12)

Collins English Dictionary (1994) defines the "dynamic" part of the name as:- "of, or concerned with energy, or forces that produce motion". (This comes from the Greek meaning "powerful" or "to be able").

Dynamic psychology is any system of psychology that emphasises the fluidity and energy of mental life and the motives, emotions and drives of the individual that underlie it. It embraces continuous change or advance.

The model is a tempered one, and an eclectic one. Some of the parts of the model will be well known to some of you ... perhaps, though, not all put together in this order.

Therapeutic Methods and Theoretical Underpinning

It is necessary to mention something about the therapeutic methods that are used, and **how** the component parts **fit into** the therapy so that points raised by both client and therapist in their statements can be understood. The therapeutic method is described in the following pages.

Mnemodynamic Therapy is a holistic and fully interactive model, with therapist and client working as partners, using the power of the client, guided by the therapist, to get better.

The actual source of this thought is quoted and explored later – but Freudian psychology implies that the unconscious mind is a cesspit of dreadful things waiting to consume the individual. However, we take the Humanistic view - that here, in the unconscious, is the powerhouse, the total resource bank that we have in us to get better from whatever is our complaint.

Assumptions of the model for a successful session

Firstly that the client is open minded and will "go along" with the process as outlined by the therapist. (The therapist needs to use his/her skills to present the work in a form acceptable to the client).

Secondly is the necessity that the client does not sabotage the process. (Of course the therapist must never say this in advance of the process. A skilful practitioner will be able to check after one session of working with Mnemodynamic therapy the amount of "improvement" the client is showing, and should be able to, sensitively and gently challenge any sabotage in the very rare instances should is happen)

PART 1

CHAPTER 1

Model of the Mind – How problems arise

Frozen in time

Life is full of pain. The only way we seem to learn lessons is the hard way. Empirically we know this. How many times have we seen a loved one, be it adult or child, about to embark upon a course of action that we know in our own minds will lead to pain for them. We attempt to 'correct' them, or to challenge them, only to have our attempts to 'save' them the pain that we consider to be a negative experience, rebuffed! There seems to be no 'saving' another person from themselves.

There are painful experiences, however, that fit into a different category than these, the everyday lessons. These are experiences, usually un-called for, or gratuitous, that happen in our lives usually when we are a lot younger, and by that, perhaps as a teenager, a junior school child, or even an infant. Because our coping mechanisms during our earlier years are not as well developed as they become later the events become "shut off".

David Groves, a well-known psychotherapist and trainer at the time of writing, speaks of these events becoming "frozen in time". We survive the event, but to protect us, feelings connected with the event become shut out, encapsulated. We have perhaps spoken to our clients about 'microchips', pointing to the solar plexus to demonstrate that it is the body where these things are lodged. This 'lodging', or 'freezing' in itself is not a great problem. Certainly, both biologically and emotionally, it is a "good move" our systems make, in looking after us this way. Emotionally, we survive to live and fight another day of course, and if we use a biological model, we get nearer the time of maturity to spread our genes and be biologically fit by producing children and grandchildren.

When clients come to see me they are usually pretty clear about what they perceive the problem is. They come with a specific reason! Other symptoms may have onset with less of a specific start. It is common for someone to say "It all started when I married" (that statement normally raises a laugh in public presentation); the recognition is pretty universal that whilst many of us feel that it is the best thing we ever did, there is still a price to pay for living with another human being in close proximity this way. "It all started when I was promoted at work" could just as easily be another such onset. It seems that we can pinpoint that from this certain time, everything went wrong.

Experience over the years has shown that this is most likely NOT the whole problem. Problems usually arrive much earlier in our lives when our coping strategies are much less developed. Take rationalisation and reframing for instance; "making best sense" or "looking on the bright side" of things, as a coping strategy. When we are young, rationalisation is hard to do. The younger the age, the harder it is for the individual to rationalise. According to the great child psychologist Jean Piaget, developmentally, a child cannot rationalise under the age of ten years – therefore information is processed at a feeling level and cannot be intellectualised or 'turned to good account' in our lives. The event is often registered as pure pain.

The onset of the symptom, then, can also be likened to the full cup model which is described below. We fill up our cup slowly over the years until overflow happens - once more into a symptom. There is also a difference in sensitivity between human beings. What seriously affects one human may be "water off a duck's back" to his compatriot. There are disagreements between thinkers and intellectuals. I was at an Open University seminar when the tutor said that ill people don't actually know what has caused their illness or problem. Here I have to disagree. People may not want to know, but we think that they do, somewhere, actually know!

Most of us recall the kind of incidents that I'm talking about here. If you imagine looking back over your life that it is a beautiful Persian carpet. Picture the warp threads down the length of the rug as the given genetic inherited traits and possibilities from our parents and ancestors before them. You have woven the weft at each point in time, and along each weft doing the best you knew how, you will recognise bits of the carpet that you wish were not there. It may be that bits of the carpet appear to have bumps under it sized from something as large as a house brick down to a beach pebble. We put it to you that the carpet would lie better without the pebbles and bricks under it. To mix some images, the "cup" would have been better for regular every-day use if it had not been full to the brim to start with. The poor old camel could have done with a bundle or two being lifted off him rather than having been given that final straw!

Given, then, the fact that material does become locked off, frozen in time, and that being acknowledged, we need to find a way of relieving the suffering that this history gives, and as easily, quickly, efficiently and

2

painlessly as we possibly can. This is what, at Mnemodynamics Unlimited, we have spent a long time doing. To put this in its historical context, I worked in practice in Chester and Liverpool for many years during the 70s and 80s. There was often the problem of economics as I worked with individuals funding their own therapy sessions. People needed help but could ill afford to pay for much. I felt the need therefore, to learn to work faster and faster, still acknowledging the vital theoretical bases underpinning my learning so far, the main one being the Freudian psychodynamic model, which seemed to me to be so very important. My old teacher that I started training with in 1968, Peter Blythe, quoted Freud as saying that it was only by "re-living with feeling" that someone got better. It was out of this economic necessity that Mnemodynamic therapy was born and is hereby wholeheartedly and unreservedly presented to you.

Why this symptom?

The problem, however, apparently arises often much later when a series of suppressed/repressed bits of material, seemingly unconnected except at a feeling level, erupt as a symptom. It is often later in our lives when we feel safe enough to deal with whatever it is that these earlier items manifest themselves in this particular way. As a practitioner you will have no doubt seen this many times! We may ask why a certain symptom arises in a particular person. Why that symptom anyway? It seems to me that like a chain, we 'break' at our weakest link.

If the large organ of your skin is weak, you will be likely to be susceptible to acne, eczema, psoriasis and so on. If it is your digestive system, then you will be more likely to get an ulcer, colitis or some other irritable bowel disorder. If it is your eyes, you may suffer from frequent headaches, migraine and so on. So the answer is fairly simple. We learn at school that a chain will break at its weakest link. Humans as a species follow this basic law. It is the part of us that is the least strong, which gives way first.

You will have heard this model called "the full cup theory". It's simple enough, and is shown on the diagram on the next page. The symptom, then, often seems to start for what possibly can appear to be a small reason. Sometimes, there is, apparently, no reason at all though from my experience, there is always a reason for the onset of a symptom. The onset of the symptom is actually the straw that broke the camel's back, rather than being "the problem" that a client presents. There can be the understandable client problem of over-simplification here!

How Problems Arise, the "Full Cup" Theory

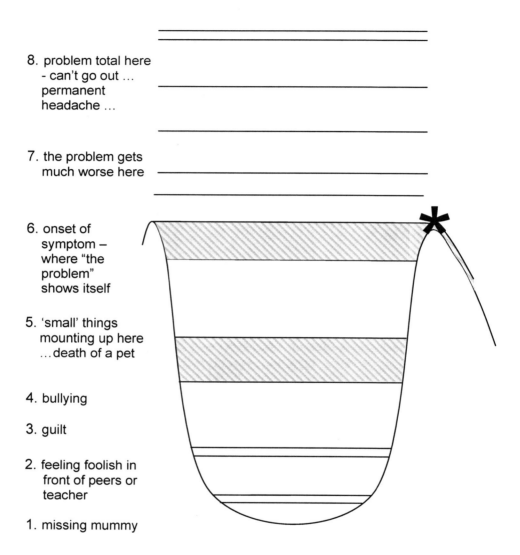

8. problem total here
   - can't go out ...
   permanent
   headache ...

7. the problem gets
   much worse here

6. onset of
   symptom –
   where "the
   problem"
   shows itself

5. 'small' things
   mounting up here
   ...death of a pet

4. bullying

3. guilt

2. feeling foolish in
   front of peers or
   teacher

1. missing mummy

Explanation of the diagram

The above diagram is pretty self-explanatory, but here is a little more detail. I am starting at the bottom. See how much you can identify with:-

Missing a parent can be difficult for an infant (1). I had a 60 year-old client just yesterday at the time of writing. Brought up just at the end of the

Second World War, her mother was a hard working nurse. She said that although she felt neglected at the time she knew that this was not the case. "Missing mummy" was certainly where it was at for her! Post war parents with Victorian parents themselves were modelled that if you paid too much attention to your child they would grow up to be a wimp and weak minded!

Do you remember times of difficulty at junior school? It may have been your first time of being away from your mother, for instance, or the first time in a crowd. The new environment may have been great fun or, on the other hand, just too much. (2)

Did you ever feel guilty for something you did (or didn't do) at home or at school? Both teachers and parents can be good at prodding our softest parts in the attempt to get us to not do something any more. I remember learning during my first degree that according to the research at the time, neurotic introverts performed best at secondary school level! (3)

Bullying is frequent at school. This can be physical or verbal. It may be that you felt left out and excluded from a peer group for some reason. The client mentioned above had always felt 'left out' and 'different'. This is hard for a child, particularly at junior school and during early teenage years when all we want to do is to fit in and be the same! Remember also that the pre 10 child cannot rationalise (4).

In real life, things happen that are difficult … death, abuse, loss, even moving house to a "better location" can give a youngster loss both of peer group support and everything familiar (5).

We may carry on like this for years or in some cases for our whole lives, no longer quite knowing what we feel, why we feel it or who we are; dutifully believing what we were told, perhaps decades ago. Until 'something' happens! Perhaps one day we are faced with the distressed cries of a hurt child, and these cries reverberate deep inside, and suddenly we hear the cries of the small child we locked away all those years ago by not believing its hurt - the small child we once were. In that instant we experience not only the pain of the time we hurt ourselves and were not acknowledged, but also the pain of all the tears of hurt that we shed throughout our lives, from all the times we felt ignored or insignificant.

This is the straw that broke the camel's back, number 6 on the diagram. Overwhelmed by this unexpected wave of emotion, we know we need to shut it off quickly. So we turn to the reason for the way we feel now, the precipitating factor - the crying child in front of us. We 'shush' the child, just as we were shushed, or smack the child as we were smacked. We know it's the only way; that it's for the child's own good, just as it was for ours. We do the best we can, just as our parents before us did the best they could at the time. We press the censor to push our uncomfortable or distressing feeling back under lock and key in our storage system, though the censor would do it whether we asked or not. At this point of too much strain, we start with a symptom. Why that symptom? Remember, like a chain, we 'break' at our weakest link.

Many readers of this volume will be British since this book will be published here first. People of my generation will recognise that they and their parents were probably brought up 'in denial' of many very real things. My maternal grandmother, a great influence on my life and born in 1899 was well and truly Victorian. These were the people who covered up the shape of Cabriole chair legs as the curves on them were too suggestive. We were taught, or rather modelled, this denial of feelings. Little boys were taught not to cry. How else would they be able to go to fight in war and kill other humans who, according to the latest evolutionary ecological research, we are all related to anyway? In general terms, we button down the stiff upper lip and carry on as if nothing has happened (7).

The symptom can become permanent as is the underlying problem. If the symptom was migraine the headache will become permanent. If one had an anxiety attack that developed into agoraphobia, by the time one gets to point 8 it is sometimes not possible even to go out and put washing on the line. The disability is so total.

Sometimes a client will arrive for a first session being very specific about the onset of the symptom, seeing that as the problem. I remember seeing a man many years ago who was specific to the minute ... "I remember, it was the seventeenth of March in nineteen seventy two. I was waiting for the number three bus, second in the queue, at ten in the morning. The bus must have come and gone, because I found myself standing there two minutes later and the queue had gone! I've felt panicky ever since".

My personal good news about the 'Full Cup' diagram is that since my first starting hypnopsychotherapeutic practice is 1968, clients are arriving for therapy saying something like "I've had this for 40 years (20 years) can you help me?" Now the tendency is more: "I've started to feel anxious and whilst I know that I could go to the doctors, I would rather do something about it myself if you can help me". Sociologically, we are getting much better at looking after ourselves and this is a much improved and noticeable trend.

Looking back at the diagram a few pages ago, there are two fairly obvious solutions to the overflow problem. Either one makes all the material fit better under the overflow level, the asterisk at point 6, or, another possibility would be to put a tap on the cup to allow the level to drop. How, then do you do that? Let us continue with some options.

"The Dynamic Model" - How the Mind Works

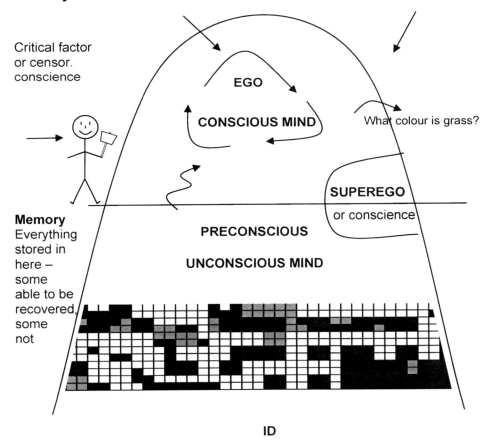

Unavailable unconscious

The model, overleaf, of how the mind works, was given to me by an American[1] mentor over thirty years ago. In all the years since I have not seen a better explanation.

It is a Freudian model, though it is perhaps easier to explain to your clients adding these Freudian labels (on your diagram overleaf in bold capitals) until the end of the drawing and description that follows. On the diagram, below, the commonsense English words are in small case and bold. The Freudian terminology is bold capitals.

Explanation of the "Dynamic Model" diagram

Material comes into the conscious mind through all the senses. Opinions of psychologists differ as to what material is filed in the unconscious. Some of that material we actually 'log' and think about, some we do not, it goes straight into the unconscious.

In my early days of doing my first degree I met Professor Donald Broadbent through the Open University. He was a pioneer in the field of psychology and argued that its starting point should be about practical problems in the real world. He helped with stresses at work and was influential in helping set up systems like our GB postal codes. He was clear in his mind that there was a short-term memory and here material was filtered, some being permanently thrown out and not registered in the memory or unconscious at all.

Contrary to Professor Broadbent, many hypnotherapeutic and psychoanalytic practitioners think that all material is recorded here. I'm pretty sure that happy memories as well as traumas come into the mind this way and are also filed in the unconscious.

Some of this material you may well recall on demand. For example, what colour is grass? What did you have for breakfast? We can usually recall these things as and when necessary. It is usually pleasurable to recall and tell one's own story. Television shows illustrate how we love the game of recall, when they feed our need and enjoyment of recall, in the many hours of quizzes available at any one time of asking.

---

1 I met the American Professor Leonard Cohen in England when he was Dr Cohen who lectured at Chorley College of Education in 1969 and he gave this description at a public lecture. He later went to Texas University of Arts and Industry to be Professor there

Material is also 'logged' or filed that we haven't necessarily thought of but may well have experienced or observed at some level or other. This is the kind of material that a forensic hypnotherapist would attempt to get a client or witness to recall in the line of helping to solve a case. There is a bank of evidence and case history in this field.

In the 1980s I was involved as a hypnotherapist in a couple of murder cases for Cheshire police. The process was very strictly guided. Scotland Yard had gone as far as drawing up a set of guidelines that enabled evidence gathered in this way to be admissible as evidence in court, and of course, this was adhered to very strictly. Interesting from the therapeutic point of view that I was given no lead at all as to what it was that the police were looking for … not even "will you see if you can find out the make of that car". Nothing!

The Mind according to Sigmund Freud

Let us work out what happens in the mind. According to Freud, the mind (psyche) has **three** levels: the **conscious**, **pre-conscious** and **unconscious**. In *"An outline of psychoanalysis" (1940)* he starts from the 'fact' of consciousness.

Of course we are aware of some part of our mental life. Kerry Thomas in "Introduction to Psychology" edited by Ilona Roth for the Open University says …

> *"…this is the conscious level. Introspection makes it clear that perception, thought or memory may be conscious at one moment and 'gone' the next.*
>
> *Freud argues that these gaps in our conscious awareness make it necessary to have a concept such as the unconscious"*

So, therefore the unconscious, as a concept, has its start. Within the unconscious Freud makes three distinctions. Some material from the unconscious can become conscious easily, as in the for-instance about the quiz show above. The unconscious mind is 'filed' in a strange way. Look at your bookshelf just now. How do you file it? By colour? By size as the easiest way for you to make a retrieval? You may know that the book about Evolution has a black spine and is taller than the normal paperback book. The rest is easy.

Your local library files alphabetically by subject and author surname. The unconscious mind is different. It places memories by **association.**

Association and the mind

It is useful to understand a model of what happens in the mind. As already stated Freud, says that the mind (the psyche) has **three** levels: the **conscious**, **pre-conscious** and **unconscious**.

Preconscious

Have you ever been thinking of something, and your mind has wandered off on to something else, and then something else again. You may sometimes wonder, "Good heavens, how did I start thinking about that!" An old-fashioned phrase for that process is 'wool gathering'. Some people spend many hours doing this. You perhaps will recall doing it at school whilst trying to look as if you were paying attention!

Both the material recalled for the quiz show and the 'train' of thought described above Freud would say is from the **preconscious**. These things would not be normally conscious but could easily become so.

Parts of the mind: UNCONSCIOUS - the ID: basic, strong drive

In Ilona Roth's (ed.) earlier work for the Open University psychology department, back in the 1980s, she stated that the unconscious mind's "id" urges strove to be satisfied "**no matter what the consequences**". Think about it. Drive does not come more powerful than that. Do you remember that drive from your earliest sexual experiences of yourself or peer group? If two people decide to get together for the purpose of sexual encounter then nothing will stop them!

As time has gone on through the field of psychology though, the Humanistic branch of psychology's point of view has become much more in vogue; that point of view is that here, in the unconscious mind, is also the power to cure and heal.

As well as these levels of operation, then, Freud elaborated his model of the mind to contain three structures, the id, the ego and the super-ego. The **ID** he said was the instinctual force of behaviour driving behaviour in the direction of instant gratification of the biological needs of the individual, the instinctual drives of hunger, thirst, sex and so on.

Secondly, he said that in the unconscious proper was material which can "through our efforts be made conscious and in the process we may have a feeling that we are overcoming very strong resistances" (Freud, 1940 p160).

Thirdly, he said that there was a great deal else in the unconscious that can perhaps never become available to consciousness.

The EGO, or consciousness

The **EGO** he said maintains the individual as a whole whilst adapting to external reality at the same time. It compromises between the id urges and the demands of the super-ego. Its functions include things like memory, learning, perception, motor skills and actions.

To put it at its simplest, EGO is US – that is you and me in the here and NOW.

Cesspits?

As stated earlier, many of us were brought up on the idea that the Freudian model portrayed the unconscious as a cesspool of nasty things waiting to get out and gobble us up.

He was a man of his time and his viewpoint is unfashionable with many now. His views were, indeed, very negative. Freud believed that the contents of the unconscious are neither conscious nor easily available to the conscious because they are painful or dangerous in some way.

He said that the unconscious contained memories, perceptions, fantasies, conflicts and impulses that must be pushed out of the way or repressed to make life in the real world contain less pain, threat and conflict.

About the unconscious mind, he says (Freud 1933):-

> ...is the dark, inaccessible part of our personality ... and most of that is of a negative character and can be described only as a

contrast to the ego. We approach the id with analogies: we call it a chaos, a cauldron full of seething excitations.

SUPER-EGO

Freud later added the **super-ego** to his theory of the three levels of conscious, pre-conscious and unconscious. The super-ego can be thought of as conscience. You will see from the diagram of a few pages ago that it straddles the line between the conscious and unconscious minds. It represents the internalised demands normally generated against culture, society and family. For a child, it can be as if parents are carried around inside his or her head. Freud (1940) says about the superego:-

> *"The long period of childhood, during which the growing human being lives in dependence on his parents, leaves behind it as a precipitate the formation in his ego of a special agency in which this parental influence is prolonged…. it constitutes a parental influence of course includes in its operations not only the personalities of the actual parents but also the family, racial and national traditions handed on through them …*

> *"It will be observed that, for all their fundamental difference, the id and the super-ego have one thing in common: they both represent the influences of the past – the id the influence of heredity, the super-ego the influence, essentially, of what is taken over from other people – whereas the ego is principally determined by the individual's own experience, that is by accidental and contemporary events".*

He is really clear, then, about the function and purpose of the super-ego to the individual. You will recognise some of the qualities of the super-ego inside yourselves. It seems to me that this is much of what is addressed in Cognitive Therapy (CBT).

Dr. Albert Ellis is widely credited with being the originator of Cognitive therapy although he calls his version Rational Emotive Therapy (REBT) (Ellis 1962). One in four medical health professionals in America use this method of psychotherapy with patients. Interestingly, the Canadian Psychological Association ranks Ellis as the single most important psychologist in the last 100 years. Second for them is Sigmund Freud.

Ellis paraphrases Shakespeare and says:-

"There's nothing so upsetting in life but thinking makes it so ... Whenever (an individual) finds himself becoming intensely upset (as distinguished from his becoming moderately regretful about some loss or irritated by some frustration), he will quickly acknowledge that he is creating his own negative emotions by reacting unthinkingly to some situation or person. He will not allow himself to be deluded by the "fact" that his acute anxieties or hostilities are "naturally" caused or are his existential lot as a human being or are created by external conditions; but he will forthrightly face the fact that he is their prime motivator and that because he produced them he, too, can eradicate them. After objectively observing his acute unhappy emotions, he will think about and trace them back to his own illogical sentences with which he is creating them. He will then logically parse[2] and forcefully question and challenge these emotion-creating sentences until he becomes convinced of their inner contradictions and finds them no longer tenable. By radically analysing and changing his self-verbalisations in this manner, he will effectively change and counteract the self-destructive emotions and actions to which they have been leading".

To store or not to store?

Clearly our storage system is necessary for our health and survival in the world, and we invest a great deal of energy in making sure it's functioning efficiently. There is a price to pay, though, for having even a perfectly functioning storage system. The more efficiently we lock our feelings away, the less in touch we become with the way we feel, and also the more difficult it becomes to connect with others and to relate to what is going on around us. We can actually get to the point at which we stop feeling.

Freud is very clear, then, in the influence of the past both on the unconscious (and preconscious) and the super-ego or conscience. It is the mayhem caused by malfunctioning in these parts of the mind and other things too that Mnemodynamic therapy addresses.

Sometimes, of course, the nasty things from the unconscious mind (shaded on the diagram of the Model of the Mind) that we shut away for our own protection try out get out and be "aired" anyway. We have,

---

[2] Collins dictionary: " To assign constituent structure to (a sentence or the words in a sentence)"

though, here in place a guardian of the unconscious mind. It carries a large mallet that can be activated at will. This mechanism is called the censor, or critical factor. In Freudian terms it would be called an ego defence mechanism. This mechanism deals with the things that try to 'get out' to protect us. It happens particularly when our minds are not concentrating on something. How many of us have been 'wool gathering' as described above when a less than pleasant memory has come into our minds and we've consciously thought "I don't want to think about **that** just now", and have squashed down a negative thought or feeling? If we did shut something away for our own protection, of course it is logical that it would not be a good idea to let it out again, or at the very least would feel uncomfortable. The censor then can squash down this memory whence it came. This works very often (though not always) by conscious will, and works often without us necessarily consciously knowing.

The mechanism, like many parts of the human, does not work with 100% efficiency all the time. At night the censor (in the model of the mind diagram) relaxes and puts the mallet down - and at this point things can get out. They do so usually not in the raw state, since this would alert the critical censor even during the sleeping state, but the things make their escape disguised as dreams. Freud called dreams "the royal road to the unconscious" because he realised how important they were in terms of the unconscious mind trying to tell the conscious mind something, or, to put it another way, repressed material trying to get out.

So often, we can awake and recall a dream, but after a few minutes the censor puts its guard back and the memory is lost. You will, I'm sure recall this phenomenon in your life. It was no wonder that Freud gave dreams "the royal road to the unconscious" description.

Denial

Let me give you another explanation of the working of the mind, repression and the critical factor.

It is so easy for stereotypic words and phrases to be passed from one generation to another. We can so easily feel not good enough, not OK. When a parent or someone important in our lives uses stereotyping or labelling words, it invalidates the way we feel and a little part of us begins to doubt ourselves and our ability to know ourselves. We begin to think that we must be wrong and these other voices must be right, but still we feel what we feel. The hurt still hurts and the anger or frustration still smoulders, but it becomes easier to hide it away, to store it somewhere where it doesn't bother us.

We can learn to deny both our feelings and things that have happened in our lives. Two other things that happen when we deny a significant portion of the way we feel are these; in the first place, we start to believe that we must be totally insignificant and unimportant because there is no-one 'out there' able to validate us. Secondly, we assume that as 'out there' is right, and as it does not agree with our experience 'in here', **we** must be wrong.

By logical deduction our perception and/or information processing system must be faulty. This means that we are unreliable, and unreliable, as we know, means 'no-good'. We no longer feel good about ourselves, nor trust ourselves. We can grow suspicious, and we also can stop loving or even liking ourselves much at all.

A small incident as a child - say of a grazed knee (because, as you already know, the unconscious mind stores things by association), may be stored in the same 'file' or 'box' as a traumatic motor accident in which we were made to feel insignificant, and a shattered love affair, in which our feelings were denied. When the box or file is opened, not only will the feelings associated with the grazed knee emerge, but also the associated feelings from the other 'items' stored with it …

Fortunately, however, most of the time these 'files' remain password protected. It's usually only when the whole storage system gets too full and overflows, or our system in general does because of reality things like stress at work, or even physical illness, that a little leakage occurs.

This usually shows up as one of a whole range of symptoms and we have a clear message that something is wrong. If the illness or sense of 'wrong' persists, we usually do something about it by seeking help from the professional we believe will be able to solve the problem for us.

There are many different events that can trigger a response from our storage system. Sometimes we recognise these times retrospectively, when we realise that we have over-reacted in some way and dumped a huge load of anger, sadness, or some other emotion onto a relatively minor incident. The insight of knowing that you have had the over-reaction can be a point for realising that you need some kind of professional help.

Our storage system is vastly complex, but has a certain logic to it - the logic of association - and you know by now that this is the way the unconscious mind files itself.

Hypnosis

The name, hypnosis tends to scare people. Perhaps we have watched too many late night movies where the villain – a Dracula type figure, stares into the eyes of the fair maiden who becomes his prey. Another old film had the character Svengali, a musician and hypnotist, from the novel "Trilby" written by George du Maurier. In the story, Trilby is an artist's model. She's tone-deaf, but Svengali transforms her into a singing sensation under his hypnotic spell. Another eponym to come out of the novel is the word for a man's hat: trilby. A trilby was a soft felt hat with a narrow brim and an indented crown. The word arose because such a hat was worn in the stage production of the novel. The descriptive word 'Svengali' has also fallen into common usage to mean someone usually maleficent.

When describing anything to do with the hypnotic state, my old teacher, Peter Blythe always used to say "the state we mis-call hypnosis". This was a good and helpful thing to say. The Greek god Hypnos was the God of sleep and all of you, as practitioners, know that there is no sleep in the hypnotic state we use and work with very often. It IS though, an altered state. It is also very useful when using Mnemodynamics because asking people to "close eyes and picture …" seems to be a method which allows instant access to what people need to find. It is here that hypnosis can come into its own by helping to bypass this critical factor.

Essential is co-operation. The client person must want to go along with the therapist. The critical factor then puts down the mallet, and providing due care is used by the therapist, a two way passage is made to the unconscious. Material can be put in the mind to help, and previously repressed or suppressed things can be released to help find resolution.
Whilst the censor is co-operating, for example, in the direct or indirect suggestion method of hypnotherapy, the therapist can say to the unconscious "You're feeling better, stronger, fitter". The therapist could not give a suggestion that would be against someone's moral code - "you will now go out and rob that bank". Here the censor is consenting for the by pass to occur.

The above example underlines a problem with the whole subject of hypnosis. Over the years, claims have been made that it will 'do' anything for anybody, a little like a magic wand. As time passed, and of course it was found not to cure everything for everybody instantly, the subject fell into disrepute.

A small illustration of this can be shown in the prospective stopper of smoking. Quite often, a person will call in and ask, "Can you make me stop" or "I think I ought to stop". Would you take on that person? Would you? Think of the question in terms of the information above. Any hypnotherapist has never stopped a person smoking in their lives, but has merely facilitated the person's own decision-making process.

Mind domination?

What we do is help many people who have decided in their own minds that this is what they want to do. If the person did not WANT to quit, the critical censor would knock my suggestion well out of the way.

The examples given above are not totally cut and dried however. At the time of Bobby Kennedy's assassination, for instance, the 24 year old assassin Palestinian Sirhan Sirhan, claimed that he'd committed the murder of the late United States president's brother under hypnosis. (Sirhan since recanted that claim, and later in 1998 sought a new trial).

The Organ of Choice

Usually someone comes along because they have a symptom that needs some relief. Why does a symptom occur? There are also times when the unconscious mind needs a symptom. At last the strain is all too much. We start with a symptom. Why that symptom anyway? Part of that (the weakest link in the chain) has already been mentioned. There is another aspect too. The German psychoanalyst Georg Groddeck spoke about illness occurring in the organ of choice. Felix Deutsch (1939) in "The Choice of Organ in Organ Neurosis" wrote the following:-

> *An organ neurosis is the necessary expression of a neurotic conflict in terms of an organic disorder which has a specific character. The organ involved is determined by the fact that it was originally affected at a time antedating the full evolution of instinctual life. The instinctual response at that time to the organic*

dysfunction created a psychosomatic unit, i.e. an active or latent co-ordination of, and interaction between, a given organ and a psychic conflict. This psychosomatic interrelation will be used under certain somatic or emotional conditions as the pathological solution of a psychic conflict and will lead to a certain symptom complex. Thus when the old psychic conflict becomes active, the organ originally associated with the conflict is called upon to produce those symptoms. In the case of certain specific conflicts, we shall witness manifestations of both components whenever one is stimulated, reproducing the other component of the original situation.

Freud and conflict

To return to Freud for a moment, he put conflict as the cornerstone to his work. He thought that maladaptive behaviours and distressing symptoms served as a goal of the person's situation and personality.

We have already heard how Freud says that it can be as if parents (and society in general) are inside a child's head. It isn't only that we were taught this or that – we were non-verbally modelled it. We spend the first few years with our parent(s) or caregiver alone before many years in formal education, learning what society and the education system thinks is the appropriate use of our minds.

We learn social interaction through all this time by trial and error, by feedback from our families and friends and society in general. The little we do learn about our feelings and how to deal with them is governed by general assumptions and stereotypes such as 'boys don't cry', or 'girls like dolls'. We don't learn how to deal with the rage we sometimes feel towards our parents when we are even young children, let alone teenagers.

Neither do we learn to deal with feelings of jealousy towards a younger brother nor sister who appears to have what we want. Parents, never having had help dealing with these issues themselves are unlikely to know what to do for their children. Generation after generation of us end up feeling uncomfortable and incompetent when faced with the emotions of others.

Given, then, the fact that material does become locked off, frozen in time, and that being acknowledged, we need to find a way of relieving the suffering that this scenario gives, and as easily, quickly, efficiently and painlessly as we possibly can. This is what I have spent my working life attempting to perfect.

I began work as a hypnopsychotherapist in 1968, having trained as a school teacher from 1965 to 1968. Sixteen years later, working in the economically needy area in Liverpool, my client group was made up of individuals who reached into their own pockets to pay me. This was difficult for many. Because of this ever-present economic dynamic I pressured myself to work with my client group more and more quickly, at this time learning Neuro-Linguistic Programming (NLP), a Behaviourist model. This was, mind you, over my training of the Freudian psychodynamic model. The denial, or non-acknowledgement of feeling inside the NLP model at the time did not sit comfortably. Eventually, Mnemodynamic therapy evolved. It is this model which is explained in these pages.

It is out of this necessity that Mnemodynamic therapy was born and is hereby wholeheartedly and unreservedly presented to you.

It is necessary to mention something about the therapeutic methods that are used, and how the component parts fit into the therapy so that points raised by both client and therapist in their statements can be understood. The therapeutic method is therefore described below.

Mnemodynamic Therapy is a fully interactive model, with therapist and client working as partners, using the power of the client, guided by the therapist, to get better. Here, Freud and I parted company.

Pre-suppositions of the Mnemodynamic Model

As already stated in the introductory pages, there are only two prerequisites of the client:-

Firstly that the client is open minded and will "go along" with the process as outlined by the therapist. (The therapist here needs to use his other skills to present the work in a form acceptable to the client).

Secondly is the necessity that the client does not sabotage the process. (Of course you would **never** say this in advance of the process but keep it at the back corner of your mind. A skilful practitioner will be able to check after one session of working with Mnemodynamic therapy the amount of improvement the client is showing, and should be able to, sensitively and gently, challenge any sabotage in the rare instances should it happen)

As required by Holistic medicine, and as already stated, this is a fully interactive model. The client is actively involved in his or her own process of getting better. The older medical model would have the patient passively sitting / lying there waiting for something to be done to them – an injection, a tablet – even amputation! You may remember it from your own childhood days.

The therapeutic methods that are used, and how its component parts fit together are outlined below so that points raised by both client and therapist in their statements can be understood. You will recognise many of the elements. The therapeutic method is therefore described next.

CHAPTER 2: The Therapeutic Sessions

The first session

1. LISTEN and find out positive details about your client

Regarding my working session, on which the process below was modelled, the first session would contain the Mnemodynamic process.

Of course it is necessary to listen to the client initially, to hear about the set of symptoms the client has, how they feel now, and when the problem first started. It is important to find out some POSITIVE details in the life of your client if you don't already know them - family, career, personal strengths, achievements and so on. One can at the very least commend the bravery of the client in getting to that part of their life to enter therapy and look at some issues also!

Positive details are pretty obvious – but these few pointers may help you: are they partnered or married? Children? Job? Qualifications?.... These will be things I'm sure you find out as rudiments in the taking of your case-history.

I suggest that you then relate the proposition that the client feels THIS, (their set of symptoms or feelings) NOW because of things that have happened in their past.

I suggest that you put forward the case that we have done the most difficult part of our lives. The early years of birth to ten years is the hardest part with 10-15 coming as the second most difficult period.

Ask for 5 minutes co-operation as described below.

I suggest:-

> "**So** often when we have a problem like this, it is there because of something that happened to us in the past. We have a way of finding that out pretty quickly.
>
> Would you be prepared to go along with me just for five minutes, so that you see how I work, and we can see if what you're feeling in the here and now is to do with past things?"

2. 5-MINUTE CONTRACT, consent, setting the scene, & distance

People will usually, though not always accept this five minute contract. Five minutes seem a reasonable time frame for people to accept, and usually, the client will do so.

Put to them that there is a really quick way of finding out if the roots of the problem lie in the past or not, so we may as well do it and see. The client will usually agree. (If they don't assent then I suggest that you use the session to reflectively listen).

You therefore have **consent.**

Good words to use are:-

> *"If I were to ask you to close your eyes and picture a TV screen out here with a picture of you (Jane aged 37) on it, could you do that?"*

To ascertain this is your **only** prerequisite.

If the answer is "yes" then:-

> *"Close your eyes to shut me out, and put a picture of you, (Jane) out here on a TV screen, and say 'yes' when you've done that".*

The reason for asking the client to place this image "out there" is to distance the client from the feeling of anything that went on in the past.

We all know that it is far easier to solve someone else's problems rather than our own. By making a distance between ourselves and one of the precipitating events therefore, this very element of distance is introduced.

We can also protect our clients from feelings and 'divide up' a scenario in an objective fashion if it is kept at a distance. This is detailed in the numbered paragraphs below.

3. DISTANCING the client by space and language

Distance helps in terms of protection, and as well as keeping the feelings connected with the event "out there", the client can release feelings a small part at a time. They can make other interventions too as well as make better cognitive sense of what is happening to them.

There are two ways of distancing. The picture 'out there' is one way - also you may have noticed the language used above is the start of making the client *'Jane'* not 'you'. To use this, the third party tense, helps with making the distance between the 'then' and 'now' in terms of another layer of third-party protection for your client. This linguistic change also suggests and offers distance to the client in terms of using the third party (to be moved to the past tense in the next stage) as well as the distance of the television screen. Be clear that there are two ways of distancing together. Your client may well return to the first person. Don't worry or challenge but just maintain your third party stance.

Think for a minute. How many people or working places are now in your session? Three I would suggest; (i) you, the therapist, (ii) the client in their chair, and (iii) the younger part of themselves some feet away.

Focus hard to do this. It is very important. My tip for doing this is to speak to the client and then to turn to the younger client in the position 'out there' to get the client to address them. When you are doing this and speaking with the client they will hear the subtle movement (as you move your head) in your voice and this will also help them keep the image of the younger person separate.

Next comes the part of the process where the therapist asks the client to find an event or period of life to work with by using the following verbalisation:-

> *"Imagine there's a videotape machine or DVD player under the TV and a remote control right next to you. Re-wind the cassette recorder.*
>
> *Take the picture back and back and back and back and back.*
>
> *I want you to look for a time when a younger (Jane) than you was in some situation or other of difficulty and when you've found the picture, freeze frame it and say 'yes' to let me know you've done that".*

4. THE ALTERED STATE

By this time, merely a few seconds, the client will have put herself in an altered state, often a deeply altered state.

"Yes"

Remember, the screen and image of the younger self now is at a distance. As the image is rewound, keep the language in the third person too.

Next the client is asked for the age of the client and to describe the scenario.

"How old is our Jane here?"

"Seven"

"What is happening for her here in this scene?"

5. THE SCENARIO

Ninety nine times out of a hundred, the client will describe the scenario – not to do so is extremely rare. If she can't describe the scene, then the therapist can work content free. Details of this will be given later.

Do your best to write down the scene word for word. The client will usually go slowly enough for you to be able to do this. If the client description is fast, it is vital that you write down **every feeling word** that is included, though usually the therapist is not overwhelmed with the amount of feeling words that get stated at this point. (Sometimes a lot of feeling words are stated in the 'narrative' and this will be covered later).

"What is she feeling?"

Wait for an answer. The client will normally tell you how the younger person felt.

For your part as the therapist, **reflectively listen** to the feelings and list them exactly as they are spoken to you. Prompt if necessary by imagining yourself in the client's shoes. Be brief and to the point, but explore corners. You will of course improve with practice.

List the feelings. Build on the reported feelings to find strength of the feeling. As in reflective listening in some counselling models, if the client says 'angry', you may offer back, in a reflective listening way the next deeper word *'furious?'* and then if confirmed, *'enraged?'* (See Appendices

5, 6 & 7 for support on reflective listening). How do you reflectively listen? Think about it!

Leading the client?

During one Mnemodynamic Master Class it was put to me that I could possibly have been 'leading' the client.

This is something you must make your own mind up about. Having watched a lot of "Perry Mason" (the American lawyer in court cases bought by British TV) programmes in the 60s, in my mind the boundary between leading and not leading is so clear that I would be hard pressed to do so at the point of a gun!

Skilful reflective listening where you "feed back the gist" (see Appendices 5, 6 & 7 again for these refinements) is a skill so subtle and observant … Of course it is possible to make a mistake, or go too far down a line of depth of feeling:

Client:	"annoyed"		
Therapist:	*"angry?"*	client:	"yes"
Therapist:	*"furious?"*	client:	"yes"
Therapist:	*"enraged?"*	client:	"yes"
Therapist	*"murderous?"*	client:	"no, not that strong …

From my experience, the client will always draw a line – their line, in the right place for them.

6. ANCHORING

The client may well have disclosed to you something which for them was difficult if not traumatic. Even if it appears, in our grown up world to be not THAT bad, remember though, it was probably pretty bad for the child in the picture.

To contextualise this and quote the Freudian context again:-

"In the end, if the situation of repression can be successfully reproduced in his memory, his compliance will be brilliantly rewarded. The whole difference between his age then and now works in his favour; and the thing from which his childish ego fled in terror will often seem to his adult and strengthened ego no more than child's play". (Sigmund Freud, 'The Question of Lay Analysis', 1926)

This is the nub of how Mnemodynamic therapy (and many other therapies) works. The younger feelings and cognition brought into the world of now and adulthood, with guidance, are so much easier to deal with.

As with someone in an accident or someone drowning, the most important thing is to throw in a life raft. There are many ways of doing this and every client and every scenario is different.

This can be done, for example by using **Anchoring** from the NLP model. Anchoring 'now' resources can offer an element of stability. Whilst, at first sight this may seem obvious, I remember for the first time this came into my consciousness and for this I acknowledge my old teacher Peter Blythe.

Whilst using the old, crude "remembering, reliving re-feeling" words that I was taught to use in therapy (Washington 2010), Peter had a client with a stammer who, having taken himself spontaneously back to his birth, brought himself out of any altered state and locked himself into a position a little like a begging dog whilst he shouted "I can't breathe" over and over again.

It is not telling tales out of school to say that Peter said that he had been very frightened at that moment. It crossed his mind that his client may even die! After the initial panic having never seen this before, he quietened himself down and realised that the man had not died at birth, he was there and sitting in the consulting room, so he really wasn't going to die now! Obvious? Well, maybe. However to reinforce this to the client is a helpful thing to do. That was, however, a small piece of this large jigsaw model that has been passed on hundreds of times and which has facilitated thousands of clients.

> *"Acknowledge that this was a difficult time/situation but (s)he DID survive or you wouldn't be here now! And tell me when you've done it"*

> "Yes"

Some counselling models talk about reflective listening being the only way of working. The therapist is an instrument of reflecting back and no more. The Mnemodynamic model is different. I have learnt to be much more definite and authoritative about right and wrong. (Please see the case of Janie in Appendix 13).

Sometimes at this 'anchoring' stage of the therapeutic process we would use the technique of sending back the adult cognition here by saying:-

> *"I guess if she knew back there about (the positive things you ascertained earlier) she'd feel better about where she's at now. Is that so?"*

The therapist would have to wait for a reply to the above which common sense says is going to be affirmative because of how you have asked the question before saying:-

> *"Let her know this. I know that you'll find a way, and tell me when you have done it".*

The client will, of course, let you know.

By this stage of the proceedings, the client will have:-

1. Let you know the scenario

2. Let you have a list of feelings such as: shocked, frightened, terrified, petrified, panic, guilty, really responsible, upset, trapped, helpless and powerless AND

3. You will be starting to help the client by anchoring the 'now' resources. In here can be put many things – so it so alright to be creative. The following are for-instances I have used which may help you:-

I want to declare more about being opinionated now. The client is coming for help with something, and may well have exposed something that is very difficult for them to deal with. It is no time for you, the therapist to set up a debate. Let me give you some for-instances:

- **Child Abuse**. In our society sexual contact under the age of consent is forbidden. Between an adult and child the perpetrator would be jailed. The child, who may well have been "groomed", most likely was, will have feelings of guilt and responsibility.   Janie's grandfather (described in the later case history) used to ask her to ask for sex and approval aged 7!   "Let's hear it for Grandpa"..... To use ones adult neediness in this fashion for me is more than out of line. Here I would say what I thought in terms of boundary issues:-

"What Grandpa did was way out of line. He was the grown up and she was the child and he should have known better, so please tell her that in terms that she will understand" ...

This can be enough to guide the adult to help the younger version of themselves.

- **Normalising: "That's what 10 year olds do".**   Sharon was devastated as a 10 year old. Treats were few in her day (now middle-aged) and mum had promised to take her to the pictures. Somehow she had transgressed though she knew not how. Mum was punishing her by not taking her out. Not only did she feel punished, but unloved and unlovable into the bargain!

   "Let her know two things – mum's reaction is about mum, not Sharon (problem ownership App. 3). Also the youngster didn't even know what she had done! Whatever it was couldn't have been too serious – so say to her 'That's what 10 year olds do!' as they live and learn and let me know when you have done that"

- **Intention:**   You can also take the heat and resentment out of a situation at this point in the process. Kevin had felt disconnected most of his life ... "there's a bit missing from my jigsaw"... In our session he used Mnemodynamics to go to an incident aged 4. Mum was "up high, singing to herself". Kevin was feeling distant, separate, alone, resigned, bamboozled, confused and wanted to play".

   "What was mummy's intention?... Did she think 'here's my Kevin and I'm now going to damage him for the next 43 years'? I thing not ... (Kevin, too was shaking his head). Please tell the little chap that mummy is being care-less, rather than being neglectful with malice aforethought - and let me know when you have done that"

- **Cognitive Connections:** Jennifer came to see me just before Christmas 2009. She was an amazingly hard worker, had done a great deal of personal growth and was intelligent and articulate. It's always a difficult time of year with pressures of home and work taking their toll. She worked for Virgin Trains. Her old male boss who had helped and supported her left and a new woman, Sue came in. She had a lot to get off her chest and we spent several sessions doing this. The new boss was both unclear and bullying. Gradually, Jennifer realised that other people were aware of the boss's shortcomings.

  At our first Mnemodynamic session, Jennifer put a montage together of all the incidents during the months that Sue had been the boss, as described earlier (see 5 The Scenario). During the previous months she had felt anxious, uncomfortable, judged, unclear, confused, unsupported, criticised, trapped, undermined, powerless, frightened, intimidated, bits of panic, and upset.
  During the anchoring stage I said to her

  "Let her know that she gradually becomes aware that other people have become aware of Sue's behaviour and she is told that Sue's manner and treatment of others has been noted by both her peer group and up line"

  For the bright woman that Jennifer is, and without my saying more, she realised that Sue would not be allowed to carry on in this manner forever and management would, in its own good time, deal with their problem. This joining up of thoughts in this way, even before the release of feeling, can bring about enormous relief.

- **Bullying and Intimidation:** My colleague and friend, the late Geoff Grahame BDS (1932-2006) was a dentist from Newcastle-upon-Tyne who became the President of the British Society for Medical and Dental Hypnosis (BSMDH) had a wonderful technique to which I can attest the efficiency. (We can put you in touch with an original video of this). He made this strong suggestion to the client in a totally waking state:-

  "When your father and mother made love to conceive you, your father deposited 370,000,000 sperm in your mother's birth canal. The sperm started swimming and one of them won the race. It won the race against three hundred and seventy million. That sperm plus egg was

what made you. **YOU** *won the race … YOU HAVE AS MUCH RIGHT TO BE HERE AS* **ANYBODY** *ELSE!"*

"At this" he would say, "a smile starts to cross the client's face, and often into a grin. You can just see it happening". It's true! Try it!!

- **Put the old head on the younger shoulders:** You may like to tell the younger person they once were his or her present day cognition of what that entire visualised scenario is about. A verbalisation can be as follows:-

   "After something like this has happened one can spend a great deal of time thinking about it. I want you to let him/her know what those present day views are … and let me know when you have done it".

- **Mental instability.** Joyce was a trainee of mine from Edinburgh. She volunteered to be a client for me to demonstrate on. She instantly went to the most awful of scenes where aged 7 she was locked in a cold and dark attic overnight as a regular occurrence. This was both moving and difficult. I could not work as I did with Kevin above using the word intention. This parent had intended to hurt and punish her child very much – behaviour for the adult part that was most inappropriate.

   Joyce of course had survived but was searching for answers in coming to terms with her difficult past. After assuring the little girl of her own survival in the anchoring part, the best I could do was:

   "Please let Joyce know that there must have been something really wrong in Mummy's mind to behave like this. I actually think that mummy must have been poorly to behave like this …. Please let little Joyce know this and tell me when you have done it".

7. RE-FEELING

Next in the process comes **Re-feeling.** This is to be done with the words the client has given you and in the order that they have been given.

"She's younger/little/smaller, over there, and you're big/grown-up here, and besides which, I'm supporting you. Help her by lifting/taking/feeling that feeling of (number one off the list, say "shock" as above) and feel it for her, here, where you're safe with me, and let me know when you've done that".

Repeat this phrase for each feeling from the top to the bottom of the list. You need to be firm, strong and commanding here rather than permissive. Do NOT be polite uttering something like "do you think you might possibly lift ..." as this gives the freedom of whether to do the task in hand, or not do it, back to the client and it is your job to facilitate them through the process as elegantly and fluently as is possible. It is not a good idea to give un-useful choices here. This is the part of the process that Freud says will make the client better (Please see appendix 3) ...

What if the client says "I can't"?

In the unlikely event the client *"can't,"* with a particular feeling, then leave that feeling out for the moment, and return at the end. If there is still difficulty, then you can ask the client to divide the feeling up by using a verbalisation like:-

"Imagine that feeling as an apple-pie. I want you to take a small section of that apple-pie of feeling and feel it for her, here, where you're safe with me, and let me know when you've done that".

The therapist may have to repeat this perhaps many times before the client says that there is no material left. To have to use this refinement of the technique is exceptional, but can happen now and again.

Be careful not to put your limits on this bit of the process. I draw my apple pie in pieces on the client's note sheet that I am working on and the process isn't OFTEN finished in one 'pie' full of say eight slices!

I have been known to draw three 'pies' of ten slices each before asking the client softly and gently:-

"How is she (he) doing?"

This facilitates the client lifting themselves a little out of what may have become quite a deep trance state (which is not the most useful to you or them).

So often the client will come back with a phrase like:-

"There are just a couple of slices left"

Trust your client to tell you when they are through with this part of the process. Paul Birley, a colleague, trainer and well-known therapist in the Midlands, called this 'the incremental stage'. Your client will very surely tell you when they have finished.

What if the client gets upset: is 'flooded' with a feeling or feelings?

The NLP model does this very well. The NLP practitioner would ask the client to put themselves behind themselves in a projection room watching the client looking at the screen in front. For myself I am happy to ask the client to push the screen through the wall to the far wall of the next room. This seems enough from my experience in terms of distance.

To take away a positive feeling?

What do you do if there is a positive feeling in the list of the negatives? Just yesterday James felt 'relief he's gone' that after years of arguments his father had actually left. The positive can so easily be there inside a list of feelings that surely **do** need to be relieved.

I usually verbalise like this:-

*"Take away from that younger (name) any parts of that ('relief he's gone' or whatever the feeling is) that may be **un-useful** to him in the future, and let me know when you have done that"*

This approach leaves the decision and power with the client and from my experience works perfectly well.

8. Your most creative and exciting part of process

Dissociation

The two steps below can be done in a quite intellectual and **dissociated** way – you as the therapist talking to the client who is helping the younger person 'out there' but separated by the distance between the client and the screen as a means of protection for the client.

8. (i) Validation

The next part of the process involves an extra much more cognitive 'layer' of reframing, validating and so on. Several of the Appendices in your Mnemodynamic Training Manual explore how people need to feel validated, normal, acknowledged, loved, that this incident was not necessarily their fault; that the apparent 'blame' or 'problem' was much more to do with the adult person in the scenario, and several other things that you will have discovered for yourself.

When the client looks back, the therapist can usually see exactly why the client felt the way they did at the time and it can facilitate the client very much to say so:-

> *"Validate, the younger Jane. Tell her what she's feeling is perfectly reasonable under the circumstances, perfectly valid, and tell me when you've done that".*

Do we not all have the need to feel that what we were feeling at the time was perfectly reasonable?

Next we need to normalise.

8. (ii) Normalise

> *"Let her know that there's nothing odd about her, any other (age year old) would feel give or take a bit the same under those circumstances too! And let me know when you have done that"...*

So often the younger person feels that they are peculiar or even going mad it is SO reassuring that, with the knowledge of hindsight, they are not mad and never were!

Dissociation v Association

All the above is done in a quite intellectual and **dissociated** way.

NOW It is appropriate now for feelings in the next part of the process to be worked with in an **associated** way, and from this point of view, I suggest that you as the therapist will need to prioritise from here. Think about how YOU would feel in the scenario in terms of what to do first. During Mnemodynamic Master Classes it has been amazing to me who has prioritised with what at this point. However, there is only you, the therapist in the therapeutic situation. You, and only you, can decide what feelings to prioritise with.

My prioritised list is here:

8. (iii) Trapped

If the client has a long list of feelings with a word like "trapped" in it, then for me, "trapped" is the number one word to work with – and who better to lift the younger person out of the trap than the person themselves. I am mentioning a real case here, Janie, who's grandfather would 'baby-sit', bath the little girl and perform oral sex on her then ask to be thanked for it,

> *"Go to the seven year old Janie in the picture and lift her out of the scenario. Scoop her up on to your hip and take her away from her bed that grandfather intruded upon. Take her to where she's safe, perhaps to your bed now so that you can watch over her, and let me know when you have done that"*

It would be very appropriate to choose to use problem ownership here. It IS OK for you to have an opinion, and to come down on the side of RIGHT. Janie's grandfather should not have been behaving like this!

> *"That man should not have done this to you. He was a grown-up and you were a child and he should have known better."*

My interjection with Janie was too strong at that point and I almost frightened her away ... but it is clear to me that Grandfather's behaviour was SO much more about meeting his own needs than those of nurturing and looking after the child for whom he was responsible.

I've been heard to say:-

> *"Hop over all that trouble, take him/her by the hand and bring him to 'now' and let me know when you've done that"*....

Other 'rescue' strategies can come in here also.

Give or take a bit I have given you the rough order I would use below ...

8. (iv) Dirty

Anne was a little girl in hospital and left by her mother for the first time. Put into her hospital bed she found that she was desperate to go to the toilet. The nurse was in the corner on the far side of the ward and brushing her hair over her head, completely absorbed in herself and taking no notice of her charges. Anne put her hand up, as the only way she knew to ask for assistance. The nurse didn't see her raised hand and, getting more and more desperate, she eventually dirtied her pants. She felt both dirty and also guilty (plus trapped of course). It was really important for one of the first actions between the grown up Anne and the child, for the grown up Anne to take and clean up the youngster, once again, an associated task:-

> *"Pick up little Anne and take her to your nice bathroom. Shower her down initially, then give her a lovely bubble bath".*

Anne is now in her late seventies. There wasn't such a thing as bubble bath when she was a child as there wasn't when I was a child either. We used to see bubble baths on films from America and long for them. Here was a way of Anne making up that deficit for the little girl which she was able to do with love, humanity and kindness for her younger self.

8. (v) Problem Ownership

For her also in that scenario came in the subject of problem ownership, as it did for Janie on the previous page, though in a different context. The hospital nurse for Anne had been in the corner of the ward with her head down and brushing her hair over it. I verbalised:-

> *"The nurse was in charge and should have been giving best attention to the children in her ward. Her not taking notice was about HER and nothing that the little girl had done wrong or omitted. She SHOULD have been doing her job properly and attended to the little girl ...*

Janie in her clinch with her Grandfather felt a myriad of feelings, not all bad ones. Re the inappropriate sexual behaviour I said to Janie:-

> *"Please let young Janie know that Grandfather was meeting his own needs here – his behaviour was all about him and nothing at*

all to do with her. His behaviour was, in fact, his problem (even though it gave her a problem to deal with)."

As Grandfather performed oral sex on her genitals she felt 'excited' and then 'guilty' and 'responsible'. At the time, I knew that Janie was a Christian and that it was therefore alright to use a Christian model. I said:-

> *"Tell her that God gave us nice feelings in our bodies so that we would want to get together with a partner at the appropriate time and make love and have a family by making babies of our own. It is really appropriate, OK for Janie to be excited when she is touched in this way – that is how God intended to get the next generation. The inappropriate thing was the person who was doing the touching … Please let her know this, and tell me when you have done it"*

I refer back to the debate mentioned under the "**To take away a positive feeling?**" above.

8. (vi) Listening - for "Sad" or "Upset"

Most counselling books talk about listening. The phrase I hold and cherish from these books is **"Listening is often enough"**. Of course that doesn't mean that listening is always everything, but that it is often enough.

Who do you think is best placed to listen to the young person?

In my mind, it is the older client who has brought the problem who is in pole position to listen to their younger self.

Regarding feelings such as 'sad', 'upset' and so on, and in the case of Janie and Anne above I would have said:-

> *"Listen to her – proper, good quality 'deep' listening, the best you've ever done, whilst you 'hold' the situation for her whilst she works through it in her own way … whilst she works it out for herself the best she can …and tell me when you have done it".*

As the text book says, this often has the desired effect.

8. (vii) "Shock",

Shock is another common feeling often expressed by the client about the event they are relating which happened often years earlier. Feel free to offer it.

We all know the treatment for shock don't we? It is the same for the child or younger person in the scenario that they have brought to you. However, the client will need the strength of your guidance:

> "She may well have become chilly even if the weather is good. Wrap her up in something warm and give her a cup of hot sweet tea – even if she is not awfully keen on it. It will help her in her recovery process"

8. (viii) "Confusion", "bewilderment"

These feelings will often be around too. If there has been "confusion", "bewilderment" use the here and now cognition to help the person, for example, use the words:-

> "I can imagine you've spent a long time getting your head around this event ever since it happened. Help her by sending back that cognition you have now as an older person, back to her in the picture, and tell me when you've done it".

8. (ix) "Lonely", "alone", "unsupported", "unloved", "unlovable", or "rejected"

For words such as 'lonely' or 'alone' or 'unsupported' or 'unloved' or 'unlovable' or 'rejected' say to the client:

> "Go to her now as a (mum, aunt, granny, kindly godmother) and acknowledge what she did for you, to help you be all you are now. Thank her for it and say to her 'I know you feel (alone) but you're not.
> * I'm from time future and you and I are one and you are not alone.
> * I will always watch over you. I will always be here for you.
> * I love you and will never, ever leave you.

Let her know all that until she knows it through to the middle her bones. Tell me when you have done it".

For issues to do with abuse, it is important to help the youngster to shed their feelings of responsibility by helping feedback **your** common sense and **their** grown-up cognition.

8. (x) Intention

This word and concept can be used at this stage in the process too as well as in 'Anchoring' described earlier. The older person will have often done something odd, mean or whacky in the presence of the younger person, now the client. The client will often keep this thing for the rest of their lives. Even Mr Shine in the Preface, probably thought he was doing the right thing and you had "to show the boys".

I remember speaking to Sue. She lived with George. I think that even George thought he was doing the right thing when he said to Sue after first hitting her; "I just want to knock some sense into you".

Thank goodness she had the confidence to stand her ground and defiantly say "You will NEVER, EVER KNOCK any sense into me". That, though, must have been his map – the behaviour that he was modelled as a youngster himself.

They did part pretty soon after this incident and a few years later he died a premature death from a heart attack in his early 60s. Even so, his model must have been that this behaviour was, actually, how to teach someone else something!

I remember hearing Oprah Winfrey being interviewed. She had been a beaten child. The simplicity of her reframe was awesome. She said, very simply, "They did the best they knew how" …

8. (xi) "Drained"

This has been used as a feeling word too and is not uncommon say in the context of someone, say in the lengthy parting of a relationship as things go wrong. To let people know that it will all be alright in the end with the benefit of the adult hindsight, and to give the younger person something to replenish them too is useful (though this is routinely dealt with at the next stage).

8. (xii) "Manipulated"

This also is not uncommon. Most people have felt this at some time. My verbalisation would be something like

> *"Let him her know that she got through it OK. Please ask her not to be blameful of herself. If we lived life backwards wouldn't we do it differently! We don't though. We live it forwards and she did the best she could at the time.*
We live and learn and get wiser as we do so…"

8. (xiii) "Insecure"

> *"Actually I know he doesn't know who you are, so tell him:*

- 'Hello… I know you don't know who I am but I am you from time future. You and I are one'…

- 'I will always, always look after you and watch over you'…

- 'And I love you' ….

> *"Make him know that so that he knows it down to the middle of his bones and tell me when you have done that"*

8. (xiv) "Guilty" or "Responsible"

To continue with the thread of Janie 8(v) above, she seemed able to take all the reframes given above in her stride. She was able to accept that her feelings were normal – but there was a twist to come. After a few sessions, Janie started to peel back another layer of disclosure. She was able to accept that she felt sexual pleasure as a seven year old.

Grandfather knew that she felt sexual pleasure of course. She told me how her Grandfather would get her to **ask** for the contact "Let's hear it for Grandpa" he would say. What a fragile adult ego to need this kind of accolade from a child! Janie, understandably, felt guilty and responsible – both emotions of which he had maximised for his own outcome.

8. (xv) Acknowledgement

I once gave an exercise to two groups of people. One was children in a school who had chosen to come to a group session. The other, on the same day was a group of teachers and support staff who also had chosen to come. The exercise was:-

> *Remember a time as a child or teenager when you told your parents how you were feeling and got a response from them something like - 'Don't be silly darling it's not that bad'.*
>
> *1. Please write down how you felt in such circumstances.*
>
> *2. What would you have liked to have heard or experienced instead?*

When we looked at what each group of people actually needed, the needs were remarkably similar! Validation, to be normal, and acknowledgement were the ones which stood out.

We all need acknowledgement. It is important that the grown-up client person acknowledges their younger part, even if that younger part and the event related to you is something that happened only a fortnight previously.

> *"Say to her, 'Thank you for going through all that for me, because without doing that for me I wouldn't be me now, and I'm really rather glad I am me now'."*

9. Re-resourcing

After that, do your best to **Re-Resource,** a well know technique from the NLP model:-

> *"I know that you have had a problem with {whatever it is ... be specific}), but I can certainly see your (capabilities, strength etc.). Send back to that younger (name) a jolly good dose of that strength, togetherness, and resourcefulness, that you have now,*

back to him/her - enough to help not only with THAT situation that (s)he is in, also with any other difficulty which might arise in the future".

This phrase "also *with any other difficulty which might arise in the future'* is the equivalent of Dr John Hartland's ego-strengthening. After that comes 'checking-out'.

10. Checking out

After that, **Check out** how the younger person in the picture is:-

"What sense do you get of him/her now?"

The word 'sense' was highlighted to me by a client. When the following happened I said to myself 'of course … but of course'. It was many years ago in Chester and Mnemodynamic therapy was in its infancy. The client did an excellent session from a standing start.

At the end of the session whilst I was 'checking out' I said to my client:-

"How does she look?"

"Exactly the same" came the reply. **That** was the 'aha' moment.

*"Oh I'm so sorry, how does she **seem**?"*

"Oh much, much better. She feels happy and serene"

This following extract is from my 2008 book "Peace of Mind Pathways to Successful Living" and the extract below starts to tell you something of Representational Systems from the NLP model:-

"Representational Systems

"Our internal representational system or 'rep' system can be compared to a map. Just as a geographical map is made from observation, measurement and experience, so an internal rep system is constructed from past experience. At any moment in time we have a number of sensory experiences available to us. Many of these we don't need, so depending on the situation, we learn which messages to respond to, and which to ignore. We delete some of the information, we may distort other information, and in this way we build up a conscious picture of the way the world appears to us. From the array of information available, we may find that what we see is most useful, or what we hear, or we may find the way we feel to be the most useful information. Over time we come to rely more and more on a particular way of gathering information. If we favour visual information, for example, we will probably ignore at least some of the sounds we can hear at the time, or we may pay less attention to how we feel. This also represents the way we remember an event - in terms of the information we have about it. NLP teaches that people fall into one of a combination of categories based on which of their senses they use the most.

"As language is a representation of our world, the words we use to describe it can be an indicator of our rep system. So if we are **visual** we tend to *see* what someone means or things will *look* or *appear* this way or that. If we are **auditory** we may *hear* things loud and clear, things will *click* into place, or *ring* bells for us. If we are **kinaesthetic** we will *get in touch with* someone or something, have a *sense* of something or find that things *fit* nicely. Although we do gather information via taste and smell, it is less common for these senses to be dominant, although many of us will remember a situation that *left a bad taste in our mouth,* or when something *smelt fishy*!

"The simple exercise below will give you a good idea of your own representational system:-

"EXERCISE 18: PREDICATE WORDS (This should take you 10-15 minutes)

1. Write down in story form, what you did this morning from the time you opened your eyes.
2. Stop when you've filled about half a page, and divide the rest of the page into four columns, under the headings of, Visual, Auditory, Kinaesthetic, Unspecified.
3. Then go through the passage and classify the words you used in terms of the sense they relate to.
4. Visual words will be any visually descriptive adjectives, such as "look", "see" and other words relating to vision.
5. Auditory words will cover aspects of sound, from "crunch", "hoot" and "tweet" to words describing sounds in terms of volume, tone, pitch, timbre and so on.
6. Kinaesthetic words relate to inner feelings as well as to the sense of touch, temperature, texture and also to movement. So here we have

"slip into", "turn around", "soft", "rough", "keep abreast of", and so on.

7. Unspecified words and phrases are those such as "process", "make sense of", "think", "consider". You may find that one of your lists is longer than the others. If so, you may have identified your rep. system. Try to become aware of the words that you use in everyday language until you are sure. It may be that your words are divided evenly into the different categories, or that two are stronger than the other.

"Some examples of the types of words that you may have identified in the above exercise and the categories that they fall into are:-

VISUAL	AUDITORY	KINAESTHETIC	UN-SPECIFIED
See	Hear	Feel	Sense
Look	Listen	Touch	Experience
View	Sound(s)	Grasp	Understand
Appear	Harmonise	Get hold of	Think
Show	Tune in	Slip through	Learn
Dawn	Be all ears	Catch on	Process
Reveal	Rings a bell	Tap into	Decide
Envision	Silence	Make contact	Motivate
Image	Be heard	Throw out	Consider
Picture	Resonate	Turn around	Change
Clear	Deaf	Hard	Perceive
Foggy	Talk	Concrete	Distinct
Focused	Speak	Scrape	Conceive
Hazy	Whine	Solid	Be conscious
Sparkling	Chime	Cemented	Know
Flash	Chatter	Soft	Wonder
Frame	Call	Keep abreast of	Realise
Vague	Tell	Fuzzy	Convince
Watch	Noise	Stiff	Plan
Colourful	Echo	Firm	Create
Sight	Sing	Cool	Identify
Dim	Volume	Flowing	Motivate

"Whatever the outcome of Exercise 18 for you, it should have provided some valuable information to you. Imagine what might happen when a person who is visual tries communicating with someone who is kinaesthetic? A useful example of this is provided by Steve Lankton, who describes a client - therapist conversation in his book "Practical Magic" (1980, p.19):

"The following example, perhaps familiar to you, demonstrates how two well-intentioned people fail to make contact on the first, and therefore most vital, step of communication.

*Client: "I'm so **hurt**". My husband left and I **feel** so helpless ... so alone. I've never **felt** so much **pain**, do you know what I mean?"*

*Therapist: "let me **see** if I understand this; I want to be **clear** on the source of your pain. Would you **focus** in and get a **picture** of your pain and we'll see if that tells us how to deal with it".*

*Client: (pause) "I just tried to get **hold** of a picture but I just **feel** worse. I don't **feel** like you're in **touch** with my difficulty".*

The therapist may conclude that the client is "resistant" and the client already considers the therapist insensitive. Now this is a slight exaggeration, but not much."

"It is like the two different maps I described earlier. If communication is to be effective, we have somehow to 'get inside' the world of the other person. If we can see the world through his or her eyes, even for a few moments, we are in a better position to bridge the gap between us. "How?" you may ask. Read on......."

By asking my client *"How does she look"* I was asking her purely for a visual response. *"How does she seem"* gave the information needed.

Depending on the answer, you as the therapist will need to repair as necessary. If there are left over feelings, then you need to deal with them quickly by reflectively listening as described above again and proceed through the stages listed and described from number **6, Anchoring** above to help you.

This whole procedure is written as neatly and succinctly as can be in the last Appendix at the end of your book.

The client may say that the younger person looks "happier". When you are reflectively listening, feeding back the gist here, 'happier' implies some sadness left. Think of the opposite of the word you have been given and offer it. As before, the client will correct you if you are wrong.

If this is not correct, then it is really alright to ask the client what he or she needs to do to make "happier" into "happy".

Do your best to get your client's younger part to a state without an "ier" on the end. Leave with as much resolution as you can, then double check:

"Is she equipped enough to continue in that situation?"

11. Is the process finished? Options in closing the altered state session

If the answer is *'yes'*, then you have options. In my opinion, the best person to look after the younger self, even if it is the younger self of three weeks ago or yesterday, is the client themselves.

On the other hand, it could be argued that this is perhaps too directive by you, the therapist, and therefore, option (ii) below can be used. I ask my client which option they prefer.

> *"Here you have a choice. S/he can go back into the picture in the video if you'd like, though my preferred option, if you and (s)he both consent, is to have you keep her/him. What would you like to do?"*

The client will tell you their preferred option, and 99 times out of a hundred will consent to keep the younger person.

Here are options:-

i) Option one is if the client does not want to keep the younger person and says they are OK to carry on in the picture.

> *"Is he/she equipped enough to continue in that situation? Good. Press the video button once again and fast forward the picture up to the grown-up person you started with, you today with me in this room. Let the picture fade - Let the screen go - Open your eyes".*

ii) Below is my preferred option:-

A 'closing down' of the session I often use is to let the grown up take the younger person to somewhere nice to be to lighten her up - a park, beach, playground, shopping (and so on).

> *"What would you like to do with him?"*

After waiting for the reply as to the preferred option and noting it, the next sentence can be adapted a little to match the client-preferred scenario -

> *"Let him play and play (do it and do it) until his heart is content and his body tired. Let him sit upon your knee and put his head on your chest and snuggle in to you. It is highly likely he will fall asleep, perfectly safe. Tell me when you have got him like that".*

When the client has replied that this is the case then:

> *"Let him melt into you, totally, utterly and completely safe and tell me when you have him there".*

One of the Centre Training trainers, Toni Lee Isaac used to say "make him very small and hold him in your heart". In helping the client to 'ground' where they now are I would say:

> *"GOOD. I'm glad you have him safe. You may find yourself doing playful whacky things between now and when we meet again – having a lollipop, or jumping in a puddle. IF that happens, I want you to let it, and indulge that part of yourself. If he feels sad or unhappy at ANY time then you can give him a squeeze of reassurance".*

When you are sure that the client is really OK and the younger part is safely re-integrated, then

> *"And whatever it is on the video out here, fast forward to where you started with you, grown-up (name) on (date maybe). Let the picture go, let the screen go and then:*
>
> *Open your eyes".* (said firmly to break the altered state)

In your **Check out** process (10), you have asked how the younger person in the picture is: *"What sense do you get of him now?"*

If the answer above is that the person that they are not quite OK, say they are "happier" or "not as angry" or any other word with an "ier" on the end, then the client is telling you, when you listen, that there is still work to be done. Go back to the reflective listening part of the process and start again. There will be much less work to do here as you will have helped the client 'skim off' many of the more intense feelings. By your patiently working through this twice, three times or even four, all client repressed, suppressed and unexpressed feelings will be lifted and resolved. The client will get better pretty quickly.

The whole session should take about twenty minutes.

At the end of the Mnemodynamic session, check out your client in the fully normal open-eyed state.

Multiple Incidents

Every now and again, it can be that the client wants to go from one session and flood into another without completing the first.
Here, in terms of protecting your client, you need to be the iron hand in the velvet glove. I would ask the client firmly to 'book mark' and literally PROMISE that or those incidents that you will return and deal with them at a future session and to thank the unconscious mind for letting the client know that those things are there.

12. Bottoming – after altered state work

You will need to listen hard to your client for a while after the Mnemodynamic session (without the altered state of course) and continue validating, reframing and normalising.

I normally open with something neutral which reflects the whole sense of the session in an open-ended and non-judgemental way in order to let the client further verbalise:

> *"That must have been a difficult time"*

I remember one session where a delightful lady, Mary, now in her 70s went back to a situation where she had had some kind of infective illness aged 7. She had lived in tenements in a Scottish city with lots of other families. It was pretty good. She had playmates her own age all around her, including Jacob. Gradually she got better but overheard her mother talking to a neighbour. One adult had said to another "of course it's not Mary's fault that Jacob died" … Jacob had fatally had the same disease as Mary. Mary was mortified to hear this and held herself responsible.

After the Mnemodynamic session she said "Do you know, I can't remember a thing about it" … I sat silently and waited. After a few more seconds she said "Oh yes, it's coming back", and we were able to level out this dreadful situation some more.

Think about that situation in terms of the Model of the Mind diagram earlier. After the session, Mary's shutters, in terms of the censor or critical factor had come down to protect her.

With physical pain, after a session, my colleague John Quigley says:

"It makes my eyes water just thinking about that!"

This part of your session is vital. For both you and the client to speak about the incident just disclosed and help get the Mnemodynamic work into some kind of order in the client mind and how their life is in the present is both appropriate and also fits in with the Freudian theory whose extract is highlighted below:

> *"The discovery that we made, at first to our own great surprise, was that when we had succeeded in bringing the exciting event to clear recollection, and had also succeeded in arousing with it the accompanying effect, and when the patient had related the occurrence in a detailed manner as possible and had expressed his feelings in regard to it in words, the various hysterical symptoms disappeared at once, never to return. Recollection without effect is nearly always quite ineffective; the original psychical process must be repeated as vividly as possible, brought into statum nascendi[1] and then 'talked out'. In the case of excitation phenomena … the symptoms appear again during this repetition in full intensity and then disappear for ever…."* (please see Appendix 15 for the whole of this paper).

With Janie, **8 (v)** mentioned earlier, I did my best with this IN the Mnemodynamic session, although we did a considerable amount of 'bottoming' after the session also. That, too, fitted in with Freudian theory as quoted above.

---

[3] The literal translation of this is "In status of birth" (Webster)

Chapter 3

Session 2

Opening the second session

At the end of the first session I ask the client to describe the image of themselves they see after all the work we have done together. The word that the person describes themselves as being at the end of the process, like "really fine" or "happy" is what I am aiming at. This is, then, the word that I expect people to come back saying they have felt in the intervening week.

Whilst I don't suggest it, experience has taught me to expect it. If that 'finishing' word is not how the client reports having been feeling in the week between the sessions, then we need to be concerned as to what is happening for the client in terms of their perception and information processing.

Percentage improvement – a measure for both you and the client

The question to be asked at the beginning of session two is:

> *"If when you came up the front pathway last time we met, on a scale of nought to ten (and nobody's at nought of course) but for the purposes of measuring, if you were at nought, and ten is where you want to be, how would you score yourself now?*
>
> *Are you still at nought, down a bit or up a bit?"*

You will note that I give three options here – level, down a bit, or up a bit. There could be, and has been, the accusation of leading the client. Be sure to use 'clean' language and offer all three options.

Most Mnemodynamic therapists will have been given most numbers of score here (not ten). One, two or three are quite acceptable, and you can re-enforce the progress the client has made back to him of course.

After the initial session, it is perfectly possible to work with more than one "incident" at session two should you choose to do that. For me, experience has taught me that one session of looking at a past incident is enough; that plus the following 'bottoming' gives work for the client between sessions which is both conscious, and unconscious.

You will need to make your own mind up on this one of course. Carefully write down the number your client gives you at the top of your 'session 2' notes and continue to do this through your agreed contract time-span. It will be a mark of his/her progress. You will learn, also, what kind of your therapeutic interventions score high, or at least show movement in terms of a person's improvement, and what do not.

I have noticed over the years, that at the first session, the unconscious mind of the client is likely to give you material that is not TOO difficult for the client, not too contentious to handle. It seems to be a perfectly reasonable strategy to me. It is highly likely that the client will not "dive in" to the heart of the problem immediately. What you will notice, though, as the sessions unfold, is the connection at a feeling level between the scenarios.

Should, occasionally, my expected outcome (of % improvement) not happen, then the word 'sabotage' comes to mind. This is a rare occurrence, but it can happen, and the therapist needs to gently and tactfully question to see whether or not this is so and if the client will 'own up' to its occurrence. If the client says they may be doing this, then you will explore why this could be so ... are there secondary gains and so on? Is there fear of living without the symptom?

Cultural differences

Cultural traits vary. In Britain, for example, we have the "stiff upper lip" which we bring down to keep all feelings firmly on the inside. Angela was a neighbour many years ago. I saw her in our village one day and her top lip looked definitely weird. After enquiring what was the matter, she burst into tears, telling me a tale of woe regarding part of her family ... One could not have missed this non-verbal cue.

Despite the symptom, the tendency is to 'soldier on' and make ourselves keep going. During this 'soldiering on', the symptom tends to get worse. Depending on where you read this book, you may well have other local differences to contend with.

A Mnemodynamic trained therapist, Tom, brought the case of one of his clients to a supervision session with me. In her culture it was rude for her, a young female, to look into the eyes of (at the face of) a man. In not looking at her male therapist, Tom at first thought she might be avoiding issues with him. Fortunately he had the sense to check this out with her, and she explained.

Irfan came this morning for the first time. From his given name as well as his family name I thought that he would probably have a different coloured skin than me. He had been born in UK from Indian parents. He called yesterday and wanted to be seen urgently. I tried to oblige.

He worked part time as a security guard. I am writing for you, in the order given to me, how his story unfolded. He was "stressed and anxious". He "wanted more confidence", more self esteem, to lose weight and quit smoking". Three years ago he had shed 7 stones. He said he was "now a bit lazy and depressed". When I asked if he has seen his GP he had. The GP had sent him to a psychiatrist who had given him tablets which he didn't take as he knew what had caused the problem. I enquired what this was and he said "money". His house had been repossessed and he had always gambled:-

> " … to get more money. Dad was always a gambler … Society always looked down on us. I was looked down on. I was bullied at school. We always got the cheapest things. I was a late developer. My parents thought I was 'possessed' and took me to psychiatrists and things. They (my parents) came from India and this was normal for them ….
>
> Why are you asking me all this? I have got over all that. I just want hypnosis…"

I couldn't help but think that there are none so blind as those that don't want to see; and hopefully his moment will come!

You will find many other cultural differences during your practice. Just be aware of them.

Client perception

Over the years I have had many clients who have got better. They have sent their friends… A typical phrase would be "Oh just go to see Sue. Talking makes you so much better!" The client has no perception that they have given themselves major surgery at an emotional level!

Chapter 4

Specific Conditions

Mnemodynamic therapy for smoking

Joyce was an intelligent and articulate, talented woman. I had met her years before when working for a well known insurance company in their employee support programme. She had been born with some kind of disability in her hip. Working in a bank, she had requested certain seating which was not given to her. She was stressed. We met four or five times at this time which seemed to help as I taught her coping strategies. Later she was to take the bank to a tribunal for ignoring her disability. She would eventually (mercifully!) leave their employment.

This was now years later and she had left the bank, re-training as a podiatrist. This life suited her much better.

She came to me to quit smoking, but was mindful, after doing Mnemodynamics last time that there "may be other things" lying about inside her. That was really good to hear as from my experience smokers don't want to know about other issues but want a 'quick fix' to get rid of the dreaded weed.

At the first Mnemodynamic session she went to be being 5 or 6 and someone had bullied her. She had always felt different because of the disability in her leg and never felt to be one of the 'in' crowd. That is always difficult for a youngster. Of course at that age we want to be accepted, to fit in and to be the same. She was hit and left with a bloody nose. Two boys came to her aid. After our work in the session she left the younger Joyce "more my old self" by the end.

Upon her return for the second visit, Joyce measured herself at 2½ out of 10. We were on the right track!

The next session involved her recalling back to 13. The family moved to the Isle of Man … "I didn't find it easy to make friends". The friends she did make were a little group of outcasts who also used to smoke together. Valerie was a dwarf and one boy had one arm. She fitted very well. Of course 'she fell' in with them and started smoking herself. After working with a lot of uncomfortable feelings that session, she left herself in a "much better" way and kept the version of her younger 13-year-old self.

She came back at 5 out of 10, though she said she had been "dizzy". She had had only 15 cigarettes in a few days and was pleased with herself. She wanted not to take on others' problems as she had been doing with her podiatry patients. It was time to refresh her coping strategies, so we did again the "Magic Garden", "Dimensional Storage System" and "Sound of Calm" (Washington 2008). I also taught her one or two other methods for 'rooting' herself to the earth and protecting herself.

She came back some ten days later at 9 out of 10 and determined to quit that day. Of her six agreed and paid for sessions, she quit at number 5 and left one session in reserve.

Mnemodynamic therapy and physical symptoms

Marjorie came to me saying "Everything is a drama. I am destroying myself". She said that she had mood swings between being "raving with anger" and "depression". She had been angry in her GP practice because of the treatment of her brother had received from them and was about to be asked to leave and go to another practice. She was now 56 and lived on an island to the North where she had retired as a secretary in a shipyard aged only 45. That was a "great issue" for her. She had had arthritis all her life. She felt generally 'dumped on' as she "had everybody's problems".

She made a considerable effort to get to me coming a long way by train then bus to the centre of my village before walking for seven minutes briskly down my lane with a stick. Because of the distance involved she stayed for a two hour session and would come less regularly.

She was looking forward however and was going to university in September to do criminology. There was a chequered history. At the age of 3 she had been into hospital in the Lake District to "have my legs straightened". This took six months. In those days parents were not allowed to stay and visited once a week – difficult for both the child and parents points of view one would think.

From 18 to 21 she had worked happily in London but came back to help look after her father who died of cancer when she was 21. She stayed in the family home. Mother died also of cancer when she was 51.

The previous November to seeing me in February she had been bending to reach something on the floor and stood up sharply, nearly knocking herself out on an open window. The back of her head "still hurt". There was also a pain under her foot when she put her foot on the ground that had been with her as long as she could remember.

At our first Mnemodynamic session, unusually, she went to 21 when she was first told that her father was ill by a lady she worked with in London. She felt all sorts of feelings as you might imagine: confusion about the decision she may have to make, upset, anxious, scared of how bad it would get, dread for father, "it had to be me; heavy duty, confusion, and later resentment, later anger and later absolute fury".

My already knowing the outcome was most helpful. I helped Marjorie help her younger self by both letting her promise her younger self that she did survive this and also that she certainly would do what she thought was the right thing. She then lifted off all the feelings one at a time before we did the next stage where she validated, normalised, listened to herself about the upset, gave herself good understanding and insight over the earlier confusion, gave herself her grown up insight and acknowledged herself before re-resourcing. She left herself "happier" which would normally fill me with doubts as to what was left, but on checking her out she said that there was 'nothing else'.

I used the rest of our session doing the concept of 'problem ownership', more fully described later and Dr Albert Ellis' CBT to help her challenge her thoughts and change them.

Marjorie returned a week later. She had "cried a lot" but measured herself as 5-6 out of 10. Half way by anybody's standards! The pain in her head had gone, and the one under her foot that she'd had as long as she could remember had disappeared also. Some weeks later I am glad to say that neither of those symptoms has returned.

I mentioned earlier about 'organ of choice' according to the psychoanalytic approach. Louise Hey (1988) continues this wonderful work in her book "You can heal your Life".

After a couple more sessions, Marjorie has made peace with her GP, given her brother his problem back and is over 7 out of 10. We still have a couple of sessions to go.

One of the themes she and I need to get to grips with is bullying. Marjorie is ashamed that as a child she bullied younger and more vulnerable people because of how she felt about herself …

"Turned Eye": getting rid of physiological constant strabismus

It will perhaps seem strange to you that something very physical, like the turn in an eye, (technically called strabismus) can be affected by one's psyche. A possible for-instance of that is shown here.

I remember many years ago meeting Martha in Chester where she came to see me with a phobia about needles and injections. She was 28 and had had the intense fear "for as long as I can remember". The subject had suddenly become important. One eye was turned inwards towards her nose and she was due to be operated on in four to six weeks. Surgeons were going to remove her eye from its socket, lay the eye on the cheek and cut the muscle to a measured and precise degree. It made my eyes water to even think about it! The procedure seemed to be a precise art because Martha told me that the hospital had measured what she called 'the discrepancy' and were ready to operate after a week's wait to give a final check to the measurement of the rate of turn in the eye. Her condition was called "constant strabismus". She was afraid to proceed to the operation because of her fear of needles and injections.

I explained how I worked and using Mnemodynamic therapy suggested that the fear was more than likely to be to do with something that had happened to her in the past. She understood and accepted the principle I was describing and consented to proceed for five minutes. During the session she remembered that she had been into hospital as a little girl aged 5 or so to have her tonsils out along with other minor ear, nose and throat procedure. She had had a 'pre-op' injection and recalled being "immediately catapulted into the feeling of being panic stricken" (not seeming to go through anxious, scared, frightened, terrified and petrified as the rest of us might do on an ascending scale!). She also thought she might die – go to sleep with the injection and not wake up!

Along with all that were feelings of being alone and parental betrayal – her mother had let her be in this frightening place and she was being hurt! She felt trapped on the operating table also (not unreasonably!). As well as all that she thought she was going mad and 'losing her marbles' as both parents and doctors had reassured her that this procedure was for her own good and she would feel much better after it! She was also shocked at the strength of her feelings.

We worked Mnemodynamically. Obviously she was sitting there with me so it was relatively easy for her to reassure her younger self, in complete honesty that she had survived the experience of the operation and was there to tell the tale! She then was able to remove the feelings from her younger self.

After that we did more levels and stages of intervention. She was able to validate herself, and tell herself that the feelings she had as a small child were valid enough. She then was able to help normalise herself as I guided her to tell herself that it was not just her, anybody in similar circumstances, older or younger, male or female, and even really grown up, people could feel give or take a bit the same! She went and took the little girl out of her 'trap' and brought her to the present day where she was safe.

She then treated the little girl for shock, giving her hot sweet tea and wrapping her up in something warm. She was able to listen to herself and 'hold' the situation whilst the younger version of herself worked through the feelings getting herself, thoughts and feelings into some kind of order. She then told the little girl that it had not been mummy and daddy's intention to cause her any grief – far from it – and I got her to tell the little girl "Mummy and Daddy love you, and that goes on forever and ever and NOTHING can EVER alter that". This jewel was given to me by Dr. Don W. Ebrahim of Coventry who was a great contributor to my training. He used this phrase as a General Practitioner in his Saturday Morning's Childrens' clinics which I was fortunate to attend once, as well as with individual clients.

She sent her own resources back to the little girl after that leaving her "happy and smiling". I suggested that she took the little girl to a place she liked to lighten up a bit. She chose to take the little girl to the park where she helped her to swing. I asked her to "Let the little girl swing and swing and swing and swing and swing and swing and swing and swing until her heart is COMPLETELY content and her body is 'plumb tuckered out' as they would say in American movies". She indicated when she had done this. I suggested that she put the little girl on her knee in my chair where she was and let the child fall asleep.

Martha indicated that she had done this. She then had a choice to make. She could either send the little girl back into the picture if she wished, but my preferred choice would be that she allowed the child to soak into herself where she, the grown op Martha, could keep giving her a reassuring squeeze and checking that she was alright. She opted to keep the little girl and plopped her inside her grown-up self. When she opened her eyes we talked about the experience and the early operation. She consciously recalled "feeling total panic" but hadn't connected that feeling with the later fear of needles. She spoke also how her fear had limited her life. She did not partake in sport for example "just in case I get hurt" ... She left the session smiling and happy and we agreed to meet in a couple of weeks after her final pre-operative discrepancy measurement.

Many years later I had a lovely letter from her. She had given birth to a little boy, Thomas and was thrilled to bits. She said "I think of you often and especially when I look at Thomas. With my needle phobia I would have not been able to consider the possibility of falling pregnant. I could not be happier".

Irritable Bowel Syndrome (IBS)

Let us take the for instance of a patient with irritable bowel syndrome (IBS). Janet was in her sixties and had had this condition for as long as she could remember. Much evidence about hypnosis says that it is useful in a case like this and that by teaching somebody to be more calm and relaxed, results can be very beneficial. By teaching somebody to relax and feel their gut calming down, a large percentage of people can be helped. It seemed to me however, that things had happened to Janet which needed a little bit more attention. What had happened to her was a long long time ago!

I used the Mnemodynamic Therapy, asking her to remember a time when things had happened to her in the past which had been difficult. She took herself to a time when aged four and a half she had to go into hospital to have an adenoids operation. Janet came from a loving home with good stable parents and had never been away from home before. She remembered the nurse standing at the other side of the ward, combing her long black hair. Janet wanted to go to the toilet. She did her best to attract the nurse's attention who came over and told her off for making a fuss, didn't listen to her and didn't let this tiny girl say what it was she wanted. Inevitably little Janet dirtied herself. She was filled with horror, guilt, shame, embarrassment, anxiety, resentment and confusion.

During our session it was important that Janet was able to resolve those feelings and get them into a grown up body and mind to process. We proceeded as set out above. Janet went along with me excellently and over the next three or four visits sorted out other difficulties. Within a short period of time she was able to lead as normal a life as anyone else. Even visits to the supermarket beforehand had been limited by her constant worry as to where the next toilet was, let alone the normal social life she had longed for. Being a pianist and singer, she sung in the local town choir and wanted to accompany people for local festivals. During the past she had had to limit herself, never being able to depend on herself for the required number of minutes that these musical activities would take.

Whilst we are growing up, particularly before the age of ten (according to Piaget), we have little or no ability to rationalise. Our experience is such that we cannot process things that happen to us that are particularly difficult. As you know, the body shuts off the feelings which happen at times like this, to protect us. We can find ourselves as grown ups over-reacting to different stimuli and situations. Our minds know we are over reacting but at a feeling level we seem to be able to do very little about it. Someone who has an anxiety state may know that it is ridiculous to be frightened of, say, going out but, maybe gripped by such feelings that stepping over the threshold cause panic. When there is conflict between the intellect and things at a feeling level these underlying issues should be resolved.

Once these issues have been resolved then the traditional hypnotic session of helping the client/patient be more calm and relaxed by using direct suggestion into the unconscious mind, and for them to be able to cope with life in a better and more efficient fashion may be given with great benefit.

Loss of libido

The case of Ann is not unusual as far as the presenting symptoms goes in that she came to me feeling that she wasn't really enjoying her sex life. From the waist down she told me her body felt "black". Mid forties and with two grown up children and one teenager, long since divorced, she lived with a partner pretty happily in Scotland. What was unusual about her case was the strength of the reaction she had when using my more than gentle Mnemodynamic Therapy technique.

I asked Ann to remember back to a time when something happened to her as a younger person that was difficult to handle. It took her only a second or two to remember a time when she was eleven years old. She was asleep in bed with her two younger brothers; two older children were meant to be looking after them downstairs. Mother, an alcoholic, and father had gone for a drink. Unbeknown to Ann, their two caretakers downstairs had found a bottle of alcohol, drunk it and passed out. The three remaining children upstairs were unprotected.

Ann awoke in the dark with a man's hands around her throat. The only thing she could do was breathe and gurgle. He was kneeling on her middle and groping her private parts. She couldn't understand why the older children downstairs did not hear the struggle and come up to rescue her. Her arms were free and she woke her brothers making them understand she needed a knife. The eldest little brother rose and got her a knife. She stabbed the man, though it was not a serious injury, and he ran away. These small children knew they had to have evidence to prove their story. The man had left his slipper, and they hid it by unscrewing the back of the radio and putting it in there. Ann then sat on the bed with her two little brothers reading them stories until her parents returned some time later.

The story seemed far-fetched but it was not. The man, a local that she knew, was given a long prison term for attempted murder and ever since that time Ann felt from the waist down fairly dead and certainly black. During our session she was able to heal her feelings which had been locked inside, and comfort this smaller child. After that one session a month or so later she reported back that she was at five out of ten on our scale of measurement. She had also lost a stone in weight going from a size 18 in clothes to a 14.

The next time Ann and I met her session was much gentler. She recalled giving birth to her eldest daughter and was pregnant with her son when her husband came in and told her he was in love with someone else. This was real love, he said, and not the brotherly love he had felt for her, Ann. He left her that night and she didn't see him until after her son was born. She felt rejected, unloved, unlovable, resentful and many other emotions. These emotions and feelings she healed, and to her insides, she brought light and rainbows.

The last time we spoke, Ann was feeling much better about everything. She told me that she had been going to break up with the man with whom she was living, but that she had changed her mind and herself. She was now able to feel sexually and her changing herself had enabled her partner to change himself too. They were both enjoying her new found feeling and intimacy so much more. Ann and I plan to meet again though I know that she has managed to heal most of these earlier difficulties.

CHAPTER 5: Variations on a Theme

Content free

With all methods of psychotherapy, it is vital that the client learns to trust the therapist as soon as is possible. We ask our clients to bare their souls and offer us the most intimate of details. It is only on the odd occasion that the client has not been able to disclose what has been going on in the image that they have found for themselves.

The way I relate to the client through the Mnemodynamic process is to put myself in the client's shoes, both the adult at the appointment date as they are with me in the room and also the younger version of themselves 'out there'.

To do this when one does not have a younger scenario to relate to is difficult from the therapist point of view. Depending on who the client is and what problem they have disclosed during the discussion when they entered the room may assist you.

Think to yourself … why would they not disclose? They are possibly embarrassed by what has come up for them. You will have to work content free. You can do only your best before the end of the Mnemodynamic session when you and the client with you in the room unpick why the non-disclosure was so.

Listening to the client disclosure as a narrative

I was watching a trainee do a session with a client in practice. The trainee listened to the client disclose a long tale of a scenario. It was fast and complex. At the end the student therapist asked the client "what did the little girl feel"? It was an entirely inappropriate question. The client had already given the student therapist about 8 feeling words, all missed because the trainee therapist was busy listening to the story! If they had noted SOME at least of the feeling words in the narrative, then at least they would have had a start to go to the client and reflectively check for depth of feeling.

Regarding the narrative, if the client description is fast, it is vital that you write down every **feeling** word that is included and work through them in the format already given even though, usually, too many feeling words do not get stated at this point.

Sergeant Pepper's Lonely Hearts Club Band

Sometimes there can be a huge patch of time where a similar type of incident happens time and time again. The client will usually have disclosed that type of scenario to you during the therapeutic interview.

I have been known to say the following during the therapeutic session:-

> "When you were at school, did you ever do a collage or montage of cut-out magazine prints? Do you remember the Beatles red album "Sergeant Pepper's Lonely Hearts Club Band"?

Most will tell you that they do remember, or can picture this. I would then suggest the following

> "Please will you visualise, out here (motioning to the place) all the little Johns from 6 to 13 out here, all linked by that feeling of being bullied by father?" (or whatever the disclosure had been)

Most will consent to do this, and then, several years' worth of difficulties can be resolved at the same session. It really does work!

Hypnotic Time Distortion

Shelly was both delightful and bright. Self-employed as an accountant, she was obviously doing materially well with a nice house and beautiful car. At 39 she had everything she would want apart from a husband and possibly a child.

Things had been difficult for her particularly early on in her life. At 6 or 7 mum had left dad after the mother's affair. Mum took her two children with her. They must have returned to the family home as Shelly's memories were of constant arguments.

When she was 14 mum had another affair, with Walter and announced that her and dad were splitting. Dad had come into Shelly's bedroom crying. Shelly was "really upset" but at the same time felt that she had "no sanctuary". At 15, Shelly's much-loved father died of a heart attack aged 44. "Mum 'went away' from us. She was very controlling".

At 16 or 17 Ken moved in as step-father. He had a son Adam who was aged 5 or 6. "Mum wouldn't speak to him – or us". "I didn't get on with him (Ken) at all".

At the first Mnemodynamic session Shelly went back to being 10 years old. Mum had promised to take Shelly to the pictures. Shelly seemed to have transgressed in some way though she knew not what she'd done and mum wouldn't take her. She begged and apologised though she never knew what for but 'twas all to no avail. She lay in bed crying. Her feelings to do with all this were "upset, devastated, punished, guilty, trapped, unacknowledged, unaccepted, helpless, powerless, unloved and unlovable". We resolved this leaving the youngster "happier".

When I reflected back *"It sounds as if she's still a bit sad"* Shelly found her second layer "sad, not even angry, weak, helpless and drained". She left herself fine at the end, hugging the little girl then choosing to take the ten year old "to rescuers". Something must have been resolved as she came back at 4 out of 10 better.

At the next session Shelly remembered back to being 15 on the day her father died. Mum was in the car distressed. This session was done with three layers of feeling words:-

1. "Helpless, powerless, trapped, upset, shocked, numb, mum's selfish, bit of resentment and confusion" which she left "calmer" after all the stages had been gone through.

2. Asking what was left, or words to that effect, she said "Lonely, alone, unsupported". At my prompting, she reminded herself that she survived and also that mum's behaviour was a lot about mum and nothing about her, also throwing in the cognitive challenge that mum's behaviour was more about neglect than wanting to harm with malice aforethought. She then took the feelings off the youngster. She left the younger girl with "not as much pain … stronger".

3. When I asked what the feelings were she said "Pain, hurt and bereaved". Of course we validated and normalised. She soothed the younger girl's pain. I decided though that she really needed more self-indulgence with the little girl than we had time for so my

verbalisation was as follows: *"Tell her you are... 'I'm from time future ... you and I are one ... I will always watch over you and make sure nothing happens to you ... and I LOVE you. Tell it her until she knows it down to the middle of her bones... Give her **time** to grieve also. This can take as long as you need in the time frame that you are in. In our time now (date) you need only take a minute or two. Tell me when you have finished".*

She left herself "better and more able to cope". Not perfect of course, but so, so much better.

Perfect?

Talking about perfect though, a colleague Dr Fran Renwick used to say "There's no such thing as the perfect Mnemodynamic session". I don't know so much. One can certainly strive for it!

Another thing she used to say, which would be echoed in the "Learning Stair" shown earlier was that when people first mastered Mnemodynamic Therapy the therapist approach had to be very cognitive - the therapist had to keep all their wits about them to proceed to a successful conclusion. As fluency and confidence grew, she purported, the working position inside the therapist altered from being head centred to becoming heart centred. It was then, she said, that works of genius did occur....

Someone who can't visualise

John came to see me at the end of 1997 wearing his Wellington boots. He killed chickens for a living at a chicken producing farm in the next village to us. He had frightened himself. Getting paid on a Friday night he would go to the local pub and get pretty well oiled with his mates. This was OK to himself HOWEVER he had found himself getting angry and violent under the influence of alcohol and he was aware of hitting someone for the last three Fridays. Last Friday was worse though. On Saturday morning he had woken up in a police cell!

He was a challenge in that he was adamant that he could not visualise. Of course, he didn't actually have to see pictures. The important part of the process, according to the Freudian theory, you will remember, is to relive with feeling.

64

Variations on a Theme

Penny Moon, a practitioner in Merseyside, had been part of the Early Years Behaviour Team, and of late has been making a chain of funded "Quiet Places" (QP™) throughout regional schools for pupils, parents and teachers. She has been a friend and trainer on the Centre Training School courses for many years. A phrase I picked up from her many years ago seems very simple - but in terms of the NLP model, opens up the chosen sensory operational mode of the client - "If you can't visualise, make sense of it in any way you can". I certainly had no boundaries, and that, combined with John's chosen way of working enabled him to complete the process.

He recalled firstly, the time when aged six, he was walking on a track through nettles behind his house with some friends. His friend was angry about something, very angry indeed, and pushed John into the nettles. As I reflectively listened him, he recalled only a few feelings; the stinging of the nettles, sympathy (incredibly for a six year old) of his very angry friend, and confusion (not surprisingly) as to why he had been pushed in the nettles. He worked in the ways described above with this scene, and left himself feeling "OK enough, undoubtedly". John the adult client in the room with me at the end of this was feeling "That a weight has been taken off my shoulders".

The part for me that was the most special was his comments with regard to his process. "I'm not actually seeing it - well I am in my own touchy-feely kind of way. I almost become part of the moment".

When John returned for his second session, he measured himself as being four or five out of ten on our agreed scale of improvement. He came one more time when we used the NLP techniques of sub-modalities, along with my reflective listening and re-framing. At the next session, he reported being five or six out of ten on the scale we were measuring. For me this was brilliant! I always wanted Mnemodynamic therapy to be universally available – and especially for the adult in the wellies!

PART 2

Some concepts that will be used in your Mnemodynamic Therapy session

Good Enough

There are many styles apparent in the way people live their lives. Many people are brought up, as I was, trying to be "good" at everything. It can be most helpful to move away from that attitude. There are risks inherent in trying to be "good" all the time which have risks and implications in the way we live.

Dr Donald Winnicott, who lived from 1924 to 1971 was a paediatrician and child psychoanalyst. He introduced the concept of a "good enough" parent into psychology (in Shapiro [1998]), working in this field for forty years. His theoretical writings emphasized empathy, imagination, and, in the words of philosopher Martha Nussbaum, a proponent of his work, "the highly particular transactions that constitute love between two imperfect people." A prime example of this is his ideal of the "good-enough mother," the imperfectly attentive mother who does a better job than the "perfect" one who risks stifling her child's development as a separate being. You will find a fuller account of him in Appendix 16 in Part 3.

Whilst we change our roles as things around us change, there are questions that each one of us must come to terms with in our own ways.

Think back in your life to what some of the commonly held views of what a good person, or parent, say, should be like? How do you think some people - professionals, neighbours, older people – may judge others as workers, or parents? Did you feel judged, for example?

What expectations do you have of yourself at work? Are your expectations realistic?

What pressures if any do you feel under from other people on how you are as a person? How do you feel about such pressures and what effect do they have on how you behave at work?

If you were freed from any expectations or pressure to be perfect, what sort of person would you like to be? How would you behave at work and in the family? If you changed, in what ways might you be different from how you are now?

What are the roles or jobs we need to take on as workers, and how do you think these roles change as the job changes? Are there, perhaps, roles that you are still taking on even though people around you could now take more responsibility for themselves?

Of course society has changed over the decades. It is no longer "authoritarian", nor "permissive". We need to think what our expectations of ourselves as workers and in the family actually are. What, for example are society's pressures on us? We all know that there are a lot of social pressures on people to achieve. Family, friends, neighbours, doctors & teachers play their part by questioning us as parents and people. We are asked what stages we are at in our lives, particularly concerning our children; what stages our children have reached and, of course, how they are behaving.

As a result, it is easy to see external things as reflecting our competence as people. We can be judgemental of ourselves. This can lead us to behave in uncharacteristic ways at work, and in our families to direct the children so that they "turn out right" to the point of robbing them of responsibility for themselves. This behaviour as co-workers and parents is well intentioned and yet it holds many risks:-

- Doing everything for others prevents them from learning to do things for themselves, and makes us feel exhausted.

- Protecting others prevents them from learning from their own experiences.

- Taking responsibility for others prevents them from developing their self-confidence.

- Controlling our children all the time breeds rebellion & discourages initiative.

- Feeling sorry for others leads them to feel inadequate & at worst self-pitying.

Examples of more useful behaviours:-

- Allow our co-workers to make mistakes. Allow children to climb up on fences and gates whilst we trust their sense of balance and knowledge of their own limits.

Some Concepts that will be used

- Ask what people want to do in different situations, instead of thinking that we need to control everything.

- Giving responsibility to people for their own "territories" of desk, clothes and ideas amongst other things.

- Not throwing ourselves into other people's upsets, with us rushing off to make everything "all right".

- You might be thinking "yes but my children continue to expect me to do everything for them". That is a natural enough argument when those around us have never known it any other way! At birth we start doing 'everything' for our children of course because they are 100% dependant and the 'everything' just gets bigger and bigger; we slowly begin to resent it, and yet how many people ever actually re-negotiate the unwritten agreement when their children reach 2, 5, 10 and so on. Maybe we could renegotiate every year!

A more useful alternative is to find the courage not to be perfect and not to have to be seen by others to be a "good" worker, or parent, but to be responsible for being ourselves at work, and at home, helping our children to grow in a way that takes in both the individual needs of the child and the world around us.

The "good enough" person:-

1. Encourages people around them to take their own decisions; (this can start with small things, like what to wear; this shows respect for the other person to make decisions and have opinions).

2. Knows that co-workers, they and their families can and will make mistakes … (milk spilled by a child or something dropped and broken). Perhaps you could see this as an accident and not deliberate, and enlist the child's help to clean up.

3. Believes in and respects their colleagues and family members.

4. Lets people do things for themselves to encourage the development of their independence.

5. Lets them do things for themselves that they are capable of doing and show enthusiasm to do. (If the job is not perfect the first time round, it

is much more likely to be with practice. This again shows our faith and trust in them and thus encourages them).

6. Allows people around them to learn from the consequences of their own actions and inactions.

7. Accepts people's feelings and helps them to express them safely.

8. For example:-

> "I'm tired." – The usual reply would be: "No, you're not, you've just had a nap".

> It is more useful to say: 'You feel tired."

If child cries when she hurts herself; usual reply: "Don't be silly, it's not so bad."

> More useful to say: "It must really hurt."

ALL THE ABOVE shows people around us that we respect them and their feelings, and have respect, trust and faith in them to make decisions and take responsibility for aspects of their own lives.

A common role to play at home and work is that of benevolent tyrant. This approach sees a more relevant role as that of "Nurturing Guide", helping people around us to grow, helping them to develop their sense of self worth as human beings, and to develop their self-esteem. Some people are not clear about the concept of self-esteem, relating it to selfishness and conceit.

One of our basic concepts is to give children and adults more and more responsibility as and when they are capable, to solve their own problems with our help if needed, make their own decisions and take us into account.

Another major aspect of being a "good enough" person (and parent) is realising that to be able to do the best for people around us, we have to be doing the best for ourselves as well. Offer the "Full Cup Theory" here, i.e. if our cup is empty we have nothing to offer anyone. Tell people that this is one topic we will particularly be looking at later.

Some Concepts that will be used

I so often give this exercise "good enough" to clients for homework after starting it off during a session. I have known this exercise alone change someone's life! It aims to help people validate themselves as being good enough. Start out on a clean piece of paper:-

> "I am a good enough""...   (client) and help people get started
>   on their lists.
>
> I am a good enough...
>
> I am a good enough ...

If you can provide pretty postcards for people to write their "good enough" lists on, then so much the better.

Sometimes things might get in the way of your putting helping skills into practise at work and at home. We can explore what people can do to have more conscious choice about how to react.

Think for yourself about the sort of things you think could get in the way of listening to people in your own practices, at work in general, and with members of your family. It may be good to acknowledge any worries you might have and begin to think about what you could do to change what you fear might happen. Perhaps also there is something you could do differently.

People could begin to break out of their un-useful patterns of reacting with others. We do not have to be perfect. It isn't possible to listen usefully all the time just as it isn't possible or appropriate to be democratic all the time. We need to practise even as we go easy on ourselves for not doing everything just how we would like to.

Sometimes, with practice, we can avoid some of these less useful things happening. Sometimes we aren't always helpful to ourselves in the ways we try to learn. It can take ages and ages to do things differently without thinking. The single most important thing for us to do is to be gentle on ourselves as we try out new ideas, and learn from the less successful times as well as the successful ones.

It is useful to look at the learning stair here to illustrate the stages we all go through in learning a new set of skills.

The Learning Stair

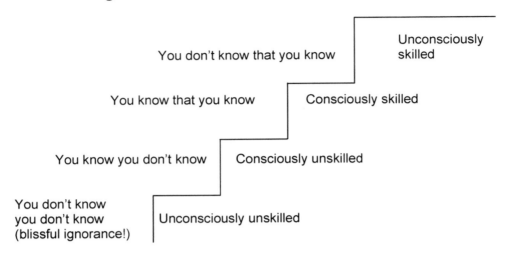

Starting from the bottom and not knowing that we you don't know (blissful or not so blissful ignorance!), the diagram moves through knowing that we don't know to getting a reasonable grasp of the idea and doing it sometimes, (that is knowing we know) through to the skill eventually all being second nature so that we forget we know!

When people haven't even heard of these ideas they are on the very bottom of the stair. Once they are introduced to it, they get to level two and it is quite inevitable at this stage that they are going to feel phoney about practising. Knowing that you do know and being consciously skilled can also be difficult at times until the skill becomes second nature. The middle two steps are the most uncomfortable though it is all worth it in the end!

Needs behind behaviour

As an introduction to the concept of meeting needs, it may be an idea to do a simple exercise. On a piece of paper, write down the answer to the following:-

(i) What do you want? And then afterwards

(ii) What will that do for you?

Some Concepts that will be used

Work through this process until you get to what appears to be the bottom line. This exercise can certainly raise awareness of how much we are looking after ourselves by doing the things we enjoy.

Somewhere in here though, is the distinction between needs and wants. Think. What do we mean by needs? I would propose that a need is equal to a necessary condition for healthy life. What, then, is the difference between a need and a want?

A want is perhaps the way we have chosen, perhaps unconsciously to satisfy a need. For example:-

- I need reliable transport; I want a new car or a yearly bus pass etc.

- I need love; I want a monogamous relationship, or I want a baby etc.

- I need to feel I belong and am part of the crowd; I want to dress fashionably, or

- I want to join a group like a church, a sports group etc.

By posing the question to yourself "What will that do for you?" or "What will that satisfy?" we can get below the want level and begin to find the need level underneath. Continue posing the question to yourself person until you have reached what feels like the bottom line. For example:-

- I need to get some qualifications. Q: *"What will that do for you?"*

- It will mean I can get a job. Q: *"What will that do for you?"*

- I will be able to earn and contribute to the family finances. Q: *"What will that do for you?"*

- I will feel more equal in my relationship with my partner. *Q: "What will that do for you?"*

- I will feel powerful and a person in my own right.

- This is a very useful process to go through. Having started with one solution, a quite different need has been uncovered at the bottom.

There are MANY ways to satisfy that need. Even if you (or the person concerned) still goes on with their original plan, they are at least much more aware of why they want to do it. Sometimes, because of the choices open to us at the time, we may have chosen a way to satisfy a need that could in fact be better met another way. Sometimes choices we made don't turn out the way we thought and hoped they would. Being aware of the need allows US to choose the most useful and fulfilling path. Many readers and clients too may get their own needs met. If they do, that's brilliant for them!

It is a good idea to look HOLISTICALLY, i.e. in broad categories e.g. - physical, emotional, intellectual, social and spiritual dimensions at the question of needs. This can enable us to make changes to satisfy those areas that weren't getting much attention.

It may be possible, of course, to brainstorm with your clients, other ways to satisfy that same need or to find some more ways to nurture ourselves. Get the client to make a commitment to make some changes.

There are undoubtedly needs that underlie all behaviour. This is further explored in Appendix 3. It can be helpful with your client to consider what the common basic needs are that underlie all behaviour. It can also be useful to make the point that all people have the full right to meet their needs, children just as much as adults. You may like to remember what it was like not to be allowed to meet your needs when you were a child or even as an adult.

Perhaps you can encourage your client to think of some of the common needs people have that lead them to behave in the ways they do. You may also think about what are some of the ways that people around you behave to meet these sorts of basic needs. The main basic needs are listed here:

- **PHYSIOLOGICAL NEEDS** food, drink, sleep, shelter, warmth etc.

- **SAFETY NEEDS** stability, protection, routine, economic security, structure.

- **BELONGINGNESS NEEDS** affection, family needs, intimacy & sex, friendship & social networks.

- **ESTEEM NEEDS** the need for recognition & acceptance, a sense of competency & achievement.

- **SELF ACTUALISATION NEEDS** the creation of love & beauty, the search for truth & understanding, personal growth, striving for equality and justice.

As far as conversation in life in general goes, sometimes we think we are saying what we mean and others don't believe us. Children in particular are very good at reading double messages. They continue to push us until we become congruent or straight. You may like to think what your children do to get you to send straight messages, or even what you did yourself as a youngster.

Here are some examples:-

- Child asking for sweets over and over again even as mother says "no". Part of mother means it and part of her doesn't - maybe she remembers what it was like to be a small child - so the child presses until finally mother loses her patience and says "No" very firmly.

- Mother asks child to stop jumping on the chairs - as an aside whilst talking to a friend. Child takes no notice until mother gets stops her conversation and turns forcefully to child and repeats it dearly and firmly.

If you do not want your child to have something, be firm and say so. Children as well as adults need limits. Be clear in your mind as to what **you** think and communicate that with conviction and love to the other.

You also might like to consider what effect your child's unacceptable behaviour has on you? Think also what was it was like when you were not allowed to do the things you had to do to satisfy your own needs. Here it is important to remember that we don't necessarily have to understand the underlying need. Just acknowledging that it exists will help us bring about changes in the behaviour.

Problem Ownership

To introduce the concept of PROBLEM OWNERSHIP so that we know which skill to use: to help people; to help ourselves get our own needs met;
- To combine those skills together when there is a shared problem.

- To explore ways to cope usefully with strong emotions that are triggered when we are faced with problems.

- To introduce the basic criteria for being an effective helper.

- To develop basic listening skills: matching, paying attention, silence.

- To raise awareness of our non-verbal communication.

- To develop further listening skills; simple acknowledgements, door openers, open ended questions as well as acknowledging feelings.

Let us consider the concept of problem ownership. It can be helpful to begin the process of seeing that getting emotionally caught up in others' problems is not the most useful thing to do.

Problem ownership is one of the most crucial concepts of your work with clients. Once you have integrated this, you have a way of deciding whose needs need meeting first - the other person's or yours, thus minimising the risk of becoming so emotionally involved in the other person's problem that you cannot be of any real use.

In choosing what to do in situations where we or others get upset, it is easiest if we are first clear about who owns the problem.

Ask yourself the following questions: -

- When you are the only one upset by something that is happening or has happened, who owns the problem?

- When someone at work is the only one upset by something, now who owns the problem?

- When something happens at work to someone that upsets a boss and you, how do you work out who owns the problem?

If the other person owns the problem, is the situation helped by you getting upset? If you usually would have got upset, what can we do to avoid this? It may be helpful to you to do the following:-

- Ask yourself the question "Whose problem is it"?

Some Concepts that will be used

- Also ask yourself "What's going on here"?

- Say to yourself: "Stop, look and listen.

- Breathe out and drop your shoulders.

- Acknowledge your own feelings.

- State to yourself "I'm feeling really upset"; then perhaps ask: "Are those feelings appropriate right now"?

It may be useful to consider the three relevant points below:-

1) Emotionally involved versus personally involved.

Being emotionally involved usually means taking on the problem and making it our own. This is not the most helpful way to respond to people if they are experiencing a difficulty. It is possible to be personally involved and yet remain detached emotionally. Of course, it does not mean you have to be cold and callous!

2) Importance of leaving responsibility with the other to solve the problem, with our help.

This encourages the other, even a child, to grow emotionally. It also encourages their development as self responsible people. It also requires our **TRUST** that the other person has the intelligence and ability to solve their problem.

Often we weren't trusted as children and this may make it very difficult to trust other people now. Remember how you felt when you were not trusted to do something you knew you could - how nice it would have been to be trusted more!

Children's dependence on adults varies as they grow of course, i.e. at 0 years old they are 100% dependent and at 18 years old maybe 0%. Giving them responsibility for aspects of their own lives has to be considered in line with their individual rate of development.

3) Examples: -

Do your best to think of some for-instances to illustrate fully this point without getting into too many more emotionally charged examples.

For each situation ask yourself the following questions -

Whose problem is it?

Whose needs need meeting first?

As stated earlier, we have used examples around children to give you quick and simple ones. You will be able to apply these principles to a host of adult or colleague examples of course.

- Your child comes home from school upset about a friends behaviour.

- Your child is playing in front of the T.V. getting in the way of your watching.

- You are worried because your child complains about being bullied at school.

- You are anxious because your child is late home from a friend's house.

- You feel bad when your older child teases the younger one to the point that he gets upset.

- Your child doesn't want to eat what you prepared for her after agreeing to it.

- Your child doesn't want to get dressed when you want to go out

- Your child squeezes another child very hard while both mothers are there.

You may like to do this short visualisation for yourself:-

Make yourself comfortable ... take a big breath and let it out ... Take a few moments to move forward in time into the near future and think of yourself being at work and in your family with the new awareness and understanding that you have gained so far. Be aware of realising that whatever people around you are doing they are doing to meet some valid need .... it is only the way they have chosen to meet it that is unacceptable see yourself staying out of the problem so that you really can help people around you in the most useful way ... I don't know which of the ways we've talked about is the most appropriate way for you ... Perhaps you take a big breath let it out and drop your shoulders, perhaps you ask yourself the question: WHOSE PROBLEM IS IT? .. and take the time you need to listen for the answer. You can use as long as you wish in your mind's time, though in real time this will take only a few seconds.... Feel the good feelings you have as you realise that you have more understanding now of what lies behind your children's behaviour and how to sort out who owns the problem .... you no longer have to solve everything for them.

Enjoy those feelings and if there is anything you need to be able to act as you would want to, bring the knowledge of what it is back here with you.

PART 3

Diagrammatic representation of the Mnemodynamic process for your note-taking

Theoretical Mnemodynamic sessions

Below are two theoretical Mnemodynamic sessions. I have put them in this book at this point to help you become more fluent with reflecting back the underlying feelings and to help you become more fluent in writing down a running record of the technique.

I suggest that one at a time you read the short background to the cases below with the scenario. Imagine yourself then in the situation as the therapist.

Next, write on your pads your 'guesses' of what the client would be feeling. It would be good if you got some of the main points I got. The next step would be for you to repeat this process in terms of how you would do the 'Anchoring' part of the process.

You might like to practice 'lifting off' a feeling each using the script at the back of the book parrot fashion, just for the experience. When you have completed this, you can repeat this process with the next column – reframing, cognition and so on. Then repeat this process with re-resourcing. See how your total 'pattern' of responses matches the original case.

Case 1: John Smith, aged 46

John had been on the Peace of Mind ™ course at Liverpool John Moore's University a few years ago and (apparently) I had partnered him when people were pairing up. He had made some disclosure to me, felt quite good about it, and had saved that in his mind until making the decision to come for a session. As the eldest of the family he has six siblings: Angela (2 years younger), Phillip (4 years younger), Tony (6 years younger), plus Julie and Christopher (twins 8 years younger). He used to get "very, very upset" about the way his parents were: untutored and "should never have had children".

He is now 46, happily married to Margaret with a daughter Ebony 21 who is studying Psychology at Liverpool University and a son James, 17 who is studying computer graphics and IT. John has a degree in music and is a therapist. He told me at the initial professional session that he has a "child's ego state". When something goes wrong, he blames himself, is "pathetic" and tearful. Whilst working in a local psychiatric/prison hospital he was "psychologically bullied". He eventually "shoved" the bully then resigned. His outcome was that he wanted rid of these feelings.

John, 46.   (Client words in *italics*)

Remembering aged 16. Left home and went to board and lodgings. 'Made that small step away'.

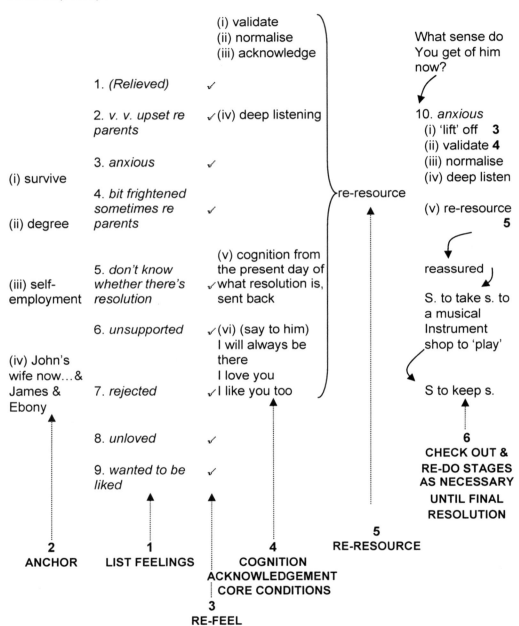

(i) validate
(ii) normalise
(iii) acknowledge

What sense do
You get of him
now?

1. *(Relieved)* ✓

2. *v. v. upset re parents* ✓ (iv) deep listening

10. *anxious*
(i) 'lift' off **3**
(ii) validate **4**
(iii) normalise
(iv) deep listen

3. *anxious* ✓

(i) survive

4. *bit frightened sometimes re parents* ✓

(ii) degree

›re-resource

(v) re-resource
                5

(v) cognition from the present day of what resolution is, sent back

5. *don't know whether there's resolution* ✓

(iii) self-employment

reassured

S. to take s. to a musical Instrument shop to 'play'

6. *unsupported* ✓ (vi) (say to him) I will always be there I love you

(iv) John's wife now...& James & Ebony

7. *rejected* ✓ I like you too

S to keep s.

8. *unloved* ✓

9. *wanted to be liked* ✓

6
CHECK OUT &
RE-DO STAGES
AS NECESSARY
UNTIL FINAL
RESOLUTION

2
ANCHOR

1
LIST FEELINGS

4
COGNITION
ACKNOWLEDGEMENT
CORE CONDITIONS

5
RE-RESOURCE

3
RE-FEEL

Case 2: Chrissie Evans 50

Chrissie is 50 and has been married to Kevin for 25 years. She says that he is neither demonstrative nor romantic. He plays golf weekly. She works at the local government offices. Always neat and smart, she is profoundly, though not totally, deaf.

She has a daughter, Jane, now 18, who was conceived after fertility treatment. Chrissie and Kevin 'tried for a long time' to get Jane. Chrissie still resents Kevin's attitude as she had to persuade him to 'get on with it' rather a lot during this time, so desperate to conceive was she. Aged 18 now, Jane has just gone to University.

Chrissie is the oldest of four siblings, Angela (18 months younger), Debbie 6 years younger and Mike at 15 years younger. She did not have a good relationship with her father who she said was 'obsessive' and also very very strict.

The family had a sweet shop in the town, and often after school, Chrissie would work in there after school, starting homework at 9pm when the shop closed. She said "I was more parent-fearing than god-fearing".

When she was 23, dad left to live with another woman. Mum died of cancer when Chrissie was 29.

She now feels 'down and depressed' and has been on anti-depressants for 10 years. She is 'deeply lonely' and resents Kevin.

The session below was our second session, 1st Mnemodynamic. She came back a week later scoring 4 or 5 out of 10 and 'not as irritated by Kevin'. More hopeful'.

Chrissie, 50.   *(Client words in italics)*

Remembering aged 11 or 12. At Secondary school. Very aware of having a hearing aid.

(i) validate
(ii) normalise
(iii) acknowledge

What sense do you get of her now?

not quite believing
lighter hearted & hopeful
Not convinced

  (i) validate
  (ii) normalise } **R**

1. *on edge* ✓

2. *anticipation* ✓

3. *self-conscious* ✓

4. *wants to be normal* ✓

5. *anxious* ✓

Kevin   6. *unfashionable* ✓ nice clothes now, snazzy dresser

Jane   7. *different* ✓

8. *worried re future*   ✓ Remind of Kevin & Jenny

re-resource

9. *bit heavy hearted* ✓
10. *doubt* ✓

more bucked up
***not** out of step with*
society

again, send back your resources to her. Tell her you love her – and thank her.

Take her somewhere nice
beach

let her play and play and play and play and play – until her heart is content … and her body is tired out – and tell me when you have her like that …You have a choice here. You can let her go back to the picture, or, if you like, you can keep her … let her soak inside you … I know she will fit … and tell me when you have got her safe …

Whatever it is on the screen out here, FF to the present day (be specific)

Let the picture fade, let the screen fade. OPEN YOUR EYES.

2	**1**	**3**	**4**	**5**	**6**
ANCHOR	LIST FEELINGS	RE-FEEL	COGNITIVE REFRAME etc	RE-RESOURCE	CHECK OUT & FIX UNTIL OK

APPENDICES

Appendix 1

FEELINGS

Feelings

Feelings can be uncomfortable. This is true of the feelings we have ourselves as well as the ones other people show us. We often find feelings difficult to cope with because we were not allowed to show them when we were little. Keeping feelings locked away is not healthy - it is much better to be able to show them in ways that don't hurt others. It is also often valuable to help others express their feelings too - especially those closest to us, like our families.

Feeling good about ourselves

We can't help anyone else feel good about themselves if we don't feel good about ourselves. We need to like who we are and what we do.

We can help ourselves by making sure that we do things we enjoy and that make us feel good. Those close to us can also do nice things for us and help us, but we can't expect them to mind read, so telling them what we like and want is important.

Another way we can improve the way we think about ourselves is by replacing the voice in our heads that tells us off with a voice that says encouraging things, and by imagining ourselves strong and competent.

> *"I never even used to know what was going on inside me physically! I would keep working around the house or rushing around after the family until I dropped. All those little warning signs other people get, like tiredness, headaches, aching joints or muscles - I'd never feel them. Then suddenly my body would collapse in a heap and the doctor would come and announce I'd got some dreaded bug and had to stay in bed for days. I'm sure it all started as a child when I was always told to ignore my feelings and aches and pains and was shouted at for mentioning them".*

We never grow up

Part of making sure we feel good about ourselves is looking after the child that is always inside us. However grown up we may be, there is always a young part somewhere inside that needs to be loved and to come out to play again.

Accepting the way others feel

Many people find it hard to cope with feelings - their own as well as those of other people. Often when we are near someone getting very upset or angry, or perhaps even being very joyful, we feel uncomfortable or awkward. Sometimes another person showing their feelings triggers similar emotions that we usually manage to keep locked away inside ourselves - often feelings that it was not all right to show when we were little. Our discomfort NOW may be related to the discomfort we felt then, when we learned to deny or 'put away' the way we felt.

Keeping our feelings locked away is not only uncomfortable, it is also not very useful. At best it makes it more difficult for us to relate to what is going on around us, and at worst, we can be so out of touch with our feelings that we don't even recognise what is going on inside us.

It is important to acknowledge the feelings those around us - those they express as well as those they try to hide. By listening to those around us, and when we acknowledge their feelings, we send out a message that says 'you are important'. We make them feel the way we would like to feel ourselves.

When dealing with children, it is even more vitally important to acknowledge the reality of their feelings, because the way they are treated in the present affects not only how they feel here and now, but also lay down patterns of response for their later adulthood. If we deny children's feelings, and criticise them for showing them, not only may it teach them to bury their feelings, it will also affect the way they think about themselves. If you acknowledge a child's pains, worries, fears and tempers, you are acknowledging them and their right to feel. If you deny them and their right to feel, you will make it difficult for them to feel good about themselves.

Most children, and many adults find it difficult to express their feelings appropriately. In these cases we can help them recognise the way they feel by saying it the way it looks to us - for example: "You look upset", "You seem sad", "Boy, you sound angry."

Destructive feelings pose a slightly more difficult problem. Feelings need to be expressed, and not denied - but sometimes creative solutions are needed, for instance: "You sound really frustrated. It's okay to show it, and I think it's unfair to take it out on us. How about going and shouting somewhere else?"

Or: "I can see that you're very angry, and I'm sure you must have a good reason to feel that way, but perhaps if you went for a little walk outside you'll come up with a more constructive way of resolving this issue."

When we were forced to deny our feelings as children, we never learned positive or alternative ways of coping with them, and this pattern can persist into adulthood. The emotions our parents had difficulty allowing us to express usually become the emotions we struggle to deal with in others. Examples of these situations:-

- A father who is frightened of his own anger may have difficulty dealing with his child's temper.

- A mother who was never allowed to run, tumble or climb freely, may have difficulty in accepting her child's physical energy.

Manipulation of Emotions

The patterns of response we have as adults were probably taught to us by our parents while we were children. For example, a dislike of insects probably came from the reaction of a parent or a significant other in our lives when we were young.

We watched others react in a certain way, and because of our love and respect for that person, we 'believed' their reaction, and adopted it as our own. Some of these patterns were very subtle, while others may have been quite overt, and in the form of clear messages.

Do you love me?

Our need for love can make us vulnerable. Love offered 'conditionally' in order to fill emotional gaps can cause great suffering. Parents who expect love from their children because of their own sense of lack of love, stunt the emotional growth of their children, who grow up to be needy adults themselves. Unable to love themselves, they search desperately for the love or another to heal them, and their very desperation drives love further and further away ....

There are two things to be learned from this. In the first place, if we have children, or deal with children in any way, we can cultivate an awareness of the way we influence their feelings, and the way they express their feelings. We can consciously 'allow' them to have their own feelings, and not 'give' them ones they don't have.

Secondly, by gaining an awareness that our original patterns of response were learned in the first place, we discover that we are able to change the ones we don't particularly want or like, and we can keep the ones we do like. We become aware of the powerful fact that we have the freedom to choose, in many cases, how we feel about things.

Accepting your own emotions

As you start to get into the habit of accepting other peoples' feelings, it is also important to become more accepting of your own.

Just as we suggested you acknowledge the feelings of others, you could usefully do the same with your own at times.

Saying "I'm fed up" or "I feel great", even without any explanation is a good way to let others know what is going on. It will not only get you more in touch with yourself, but send the message that it's okay to say how you feel, and those around you will begin to feel more comfortable about being honest about the way they feel.

Appendix 1 - Feelings

Labels and expressing feelings

Some people tend to label other people's behaviour because they don't find it easy to express their own feelings instead. They might say : "You are rotten" when they really mean "I really feel hurt by what you've just done". So when they try to stop using labels and just describe behaviour they feel frustrated.

> *When Jim's secretary didn't type an important letter he needed desperately, he bravely controlled his extreme irritation and said "You still haven't typed the letter," instead of shouting and calling her stupid, as he would have liked to have done. But he found that he grew even more angry and frustrated. He hadn't been able to express or give vent to the way he felt either by labelling the secretary or saying how he felt.*

He would probably have felt better if his response had been:

> *"That was an extremely important letter, and you the delay at getting it in the post may have serious consequences for the business. I feel very frustrated and angry the moment!"*

A sad but very true thing about labels is that they tend to be self-fulfilling. If you tell someone often enough that they are stupid, they will doubtless become stupid before too long.

The act of labelling does offer some relief to the one doing the labelling. That is because labels are usually negative, and expressed in anger. Being able to label or name something can therefore have the effect of relieving some of the stress, anger or tension in the person who feels wronged, but it invariably creates great distress in the other party. The most desirable outcome is for the angered or upset party to express how

> *"I used to think it was bad to show my feelings, so I would try hard to hide them. I dread to think of the number of times I must have been heard to scream: 'Of course I'm not bloody angry!'*
>
> *Now it makes so much difference just to admit to myself how I am feeling and share that with others. If I tell my children I'm upset about something right at the beginning. It gives us all a chance to work it out. Before I used to hold it in until I was so livid with rage that the whole thing used to explode".*

they feel without labeling or causing distress to anyone else. At first this may seem quite difficult, but the dividends in terms of improved relationships makes the effort at creativity worthwhile.

"High self-esteem is not a noisy conceit. It is quiet sense of self-respect, a feeling of self-worth. When you have it deep inside, you're glad you're you.

Conceit is but whitewash to cover low self-esteem. With high self esteem, you don't waste time and energy in impressing others. You already know you have value......feelings of self worth from the core of (the) personality can determine the use (made) of ..... aptitudes and abilities. In fact, self-esteem is the mainspring that marks every (person) for success or failure as a human being".

Dorothy Corkille-Briggs, "Your child's self esteem" Dolphin books, 1975

Self-Esteem

There is one quality above all others that determines how individuals respond to circumstances in their lives - that quality is self-esteem. Self-esteem is how a person feels about himself or herself; how much he likes being him, how much she feels good about just being alive.

The level of self-esteem of those around you is clearly not your 'responsibility' - but we would be surprised if we knew to what extent our words and actions affect the ways those around us see themselves. When it comes to children, our responsibility increases dramatically.

When thinking about the your effect on those around you, and the extent to which you can exert a positive influence, the first and most important place to start is looking at your own self-esteem. Do you have 'a quiet sense of self-respect, a feeling of self-worth' - are you glad that you are you?

Everything good that you wish for those around you, you deserve for yourself. Are you giving yourself those things, or do you think that you are not important, or that your needs can wait? How you treat yourself is a model for how others will treat you. How you treat yourself will also affect how you do your job, and take care of those around you. The more you look after yourself, the better and happier you will feel, and the more energy you will have perform those tasks you must perform. It is a little like making sure you keep your car battery topped up. If it is too low and your next door neighbour needs a jump start, you will not be able to help. Or to put it another way, only if you keep filling up your own cup will there be anything in it for others to drink.

Some ways to develop your own self-esteem

Being nice to yourself

We all need what psychologist Eric Berne called 'strokes'. A stroke is a unit of attention, and it can be negative or positive. A smile or a loving touch are loving strokes, an angry frown or sharp slap are negative strokes.

The worst thing for all people (and animals) is not to be getting any strokes at all - in other words to be ignored or to feel left out. Even negative strokes are better than no strokes at all!

Many adults are so busy stroking their children, their partner, the hamster, the house, the boss, that they forget about getting strokes for themselves. They end up tired and depressed and wonder what on earth is wrong with them. Somewhere along the line they start ignoring themselves and feeling that they are not important, and everybody else follows suit. No one is an endless reservoir of energy. In order to keep giving out love, care and attention, we all need to get something back for ourselves, and being adults, the responsibility for that lies firmly in our own laps.

There are two main ways to get strokes:-

1. Stroking yourself

This means treating yourself with love, care and attention, and is usually to do with very simple things.

- It means giving yourself something just for you, just because you enjoy it. Also giving yourself time to rest when you know that you are tired.

- It means caring for your body, wearing things that you like, having space for yourself that is warm and comforting.

- It means cooking and eating what you like, with time to enjoy it.

- It means making sure that you have something that you love to do, just for yourself. It may be painting, walking in the country, reading adventure novels, being with a close friend. The important thing is that it is for you, not for anyone else.

Make a list of the things you really like to do, even things that seem impossible at the moment. If you have been ignoring yourself for a long time this may prove difficult at first but that is all the more reason to do it. You are in real need of strokes if you have forgotten what it is you like to do.

However much we would like others to take care of us, it is ultimately our own responsibility to see that we get the love, care, attention and fun that we need. The place to start is by giving to yourself, and thereby signalling to the world that you are an important human being and you deserve nice things!

2. Getting strokes from others

We are hampered in our attempts to get what we want from others by some strong but false messages. These say things like:

- If you loved me you would know what I want!

- It isn't the same if I have to ask for it!

- "I want" doesn't get!

People are not mind readers. If they are not told what it is you like them to give you, they will get it all wrong, apart from a few lucky guesses!

Many people get strokes from others that they either don't value or don't like. Again, it is your responsibility to let others know exactly what it is you want them to do or say.

Doing this can bring up fears of rejection but, if you are asking from the stand-point of being a valuable person who has a right to get his or her needs met, the likelihood of your being rejected is small. Asking in a straightforward way for what you want doesn't mean that you will always get it but it is honest and clear and encourages others to respond in the same way to you.

Think about the following things:-

- What forms of attention do you value from others?

- What would you like them to say to you?

- How would you like them to comfort you?

- What things about you would you like them to take notice of?

- What sort of things do you like to be given as presents?

- How do you like to be touched and made love to?

Do you get these things?

Affirmations - saying nice things to yourself

Have you got a little voice inside your head? One that chatters on endlessly about what you should or shouldn't do, like some miniature critic who lives somewhere inside your grey matter? I do - and we have yet to meet anybody that didn't.

We could call this voice the tape recorder and affirmations are the tapes to put in it, tapes that say positive things about you.

If you have to have a voice inside your head it might as well be saying nice things to you!

We could call this voice the tape recorder and affirmations are the tapes to put in it, tapes that say positive things about you.

If you have to have a voice inside your head it might as well be saying nice things to you!

What we say to ourselves is important because both our conscious and our unconscious minds listen to what we are saying and act upon it. If you are telling yourself that you are fat, stupid and ugly, unconsciously you will be working away at being just that!

Remember what we said about labels as self fulfilling. You already have all the material you will ever need for your affirmations. At the moment they are in the form of negative statements that you say to yourself. All you have to do is reverse their message in a way that is meaningful to you. You will know if your affirmations are meaningful by your reaction to them. If they are difficult for you to say, if you get "funny feelings" like tingling, warmth, tears or if you suddenly "feel better" or lighter, then the affirmation is doing its work. It is changing how you feel and think about yourself at a very deep level.

"At first I found this really difficult, everything that I thought of was to do with doing something for somebody else.

Then I went back to the time before I was married and things began to come back to me. Dancing, I loved dancing, and walking on grass, and being by myself. Being alone was a luxury I really enjoyed. I didn't get much chance as a child and I certainly don't now.

All these things came flooding back to me. It was really quite a relief to find out that I did know what I liked to do after all. Now all I need is the courage to start doing them again".

The negative statements in our head are not true but they are very powerful. If we try to fight them or to argue with them we just reinforce them. Just let them be and build yourself some positive ones. Use them to help yourself instead of pulling yourself down.

If affirmations appeal to you, they work. Try it and see!

If saying affirmations seems strange or odd to you, don't you also think it is odd to have a voice telling you how awful you are all the time? The enemy within is probably the biggest any of us will ever have to fight.

Visualisation

The unconscious self not only listens to what you say, it also notices the thoughts and pictures, or images, that you have. Some of us can see very clear pictures in our mind's eye and some of us don't. This is just the different ways in which brains can work but if you can think about something and somehow "experience it", in whatever way you do it, then you can do what we call "visualise".

Think about pink snow ....

The first kitchen you ever remember seeing ....

A large stone with a bright light in the centre of it.........

There you visualised those things in whatever way was right for you!

Trust your own way and don't worry if it's not like anyone else's. It's yours and it works!

Now we can use the process of visualisation to help us build our self-esteem.

To visualise for this purpose means to close your eyes and imagine yourself or others as you want them to be.

Imagine your family is happy and at peace. Imagine yourself being as you would like to be.

When Carol gets tired and worried, because her baby always seems to be so upset, she closes her eyes and allows herself to imagine a Carol who is a warm, caring, capable mother, a Carol who knows, deep inside, that she has every right to be the mother of this child, who has every right to be tired and will give herself the rest she needs.

When John worries about his presentation to the managing director, he closes his eyes and visualises himself as a calm but alert person who can communicate in a clear, concise way, as a man with something important to say, and who deserves to be listened to.

What we think and say to ourselves matters. Use the skills of affirmations and visualisations to help yourself build a more positive self image.

Also teach these ideas to your children. They will take to them very easily because, unlike adults, they tend to believe that what they think can change reality.

The child within us

Even when we are adults, there is a child tucked away inside. Learning to take care of the child within us is of major importance. Some people can do this easily, especially if they had affectionate, caring parents. Others have to really work at it, especially if they didn't get enough love, direction and attention for themselves when they were young. The child in you is often more active when you are feeling hungry, sick, worried, tired, hurt or afraid. The child in you then feels a need for something - food, sleep, comfort, encouragement, love and so forth. If these needs are not met, then you feel worse. Whereas if they are met you usually not only feel better but are able to cope better.

One way to care for your inner child is to care for or nurture yourself. Treat yourself to your favourite things: a special food, a new book, a walk in the sunshine or the rain, a meal without the children, a visit to your friend. Give yourself the things you really enjoy and deserve because you are a person too.

Another form of nurturing is to give yourself the things that are good for you: fresh air, some form of exercise that feels right for you, proper care and attention when you don't feel so good. Nurturing also involves giving yourself comfort: cool, clean sheets, a snuggle in a favourite blanket or arm chair, a hot bath and comfortable clothing, peace and quiet or your favourite music. It can also include talking to yourself to give yourself comfort, reassurance and encouragement.

Your inner child may like playing and having fun: running on the grass, playing catch, laughing at a silly joke. Recapture your childlike fun, however that expressed itself! It's also possible to have fun alone: a walk in the woods, paddling in a stream, feeling the warm sun on your face, drawing, dancing to music. Children are able to enjoy themselves alone and that ability still lies within us as adults, however deeply buried. Recognising and fulfilling your child's inner needs leads you towards becoming a happier, more secure person, and that in turn makes you more able to meet your responsibilities towards others. Everyone benefits when you are nicer to yourself and more accepting of yourself and your needs.

If you are aware of not doing enough to look after yourself and your inner child, it might be useful to think about what stops you or what is getting in the way? What steps would you have to take to start nurturing yourself more?

You may be able to speak to others to learn what they are doing for themselves and how you can too.

"As a 12-year-old I lay in the bath with my eyes closed and my big toe under the cold tap. The tap was dripping fairly quickly and the cold water was running down my foot.

After a while I opened my eyes and saw that my big toe was under the hot tap and very hot water was running down my foot and burning me. When I thought it was cold, it was cold. When I thought it was hot, it was hot. The thought mattered".

Building Bridges

The following activity will help you get in touch with your inner child needs. You will need pen and paper and some time to yourself.

Take yourself back to your childhood and begin to remember the things you really enjoyed. The following list may help you:

weather, animals, places, nature, tastes, smells, sounds, smells, sounds, music, textures, people, activities, sights, colours, food, friends, holidays, buildings, body sensations, rituals ...

Appendix 2

LABELS

Labels are a shorthand way of commenting on a person's behaviour. Instead of describing what we have done, it is all too easy for someone to invent a name for it and hang it around our necks. More often than not the label is a direct criticism and hurts our feelings. It also tells us nothing about what they want changed. And worst of all, if we hear the label enough we may end up taking it on board for good, becoming just what they don't want.

"What was that you called me?"

We all put labels on our own and other people's behaviour. We describe someone as clever, stupid, polite, spoilt, rude, selfish and so on. It is very easy for us to get so used to hearing and using these terms that we can bandy them about without thinking any more whether they still apply. Some labels were applied a long time ago, and in very specific circumstances, which changed, but the label's stuck. We must therefore question whether we are really saying that these words apply to someone, or is there another reason? Perhaps something about ourselves?

And what do words like these really mean in the first place? Different people mean different things when they use words like "clever" or "clumsy". Many of these labels originate in childhood, and when we are young, they create a particular way of thinking about ourselves.

It makes far more sense to describe the actual behaviour, rather than labelling the person. That means talking only in terms of what we can see, hear and feel. There are several good reasons for this.

Firstly, we often use labels by way of telling someone off without actually clafifying the nature of unacceptable behaviour. This makes it difficult for anyone to stop doing whatever they are doing. If we *describe* behaviour we are supplying the information necessary to effect change.

Secondly, often using a label comes across as a criticism and results in feelings of hurt and resentful. With feelings like that around, it becomes difficult to be co-operative or to have any desire to change anything. A simple description of the facts is easier to listen to and accept.

Thirdly, labels have a nasty habit of becoming true. If we use the same labels for long enough, everyone concerned can come to believe them. We become so used to being called clumsy or stupid that we adjust our expectations of ourselves to accommodate what we take to be a revised evaluation of ourselves.

Building Bridges

Below is a list of words often used to label behaviour. Add any more you feel relevant. Take each label in turn and describe the behaviour that could elicit that label. Remember to describe only behaviour that can be seen, heard and felt, for example: selfish = your partner coming home late without warning or explanation.

selfish	polite	clever
neat	childish rude	funny
stupid	good	dirty
bad	cheeky	clumsy
grown-up		
stubborn		
lazy		

Remember to look at the labels you give yourself and your own behaviour. It can be quite a load off your shoulders to discover, for example, that you are not really lazy, you just don't want to do certain things at certain times.

Say what you want

If you say to a person "Don't drop it!" they have to make a picture or get a sense in their head of dropping it, just so that they can avoid doing so. While they are making that picture they are half-way towards dropping it, probably helped by the anxiety in your voice! It is much more helpful to say what it is you do want to happen, for example "hold on tight to it." Or if we say to our child "Don't spill the milk", they have to imagine spilt milk - and milk, once imagined spilt, is all the easier to spill.

We could consider describing the behaviour we *do* want. This can be quite difficult, because we all tend to know what we don't want but have greater difficulty in defining what we do want! Even when we have worked out the behaviour behind the label, it is still very easy to say "Don't leave things lying around" rather than "Do put things away".

Making the change to stating what we want rather than what we do not want takes extra thought and attention, but with care we can break a long-standing habit. Instead of "Don't spill the milk" we could say "Hold the milk steady".

Here are some more examples:-

>*"Don't interrupt me!"*
>>could be
>*"Please let me finish speaking!"*

>*"Don't wake me when you come in."*
>>could be
>*"Be quiet when you come in."*

>*"Don't make any mistakes with these figures."*
>>could be
>*"Take extra care with these figures."*

>*"Don't be late for the meeting"*
>>could be
>*"Leave yourself plenty of time to get to the meeting."*

Different people, different experiences

Our experience of life is uniquely our own. This means that our perspective will be unique to us as well. This is because much of the way we experience our lives originated in childhood. We came to understand and make sense of our world according to many different factors. As adults we forget that these differences exist, and therefore expect that all people see, hear, taste smell and feel life in the same way as we do. In the process of growing up, we come to imbue words with subtle and sometimes slightly different meanings. Understanding this is vitally important when dealing with children. Children have a totally different frame of reference to adults, and tend to take words at their literal meaning. If we are not careful, this can result in serious problems in communication.

It is not only with adults that errors in communication can arise. We sometimes use words that are loaded with meaning for us, and wonder why others don't respond in the way we would have responded. For example, sally's mother used the word 'fine' in a slightly disapproving sense. When she said Sally looked fine, it really meant that she didn't like the way Sally was dressed, was refraining from being critical. Sally grew to hate the word. Years later, when she was married, her husband couldn't understand why she got upset when he said that she looked 'fine'.

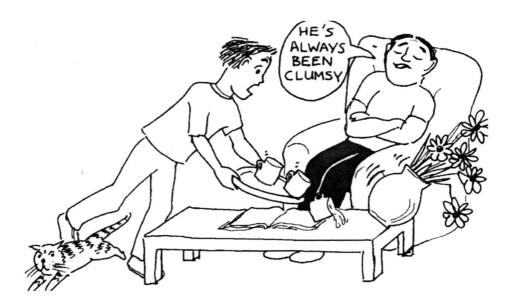

The development of self-esteem

So much of what happens in our lives depends on how we feel about ourselves - on our sense of our own worth, or what we call 'self-esteem'. Much of the development of self esteem takes place during childhood, but each and every encounter we have in our lives can influence our self esteem in a positive or negative way.

It is from our family that we first learnt whether we were lovable or not, so what we do and say to our children has a significant effect on their developing self-esteem. It is therefore vitally important to be aware of how we talk to our children.

But it is not only children who are affected by the way they are treated. At any point in our lives, the attitude of the significant people around us has an effect on how we feel about ourselves. Self esteem is not static, so although childhood influences are important, they are not all that matters.

Below is a list of some of the areas in which positive messages can be given, helping us feel better about ourselves:-

1. Being

We need to feel we have a right to be here and that we are lovable just because we exist.

We get this message when we know that we are loved, that we are important, and that people like our company.

2. Doing

We need to know that others think we are capable of succeeding in our lives.

We get positive messages to this effect directly: "you did that well!" "I really liked the way you did ...." "I love the way you do ...." and so on.

3. Thinking

We need to have a sense of our own capability on a mental level. This is very often broken down when our views and opinions are not sought, of if they are sought, they are disregarded as useless without being given any consideration. This is a common in the workplace these days.

4. Feeling

All human beings need to know that they have a right to show their feelings. Our society has made it unfashionable for whole groups to be real about their feelings. Men are traditionally not allowed to express emotion in any way other than through violence or aggression. The British people as a whole are famed for their 'stiff upper lip'. It is important to find acceptable ways to share our feelings with other people rather than bottle them up inside.

5. Learning who we are

Being strong and capable means just that - it does not mean that we somehow reach a state in which we have no needs. No matter how independent, powerful or accomplished we become, we still need love, support and care.

We need to learn that it is all right to ask in a straightforward way for what we want. We don't have to pretend to be sick, sad or angry to get what we need. It is all right to express honestly what we are feeling.

Quite often we expect others to know quite intuitively what we want, especially in close family relationships, but also at work or in friendship relationships. When we become aware of the nature of our expectation we are able to do something about it. We need to cultivate the awareness that separates us from those around us, so that we can see he dynamics of our relationships more clearly.

We need to know who we are in order to get what we want or need.

6. Learning to do things our own way

Often one of the most pervasive lessons we learned in childhood was the lesson of obedience. Hopefully as we grew older, we learned to temper our blind obedience with discrimination. This is the theory of it. Looking around in the world however, and with lessons such as the one taught by Hitler in the second world war, or some of the modern-day civil wars in various parts of the world, we can see that theory does not always manifest in reality. We may protest wildly that we would never get caught in a situation like that - perhaps not exactly like that, but if we are honest, there are probably many instances in which we follow what other say without thinking for ourselves.

> *"I had a great many messages as a child telling me not to be who I was', and now, at 39, 1 am just beginning to learn that it is okay to be who I am. I don't have to hide any longer. This is at a time when my own child is just beginning to go through the same stage for the first time, so we are learning together".*

The power of the advertising industry is an example of this phenomenon. Again all we can do is cultivate an awareness in ourselves of the reasons we do things. If we spend most of our time doing things others want us to do, then we need to look at what is happening inside ourselves quite carefully. The converse is also true. If we spend our lives doing the opposite of what others want us to do, then it is possible that we are 'reacting' to attempted control, but still not doing what we need to do ourselves.

If we deal with children, we need to give them positive messages which encourage them to think for themselves, and work out what they want to do or believe. They need to learn from an early age to trust their feelings to help them know what to do. The world has seen the tragic consequences of this failing in this lesson.

7. Sexuality

Often our feelings of sexuality are tied up in the needs and expectations of others at an early age. We may learn that our worth depends on our ability to perform sexually, or we may learn that our sexuality is dirty and sinful, depending on the influences to which we were exposed. Religion and society has many good reasons for manipulation in this part of our lives. While we wouldn't suggest that the development of a sense of morality is undesirable, we would say that it is difficult to obtain a balance in these matters, and that often we are a victim of the conditioning we received when we were young. The feelings we develop regarding our sexuality from childhood often persists well into adulthood, reducing our ability to feel or think clearly as self determining adults.

We also need to learn to discriminate between our sexuality and our need for love and comfort, because these can easily become confused and intertwined.

8. Independence

The development of independence is very much an issue of relevance to parents. Parents know that helping their children achieve independence can be one of the most difficult things to do. As parents we may have needs of our own that get in the way of helping our children along this path, or we may simply not know what sort of messages we need to give to our children. *How* we give them these messages depends very much on the type of person we are and the sort of language we use.

Even if we are not parents, the issue of independence is probably still of great relevance to us. If we didn't get the help we needed as children through the phases we have been discussing, it is likely that our sense of our ability to live an independent life may be stunted or warped. Often marriage or partner relationships engender patterns of dependency based on earlier parent-child relationships. We may either experience ourselves as dependent on others, or we may have powerful needs for others to be dependent on us. Both these patterns stem from the messages we received in childhood. To raise our awareness of these issues in our lives, it is helpful to consider the nature of our feelings around these issues. If we think about our relationship either with someone we depend on, on who depends on us, we can try to identify things that bring up strong feelings. They may be messages that you missed out on as a child and now have a chance to catch up on.

If we didn't get the things we needed at the right time when we were children, we continually get chances to make up that lack as we go on through our life.

Clearly the issue of independence is very much an issue of the level of self esteem. We need others to depend on us, because that proves that we are 'good'. It also in fact proves that we are actually exist. It may also legitimise us in our own eyes, for if someone else needs us, then there must be a reason for our lives after all.

There are two principle beliefs we need for high self-esteem:-

- the belief that I am lovable simply because I exist.

- the belief that I am worthwhile, that I have something to give and to offer others.

The deep down feeling that we are worth being loved and valued, comes about through the quality of the relationships we have with the important people in our lives. While it is impossible to fill these needs for ourselves in a direct way, we can do so indirectly by creating a wholesome climate for the significant others in our lives. It is an amazing fact that when we help others feel better about themselves, they quite literally can't help responding in positive ways, which in turn helps us feel better as well.

We can create this wholesome climate by focusing on strengths rather weaknesses, on successes rather than failures. Most of us are expert at finding fault, expecting the worst and dwelling on mistakes. This can lead us to anticipate failure from others, which creates an atmosphere of tension and mistrust.

Expectation of failure encourages failure. Just as "Don't spill the milk" makes it easier to spill the milk, expecting the worst creates increases the possibility of the worst occurring. Stating things in the positive is therefore of great importance, but going 'over the top' even in terms of positivity can have its dangers as well. If we set up expectations of a positive outcome in someone in an area where the target task or activity is well beyond present capability, the inevitable result is failure, and the result will be a double negative - dealing with he failure itself and dealing with the expectation.

Encouraging someone to do something of which they are clearly incapable (at the moment) is as great a dis-service as expecting them to fail. It may be better to focus on the individual skills needed to achieve a particular task, and work our realistic programme to help acquire them. For example if someone wants to run a marathon, we may need to encourage them to get fit in manageable stages. We would not say "You will never run a marathon". We may say "I'm sure you do well next year if you start training now".

"My father only ever gave me attention when I did something that he approved of. Because I loved him so much I ended up only doing the things I knew he would like and I hid lots of things about myself from him. I wanted to be ME and I wanted his love. Because I could't do both I stopped being me.

I wanted to be loved for me. I wanted to be encouraged and supported in my own hopes and dreams. He died and I never got what I wanted from him. Only now, years later, am I beginning to be able to give those things to myself. If only he had been as happy with me as I was".

A common danger is comparing the performance of one person to that of another. For example, we might be tempted to say "Jones manages to get through that pile of paperwork in one day, so can you." Sadly, in the real world these situations occur on a daily basis. Worse still, very often someone's performance will be deemed unacceptable on the basis of the perceived performance of another. In industry, where results are all that matter, people are expendable, and their sense of their own worth is considered irrelevant. This is a short term view, and situations where people find themselves often unfairly compared to others arise due to management problems. If people are wisely placed in positions which offer them a realistic chance of success, the increase in their sense of self worth will translate itself into increased productivity, which is the what industry wants in the first place.

Praise and Encouragement

Positive labels can be as unhelpful as negative ones. Praise, like criticism, is a judgement made from outside and imposed on the individual. It is often used to manipulate behaviour to fit a certain set of external criteria. The 'danger' of constant raise is that it encourages behaviour for external reasons, and discourages self-referral, or reliance on the self to determine behaviour. Looking around us, we can see what effect this need for external reward has done to the state of our world.

We all need positive messages about what we do, who we are and what we create. It is possible to give and receive encouragement without the use of labels. If we describe behaviour and say what we feel about it, we can give a positive message without the risks involved in labelling.

Some drawbacks of praising

1. What you are praising the other person for may not be valued by them at all; it may even be meaningless or annoying to them.

2. People know that if they can be praised they can also be blamed and, if praise is used a great deal in a relationship, the lack of it can be taken as criticism.

3. Praise is often used as a form of manipulation to try and get someone to do what you want rather than as a genuine compliment.

4. Being praised for things that aren't valuable or important to you can make you feel that the other person doesn't understand you.

5. Being praised can deeply embarrass some people, especially when it is done in front of an audience.

6. People can grow to depend on praise and begin to demand it as a way of getting attention and approval.

Children know when they have done something well or badly. You can see and hear their satisfaction when they have achieved what they have set out to do and also their dissatisfaction when they don't. As they grow a bit older they learn that if they do certain things they are "good" and approved of and if they do others they are "bad" and disapproved of. Gradually, because the approval of the people who are bringing them up is so important, they begin to lose their own "knowing" and rely upon their grown ups' judgements of their behaviour.

Often this process through childhood results in us loosing our sense of knowing altogether and we come to rely completely on others to tell us who we are and what we should be doing. We may completely bury our "selves" and constantly check to see if others approve of what we are doing or wanting. As adults may live out our lives doing what we think others want and never know what our own needs are at all.

The idea that praise may be just another form of labelling may seem a strange contradiction, because we have been taught that praise is 'good'. After all, it can't be bad to say nice things to people, can it? But, as with many things that started out as good ideas, the act of praising has become misused and misunderstood.

Praise is usually an evaluation of another person and their qualities and abilities; it does not show what you are really thinking and feeling. The next time you have the urge to praise, stop yourself and ask yourself why. What is your real intention? Do you really want to say something nice to that person? Do you want to manipulate them into doing something? Are you doing it to avoid acknowledging something else that is going on (e.g. jealousy, guilt)?

So what do we do instead?

Rather than using praise that judges, try using praise that describes. So, instead of saying things like: "You are wonderful, good, lovely, brilliant or whatever (which tell the person nothing about why you think so), be explicit about what it is you like and how it makes you feel.

Here are some examples:-

1. *I really like the way you help me wash up.*

2. *When you rub my neck like that I feel really cared for.*

3. *That cooker you have just cleaned looks spotless.*

4. *I am really happy with the earrings you bought me.*

Descriptive praise usually includes the following:-

- *An accurate description of the work, behaviour or accomplishment of the other.*

- *How you feel about or value what you have described.*

- *And, if there is one, the positive effect that the behaviour has had on you.*

Changing from judging to describing takes time to learn because praising in the old way is such a habit in our society. Be patient with yourself while you are learning this new skill.

Praising in this new way quite often brings to the surface thoughts and feelings that never get expressed when the other kind of praise is used. It lets the other person know more about you and the positive effect that they and their behaviour have on you.

A 35-year-old doctor, with blonde hair, glasses and two children, spent six months training to run the New York Marathon. The great day arrived and he finished 999th out of 1000.

He returned to the hospital on Monday to be asked by his fellow doctors where he came in the race, so he told them

"Ah! You only beat one person," they exclaimed. "But that doesn't matter, I was best in my class," he replied. They couldn't understand. "What class was that?" they asked. He explained:-

"That was the class for 35-year-old doctors with blonde hair, glasses and two children. I did my best. I can't compare myself with other people because then I am always going to lose - and I will probably get ulcers into the bargain. I gave 100 per cent and that is all I can ever do. I can only try to be the best person, runner and doctor that I can be".

Defences

Many adults and children have built large defensive walls around themselves and they ward off positive comments that they receive saying things like: "Oh, it's nothing" or "I didn't do anything really". These people are pushing away the very thing that they most need, positive attention, because they don't trust or are embarrassed by the form in which the comments are made.

If someone responds that way to something you say, try repeating what you originally said in a descriptive rather than a judging way. This may break through their defensive wall, because it is hard for them to dismiss as "nothing" something you have said about how feel. They may be able to accept and take in your words and then they may really glow!

Remember to use your voice, your body, and your heart, when you do it.

We feel good when others express their good feelings about us, and when we can accept our self-worth, we don't ever need others to tell us that we are okay or to compare our achievements to theirs.

Appendix 3

WHOSE PROBLEM

Needs behind behaviour

Everything we do in life is geared to meet some need. There are a limited number of needs that all people share. On the simplest level, these include things like the need for food, shelter, sleep, security, safety, love, friendship, exercise for the body and the mind. As we meet these basic needs so we can begin to work towards others that are more to do with our self-esteem, creative ability and being part of the world we live in a way that counts for something.

Acceptable and unacceptable behaviour

The ways people choose to try and meet their needs may or may not interfere with other people. If they don't interfere, they will be seen as acceptable, if they do, they will be seen as unacceptable. There are four factors that may affect how accepting of the behaviour of others we are:-

- how we are feeling

- who is doing the behaviour

- where they are doing it

- when they are doing it.

Who owns a problem

If everyone is having a good time and is quite happy, there is no problem. If the people around us behave in ways that affect our needs, we are displeased and have a problem. If we behave in ways that affect their needs, they are displeased and have a problem. Before we start to sort out our problems and help them sort out theirs, it is useful to make sure we know who owns the problem.

We are not our behaviour

It is very common to identify ourselves by the job we do, the way we look, the background we came from, or whether we are rich or poor, so it can be very difficult for us to be ourselves as we really are. We are individuals in our own right, regardless of our roles, our status in society or our possessions. Most of us have a deep-rooted desire to be loved for ourselves, rather than for our looks or our connections or whatever.

Yet very often we get stereotyped with a particular label and then people are no longer open to seeing us any other way. We have all, at some time, probably been treated as just a woman or a typical male or too old to understand or too young to understand or always hysterical or rational or any one of the thousands of labels that can be used to stop us being seen as complex individuals. This is the process that begins very early in life when children begin to be labelled for their behaviour.

For example - she is:-

quiet, good, studious, helpful, kind, bossy, rude, stubborn, stupid, clumsy, thick, and so on.

If the label is used often enough, it sticks, and *she* becomes a neatly labelled package from which she cannot escape; the label follows her through school, work, marriage and parenthood to her death. If we are able to distinguish between the individual and the behaviour, it becomes easier to avoid the trap of labelling. 'I didn't like the way you did that' might then replace 'You idiot! You've made a right mess of that!'

Behaviour can be learned, changed and developed. Love, on the other hand, is unconditional and says: "I might not like what you do sometimes but I love, support and cherish you."

Building Bridges

At the end of the day, when it is peaceful, sit quietly and think about someone in your life - your spouse or partner, your child, a friend, a colleague. This exercise will be particularly useful if you have been experiencing some difficulty with this person.

Let go of all your thoughts and try to see their face in your mind's eye - get a sense of who they really are. In doing this, just let any feelings that arise in you flow softly through you.

Behaviour and needs

American psychologist Abraham Maslow describes human needs as falling into five categories, as represented in the pyramid below.

Maslow believed that, until our most basic needs are met (level 1), we are unable to aspire to those on level 2.

Until we feel a physical sense of stability and safety (level 2), we are unable to form the ties that enable us to feel emotionally secure (level 3) and so on, one by one, up to level 5.

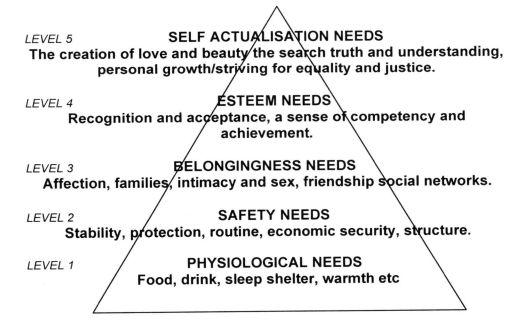

LEVEL 5   **SELF ACTUALISATION NEEDS**
The creation of love and beauty the search truth and understanding, personal growth/striving for equality and justice.

LEVEL 4   **ESTEEM NEEDS**
Recognition and acceptance, a sense of competency and achievement.

LEVEL 3   **BELONGINGNESS NEEDS**
Affection, families, intimacy and sex, friendship social networks.

LEVEL 2   **SAFETY NEEDS**
Stability, protection, routine, economic security, structure.

LEVEL 1   **PHYSIOLOGICAL NEEDS**
Food, drink, sleep shelter, warmth etc

For example, if a little girl felt unprotected and insecure, on level 2 of the pyramid, she would be unhappy, insecure and fearful most of the time and so be unable to make friends and take the first step in reaching out towards others, which are the belongingness needs on level three of the pyramid.

In other words, meeting our needs successfully at each level leads us up the pyramid to becoming what Maslow called a "self-actualised person", one who is self-motivated, successful and competent, and always reaching out into the world to grow, change and experience new things.

The same needs

As human beings we all have the same needs and we behave in ways we think will help us get those needs met. This is normal and healthy. But people who are for some reason continually unable to get their needs met may resort to more and more extreme behaviour. While this behaviour may be undesirable or inappropriate, it does not mean that the underlying need is wrong.

For example:-

- With a young family to support and things being rather uncertain at work, Thomas feels under extreme pressure. He finds himself contemplating ways to 'end it all'.

- Twenty-year-old Lorraine needs love, warmth and comfort, so she gets a sore throat and has to go to bed for two days.

- Teenage Sally establishes her independence by staying out all night without telling her parents where she is.

- Six-year-old Adam needs to develop and test out his sense of balance and co-ordination, so he climbs trees and climbing frames to heights that scare his mother.

In these examples the actual needs are valid human needs but the behaviours used to fulfil them may cause problems for the individual and for others round them.

Acceptable and unacceptable behaviour

Behaviour that interferes with us and our needs we think of negatively; behaviour that doesn't interfere with us is thought of positively. In this way, we tend to view behaviour as either good or bad, nice or naughty, quiet or annoying and so on.

It is much more useful to look at behaviour in terms of whether we find it acceptable or unacceptable, for by doing this we are not labelling the individual or the behaviour (as good or bad or whatever) but looking at our own needs and feelings at the time. Being clearer in your own mind about what you find acceptable at any given time can lead to a far better understanding between yourself and others.

Building Bridges

Consider examples of the way people around you choose to meet the following needs:

- Need to grow and learn - have new experiences
- Need for attention   Need for love and affection
- Need to belong   Need for independence
- Need for security   Need to feel useful
- Need for approval

Just what behaviour we find unacceptable at any given time depends on several factors:-

- **how we feel** at the time - when we are feeling well and happy it is likely that we will find far more behaviour acceptable than when we are tired, cross and upset.

- **who** is doing the behaviour - you probably like some people more than others and allow them more freedom with your time, space and attention. And you also have different expectations of different people. You will probably be quite happy for your partner to snuggle up next to you as you sit on the bus, but will have a different reaction if a total stranger did the same.

- **where** the behaviour is taking place has an effect on whether you find it acceptable or not; you may really like your child's gymnastic ability but not at Granny's funeral.

- **when** the behaviour takes place - jibes and teasing from your mates over drinks in the evening are likely to be taken in fun, but the same comments to next morning at work may well be offensive!

Because of these factors there is not a hard and fast rule that you can follow regarding your response to behaviour.

Problem ownership

Problems that inevitably occur within most relationships can be much easier to tackle if we are familiar with the concept of problem ownership. This means stepping back when a problem begins to arise and asking yourself: "Who is most upset?" or "Who needs help first?" and "Whose problem is this?"

If a person is not getting something they need, they will feel uncomfortable and get upset - how upset depends on the importance of the need. But if their behaviour in fulfilling this need doesn't interfere with the others, or prevent others from meeting their own needs, then the only problem is the satisfaction of the need - the person owns the problem.

Building Bridges

When, where and with whom would you find the following behaviours acceptable?:-

Eating someone's left over food,   Breaking into a house
Being shouted at,   Being sprayed with water
Dressing up as a clown,   Having your needs discounted

When, where and with whom would you find the following behaviours unacceptable?:-

Being kissed and cuddled,   Being admired and complimented
Being comforted when you're upset, Being offered money

You might like to ask the people around you to answer too, to see how their acceptance of behaviour differs from your own

---

If a person is managing to satisfy their needs but the way they have chosen interferes with others and does prevent others from meeting their own needs, then the other people are likely to get upset - they own the problem. When everybody is managing to meet their needs without interfering with anybody else, there is no problem!

Quite often we become emotionally involved in a problem that is not ours and this reduces our ability to cope, think straight or help the person with the problem. This happens more often in close relationships where our loved ones' distress, anger, confusion, and so on is more likely to trigger our own emotional patterns from the past.

WHO OWNS IT?

'Self' owns the problem

Derek is frustrated because his computer crashed, and he lost all his data.

June is upset because Sally seemed to ignore her in the canteen.

Matt is angry because his car had a flat tyre, and he missed his meeting.

Julia is in pain from a sprained ankle.

'Other' owns the problem

The family has the television up loud while Ann is trying to have a telephone conversation.

George is worried when daughter Jane doesn't arrive home at the agreed time.

Mary doesn't have the stock figures for the meeting because her secretary took an extended lunch and didn't finish typing them up.

Peter is late for work because the boys were"t ready to be dropped at school.

By asking ourselves the above questions we can figure out who has the problem and from there we can make clearer decisions about whether we need to be involved and what action to take if we do.

It sometimes happens that we 'take on' the problems of others – always with the best intentions, and because we most probably genuinely care about them. Often we have a sense of responsibility for the other person, as a parent, or boss, or older sibling. But in certain cases this is quite inappropriate. Not only do we load ourselves with a burden we don't really need (no doubt having enough of our own!) we also deprive those whose problem we take on, of the sense of achievement that comes from sorting out a problem, and we encourage their continued dependence and an attitude of dependency.

There is a fine line between truly helping a person towards finding their solutions, and thereby increasing their self-worth, and "doing it for them", which keeps them powerless.

A matter of priority

There will be occasions when it isn't clear who owns the problem. For example:-

"When I came upon a road accident, I knew the people needed my help, but I had to deal with my own distress before I could be of any use".

"A week after I had been promoted to manager, I received a list of the redundancies in my division. I was surprised, and more than a little uncomfortable, when Jed, who was on my list, came to see me. He proceeded to tell me about the difficulties he had been having in his marriage, which had finally come to a head, and he was going through a rather messy divorce. He asked for my support. I did what I could to reassure him, but felt awful, and had to see my manager for help in dealing with the situation."

"My son was upset because his grandmother had repeatedly promised him a particular present and failed yet again to deliver. Before I could help him think about what to do with what should have been his problem, I needed to unload my share of the problem - which I did by telling him how annoyed I was at my mother for breaking her promises. That freed me then to help him".

In these situations, both parties involved had a problem, and a series of solutions had to be worked out, prioritising both peoples' needs and possible remedies. In the first, the person arriving on the scene of the accident had to deal with their distress first. In the second, the new manager had to offer what support he could, before seeking help himself. The parent in the third case, managed to deal with both problems at the same time by expressing how they felt as part of the same process of listening to and dealing with the distress of the son.

Some people in these three situations would not have experienced any needs of their own and so would have been able to concentrate straightaway on the needs of the other. Others may have felt themselves being sucked into the problem and taken the decision to stay back and not get emotionally involved.

More problem ownership

The two most important things about the concept of problem ownership are firstly that it helps you to identify how to act, if at all; and secondly, it encourages you to allow others responsibility for their own problems.

The important issue is to differentiate between your own needs and the needs of others. With your own problems you need skills that help you assert your own needs. When you are dealing with others who have problems you need helping skills which show caring and support for the other person whilst also enabling them to find their own solutions to their problems.

> **"I sit on a man's back, choking him and making him carry me and yet assure myself and others that I am sorry for him and wish to lighten his load by all possible means – except by getting off his back".**
>
> *Leo Tolstoy*

A helping relationship is one in which a person helps another to develop and grow as a human being. All your relationships can have this element in them at some time - relationships with your loved ones, the people you work with, even with people you don't like or people who are complete strangers to you. We have in our society many "helping" professions in which people are trained in some way to help others in need. But many studies show that it is from within our own circle of family, friends and acquaintances that we are most likely to get the help we really need.

Most of us have known, at some time or another, someone that we could "talk" to, who "understood" us and who we felt "safe" with. This sort of person is straight, honest and open with us; we trust them to tell us the truth. They care about us and don't get sucked into our problems. They are not depressed by our depression or fearful of our fear.

They empathise with how we feel and what is happening to us and that helps us to understand ourselves and our problems better. We are not threatened by them, they don't judge us and they accept the differences and changes in us.

These are qualities that we all display towards someone at some time in our lives and they are the qualities that are most likely to provide worthwhile help and support to a person with a problem.

Building Bridges

Spend a couple of days noticing people who are having problems of some sort. Keep your eyes open at work, in the supermarket, in the street, on public transport as well as in your own house.

As you are noticing, ask yourself whose problem it is and whether it appears that somebody is taking it on who doesn't need to.

As much as possible, just notice what is happening without getting into labelling and judging what you are watching - in this exercise you are gathering information to look at, not trying to change anything that you see.

Think of problems large and small that you and those around you have and identify who owns the problem in each case.

Appendix 4

BEING A HELPER

Important points about helping others

The people in our lives will experience us being most helpful if we manage to display the following characteristics:-

Accepting them as a human being without denying their feelings, however painful these may be for them or us.

Caring enough to be prepared to help them help themselves and, if necessary, just being there to support them when the going gets tough.

Understanding that we can get a sense of what is going on for someone else without having to step in and take over.

Trusting that they are able to help themselves, with assistance, if necessary, in the form they want from us, as and when they ask for it.

Being straight or congruent with them, so that they know where they stand.

It's enough to listen

We are often most helpful when we are just listening. When others share their feelings with us, it is very easy to want to help them so badly that we give them good advice, take over their problem or - if its bad enough - try and take their minds off the situation. However, the most useful thing we can do is keep quiet, show them we care by the way we listen and attend to them and let them use us as a sounding board to vent off their feelings.

Being there for someone

One of the best ways in which we can help others when they have a problem is just to listen and act as a sounding board for their thoughts and feelings. This means caring enough about the person to put aside all thoughts of ourselves and concentrate our whole attention and awareness on them, in an open and caring way. The people we tend to find it easiest to talk to about our deepest fears and worries are those who don't talk back to us very much. Mostly they just listen and we go away feeling that we have really been heard and understood.

What these people are doing is allowing us to speak our worries freely without putting in their own thoughts and feelings to get in our way. Although they are often silent we know from the expression on their face and how they sit or stand that they are giving us their complete attention.

> *"My 13-year-old daughter came home from school one day obviously upset. She threw her school-bag on the floor in the hall, stamped through the kitchen and out of the back door. I got up and followed her out, finding her sitting on the back steps. I sensed her feeling hurt and upset and close to tears. Managing to resist trying to help in the old ways, I sat down beside her to listen if she wanted to talk. I imagined sending love waves to her so she would know I was there to help if she needed me. After 10 minutes she sighed a huge sigh, stood up and stretched and said: 'Thanks for listening, mum', before going inside obviously feeling better".*

They show their caring, acceptance and trust to us and feeling this from them, we can let go of some of our fear and share a lot more of what is troubling us than we would otherwise do. In doing so, we can see ourselves and our problem more clearly. Doing and saying nothing but just silently being there, attentive and caring, can be the most profound help that we can ever give to another human being. Yet, although we are taught how to talk, read and write, very rarely are we taught to listen, despite the fact that it is a communication skill like all the others.

Research has shown that people who are thought of as very good listeners tend to "match" the person who is talking to them. This matching behaviour includes what they do with their body and their gestures, the use of similar words and phrases and, more subtly, mirroring thought processes. Most of us do this to some degree, even if only at an unconscious level, and the skill can be developed considerably with practice. Matching has the effect of putting the other person more at their ease and making them feel comfortable and accepted for who and what they are. This feeling of safety gives them the freedom to explore their problems more deeply and productively.

> "You have two ears and one tongue - take the hint!"

The essential ingredients for a helping relationship

When professionals first started to train people as helpers, they spent years noticing how people who were naturally helpful behaved. In this way they identified five major ingredients that we can all usefully employ in helping both adults and children:-

1. Acceptance

Difficulty with acceptance is often bound up with issues of control. We may find it difficult to accept others if we have the need to control or judge the behaviour or feelings especially when they are feelings that don't fit with our picture of the world. If we can cultivate a sense of impartiality, or an awareness of a clear distance between "me" and "you", we will find it easier to accept others fully, and to accept what they say without judgement.

2. Care

Even as we are able to accept others and what is happening for them, without judgement, we need to be able to genuinely care about them enough to be able to want to help them both now with their problem and in the long term by helping them learn how to help themselves. This can be particularly difficult when dealing with those closest to us. It is one of the most difficult things a parent can do for instance, to watch while their children learn 'from their own mistakes'.

3. Understanding

We can never truly experience things in exactly the same way as someone else - but to be understanding we need to get as close to this as we possibly can. Part of being a helper is taking the time almost to think ourselves into someone else's shoes, imagining or visualising what might they be feeling like right now, not in order to present them with our ready made solution but to be able to work alongside them in their task to find their own.

Building Bridges

Watch for evidence of matching behaviour in the people around you; it is easy to see in people who are close to each other. It is also easy to see mismatching behaviour in people who are arguing, who don't like each other or who are not listening to each other.

Practise matching for yourself. At first it may seem wooden, false or clumsy to you, as any new skill does, but it soon becomes as easy and natural part of your normal behaviour.

It can also be fun to practise mismatching when you are with friends or family who won't be upset by it!

---

4. Trust

None of the above is a lot of use if we do not believe that the other person is *actually* capable of understanding their own feelings and issues, finding their own answers and looking after themselves. We need to be able to trust them to help themselves, which may or may not include asking us for assistance along the way. As we trust them more, they will come to trust themselves more and will grow - learning from their mistakes - to be more and more capable.

Building Bridges

Watch for evidence of matching behaviour in the people around you; it is easy to see in people who are close to each other. It is also easy to see mismatching behaviour in people who are arguing, who don't like each other or who are not listening to each other.

Practise matching for yourself. At first it may seem wooden, false or clumsy to you, as any new skill does, but it soon becomes as easy and natural part of your normal behaviour.

It can also be fun to practise mismatching when you are with friends or family who won't be upset by it!

---

5. Being congruent

Being congruent means that all the different parts of you match. They are all expressing the same thing.

These parts include:-

- Tone of voice.
- Facial expression.
- Posture and body language.
- Internal feelings and sensations.
- Thoughts and beliefs.
- The words that are spoken.
- The actions you perform.

For example, if you were angry, you would look and sound angry, you would be thinking angry thoughts and you would be expressing yourself verbally in an angry way. No-one would be in any doubt about the fact that you were ANGRY! Being congruent involves:-

Experiencing - having thoughts, feelings, bodily sensations, physical tensions,

Awareness - knowing what you are feeling and thinking, and

Communication - being able to communicate these things to others.

Quite often we are not congruent. For example, we may feel angry in our minds and bodies but try not to show it. This is called a mixed message and these can cause confusion in other people because they can sense that something isn't "straight".

Children are especially sensitive to mixed messages and may behave in negative ways when they are receiving them from you because they cannot cope with the confusion they are experiencing.

We can be incongruent in three ways:-

1. At the awareness level

We can experience thoughts and feelings without being aware of them. This means that others can sense that we are angry, hurt or upset but we don't know it ourselves. When someone confronts us with how we are feeling we deny it and may even become defensive about it. Hence the red-faced person loudly shouting "I am not angry!"

What happens when we're not congruent

"I used to wonder why my children didn't get their coats on to go to school when I shouted out 'OK, I'm ready to leave!' I was still clearing breakfast things and knew in my mind that by the time they were ready I could have my coat on. Now I realise that they paid attention to my actions, not my words. They knew I wasn't ready, so why should they be?"

"Whenever I tried to speak to my husband while the telly was on, he would say he was listening, and encourage me to speak, but his eyes kept flitting to the screen, and I knew he wasn't really paying attention, no matter what he said. It made me feel really angry".

In these instances the person is genuinely unaware of what they are experiencing and they may need help and support in order to "get in touch" with their feelings.

2. At the communication level

In these instances a person is aware of what they are experiencing but for some reason they are choosing not to express it to others. This includes being "polite" to someone you may not like and, also, not telling someone how you really feel because it may "hurt" them.

The choice not to express what you are feeling may be conscious or unconscious. We often learn as children that it is not safe to talk openly about what we experience and we bring this lesson with us into adult life. For instance, the little boy who is told it isn't manly to cry may grow up into a man who suppresses any display of emotion. People who learn that it isn't safe to be honest about their feelings very often keep their opinions of things to themselves, even when it would be valuable for them to express them.

3. Internal congruence

We can also experience a lack of congruence if what we believe is right is at odds with what we are actually able to do. For example, a modern mother may "believe" in breast feeding on demand. But perhaps she doesn't have enough milk or she becomes too exhausted because she has other small children to take care of too. She becomes more and more tired, irritable and run down. Her beliefs are at odds with what she is physically capable of doing.

In instances like these, the belief needs changing and there needs to be far more trust put into what "feels" right rather than what is "thought" to be right.

What is right for a person makes them feel happy, doesn't exhaust them, feels good, and works!

If you don't feel happy and comfortable with what you are doing, then it isn't right for you, whatever anyone tells you. Take time to find out what feels right! If you are happy, you will have so much more energy to live your life creatively.

Communication

Communication is the process by which messages are sent from one person to another via our senses. In our society there is a great deal of emphasis placed on words but studies have shown that often the words are the least important part of the communication.

Actions speak louder than words

If we take away the word content of communication we are left *with tone of voice*, which includes pitch, rhythm, volume, etc. and *body language*, which includes facial expression, gestures, body movement, posture and breathing.

It's not what we say but how we say it, as the old saying goes.

Spend some time just watching people, making sure that you can't hear what they are saying, and see just how much you can pick up from their non-verbal behaviour.

One interesting way to do this is to turn the sound down on the television and watch the picture alone. It is often quite easy to follow what is happening in the programme without sounds.

Most of us pick up the non-verbal aspect of communication unconsciously as we go along and only really become aware of it when there is a very obvious discrepancy between what is being said and the way in which it is said.

These discrepancies arise when we are not being congruent; on some level we are sending a mixed message that the receiver is unclear about, e.g. saying yes or no when we really don't want to, or when we are trying to hide our true thoughts and feelings.

Think of as many different ways as you can of saying the following sentences. Don't change the words, just change your tone of voice. Many can be said in such a way as to completely reverse the meaning.

"Of course I don't mind…"
"I hate you".
"Oh, stop complaining and get on with it".
"You won't get away with a stunt like that again".

Using the child as a guide

We all have some ability to sense when people are not being straightforward or completely honest with us. Our response, when this happens, can range from feeling slightly uncomfortable to believing that we are being lied to. Whatever the response there is likely to be a feeling of confusion and a lack of understanding of what is going on.

In an effort to be Mr. Nice Guy, Bob sent out mixed messages, until his internal stress reached critical levels, and he erupted. After that everyone knew what it was that Bob wanted and was happy to give it to him.

140

Building Bridges

Place a tape recorder in an unobtrusive place and tape half an hour or an hour of social interaction. General office interaction, a mealtime, over drinks at the pub - any time when you are in conversation with others.

If possible, listen for any words or phrases you use which come across in a way that is unhelpful or which don't have the effect you intended.

Then take some time to practise saying the same words in a different way. This can be difficult because quite often it means that you have to make some change in your mood and your attitude towards the person you were speaking to.

Because we can never really know another person's experience, we often misinterpret their body language. The more you increase your awareness of non-verbal messages, the more you will improve your communication with people, both when you talk and when you listen.

Here are some guidelines for improving your ability to "read" non-verbal communications.

- Spend time concentrating your attention on the most used non-verbal behaviours around you.. Notice their facial expression, tone of voice, posture and gestures.

- Notice the discrepancies in messages - when the face and body signals don't match the words.

- Pay more attention to the thoughts and feelings that you are experiencing - eg when you pick up an 'atmosphere' in a room or sense that you have to be careful about what you say. We often have an inner awareness of these things, whether we act on it or not.

- Remember that meaning can only ever be understood in context; gestures, body patterns etc must be interpreted as part of a whole and not judged and labelled in isolation.

For example, think of a few situations which could account for each of the following:-

A woman hunched over, head in hands, sobbing loudly…..

A child running wildly down the street screaming…..

A person kneeling facing the wall, eyes closed, humming and rocking gently backwards and forwards…..

A man standing in the middle of the street, waving his arms around.

Often children force us to be straight and honest by their simple innocence and directness. This quality of innocence is important in helping us remain straight with ourselves. Observe young children and get a sense of where they're coming from and apply this to your own life.

If you don't have children in your life, try to harness the innocence and directness that is still part of the child within you - the child that you once were. Pay attention to that little voice inside - it is often more honest than we allow ourselves to be, and can help us become more congruent, more 'real' in our daily lives.

Appendix 5

INTRODUCTION TO LISTENING

Silence is not enough

As powerful as silent listening is, there are many occasions when we could be more active in our listening. Even simple, factual communications can be coloured by underlying emotion, and to receive the full communication it is useful to listen not only to the words, but to acknowledge the feelings that are being expressed. Upset people don't send clear messages, there are usually too many unpleasant and strong feelings around.

Letting people know you are aware of their feelings not only clarifies communication, but also helps both parties acknowledge and deal with relevant issues. Just giving a name to what you think they feel can be enough.

Open ended questions

Open ended questions leave the person you are listening to with the responsibility as to what they tell you and how the conversation goes. Unlike a closed question they do not suggest an answer, for example: "What aspect of your job bothers you?" rather than "Are you unhappy with your salary?"

Open ended questions fall into two categories:

1. Door openers, to start the ball rolling

It is not easy for some people to express the way they feel, especially if they perceive their feelings as negative. At these times it is useful to encourage them to start talking with open ended questions like:-

"Do you want to talk about anything?"
"You seem a bit out of sorts, do you want to tell me about it?"

2. Questions to keep the flow going

Though pauses and silences are valuable in a conversation, sometimes it is useful keep people going with more open ended questions:-

"Is there anything more?" "Is there something else worrying you?"

Learning from our successes and mistakes

Children learning to walk try different ways of getting up and launching themselves on two feet, each time learning from what they do to be more successful at the next attempt. Unlike adults, they do not beat themselves up for making mistakes, but learn from experience, responding to the "feedback" that the experience offers them. We can learn to do likewise, considering what we do and the effect it has on us and others and using the feedback from other people and the environment to change things the next time.

What might get in the way of listening

Learning to really listen isn't always easy. There are all sorts of patterns that can get in the way. However much we may want to be helpful in these new ways, we may be stuck in old patterns of trying to sort things out for others, and solve their problems for them.

We may also find that feelings expressed to us trigger us into our own, often unfruitful ways of responding, and the situation becomes about us, rather than about the other person, or the problem to be solved.

Obviously we want to do it all as well as we can, and it will take time to replace the old patterns of behaving with new ones. Only doing it and learning from the feedback we get both at work and at home can speed the process up.

Building Bridges

Try to think of some of the cues you get from the behaviour of others that cause you to suspect that there is something wrong. How often has someone been able to tell you calmly what their problem is rather than you getting a sense that there is something wrong because of the things they are saying or doing?

When someone is upset, one of the most useful things we can do is just acknowledge their feelings. So often in life people criticise us for feeling 'nasty' things, or try and persuade us to push the feelings to one side. All of this actually make the matter worse because the feelings are stuck inside with nowhere to go. The person who encourages us to feel them and lets us express them is the person we are more likely to experience as helpful.

There is a common fear that expressing our feelings will make it all worse. If we just concentrate on churning around inside the feelings and getting bogged down in them, that may well make it worse. However having the feelings acknowledged by another person has the great effect of helping us actually let go of them and move on to whatever else is lying underneath - the next feeling perhaps, or the practical difficulty that caused the feelings in the first place.

Taking listening a step further

Sometimes silence and the best attentive behaviour in the world are not quite enough. Some situations need something more. At these times we can use very simple responses so that the speaker knows we are still with them. In this way we encourage the speaker to continue talking and don't interrupt the flow.

Examples:-

..... mm-hum ..... go on ..... yes ..... really? ..... oh ..... and?

Repeating key words from the speaker's last sentence may also be used as a way of encouraging someone to continue. For example:

Speaker: *'I don't know what's happening, I just feel stuck'.*

Listener: *'Stuck'.*

The listener's body language, tone of voice and facial expression can also act as encouragement.

The aim of these responses is not to interrupt the person or agree or disagree with them but just to let them know that you hear what they are saying.

Of course, we have all experienced inattentive listeners who repeat the same words and sounds, trying to mask that they are not listening at all and maybe not even caring about what we are saying. So make sure you are feeling accepting and understanding when you use these simple forms of acknowledgement.

Remaining silent is a very powerful way of giving people the space and safety to talk through their fears, worries, upsets and difficulties. If we can give our attention in a caring, accepting and supportive way, then we are halfway towards being as helpful as it is possible to be.

Trusting

In wanting to do more to help it is easy to forget the value of trusting the other person to be able to work through whatever they need to deal with, without our help. We leave the responsibility for dealing with feelings, solving the problem, or calming the worry with the person who is experiencing the feeling, problem or worry.

In this way, not only do we play our part in making sure that they do what is best for them, we are also helping them to learn how to do it in the future when we are not around to help. Particularly with our children this is a very important step we can help them take in their growing up - but it applies equally in any situation where a person is learning a new skill or assuming a new set of responsibilities.

As we said in the introduction, people who are upset do not send straight messages.

Asking questions

It isn't always easy to talk about our feelings, worries or problems. In particular it can be difficult to get started. If you think that someone has something on their mind that you could help them with, a good way to start is letting them know that you have the time to listen and are prepared to give them the time and attention that they may need.

As nice as it is to be able to help, there are times when you may well have more important things to do or to think about. It is more useful not to offer to listen than to offer and then not listen, giving all those little unconscious messages that show you would rather really be somewhere else.

'But what,' you might wonder, 'if they dry up and don't seem to know what to say?'

It is a natural response, in this situation, to feel that you want to ask questions. After all, asking questions helps the flow of conversation.

Question may well be appropriate at such a time - however, there are useful and not so useful questions to use.

Questions can be either **closed** questions or **open ended** questions.

By asking open-ended questions rather than closed, directive ones, you are firmly leaving the responsibility for the feeling or the problem with the other person, rather than trying to solve it for them.

Your open-ended questions, coupled with an accepting and attentive attitude, convey your genuine interest in helping them without taking over or prying into things they may like to work through on their own.

Closed question

These usually limit a person to a yes or no type answer. They are asked to get a particular piece of information for you the questioner, and are seldom of any practical help for the person being asked.

Examples of closed questions:

- *Do you want eggs or beans for tea?*
- *Are you feeling sad?*
- *Are you worried about your job?*
- *Do you love me?*

Open ended questions

This type of question allows a person room to answer as he or she wishes and doesn't dictate or limit their answer.

Examples of open-ended questions:

- *What would you like for tea?*
- *Can you tell me what you are feeling?*
- *What's happening?*
- *Is there something on your mind?*
- *Would you like to talk about it?*
- *Can you tell me more about it?*

Here are some of the less useful reasons questions are usually asked:-

1   To fill in silences that the <u>listener</u> finds uncomfortable.

2   To confirm something the questioner is thinking.

3   To veil some emotion or need of the questioner, e.g. 'Why are you doing that?' instead of 'I don't want you to do that'.

4   To satisfy the questioner's own curiosity or need to know.

These reasons usually conceal a statement that the person isn't willing to state out loud, or may not be aware of. Look for the statement underlying your question. It is usually better to make a statement (*'I want some peace!'*) than to phrase it as a question. (*'Do you have to make so much noise?'*)

Emotional Flooding

There is another good reason for not asking closed questions of someone who is experiencing a problem and is emotionally upset. When we are upset, our emotions tend to take over the thinking part of our make-up. The more upset we are, the more difficult it is to think straight.

Building Bridges

Start to practise using both simple acknowledgements and open ended questions.

At times when you would perhaps have asked questions about what happened in someone's life, just invite them to talk about it. Sit down somewhere. Give them a few moments of real attention and be accepting of whatever comes up for them.

Choose carefully the moment you start listening to someone's upsets. If you are busy, or likely to be interrupted, avoid offering to listen. There is little worse than starting to share something important and painful and finding that, half-way through, your listener gets distracted by the need to do something else.

If you want to listen and have other things to do, either change your priorities, or if that isn't practical, arrange a time as close ahead as possible when you can give them the attention they need.

Inevitably you will catch yourself asking all sorts of questions. When you do, don't worry about it; just make a mental note or even a written one of the sorts of questions you are asking and when. Explore these later and ask yourself: what was I trying to achieve by asking that question?

When we are upset we are **emotionally flooded.** Closed questions, or questions that demand specific information in answer, address just that thinking side of the mind which is being flooded out by emotions. The result is either that the emotional temperature can rise as the upset person struggles to find the answer and/or they are taken off track from the real issues by trying to answer well-intentioned but irrelevant questions. It can be a painful realisation for well-meaning people to discover that their best efforts to help are only making matters worse.

Learning from past experience

Young children don't make mistakes or fail at things - they do something, then do it again and again, finding new ways if the old ones don't work, until they have got it how they want it.

This is how they learn to crawl, sit up, walk, talk and achieve many of their early skills.

Children *learn* about failure. They learn because of the expectations placed on them by adults, and sometimes by older children, and the negative messages that get when they don't meet up to those expectations. As they get older they may start to have unrealistic expectations of themselves, wanting to do things that their bodies or minds can't achieve.

Our society is very goal and achievement-oriented and there is not much emphasis placed on enjoyment while getting there. We want to 'be it' or 'have it' now.

It is easy to love perfection and the way things should be. The real test is to feel comfortable and content with the way it is right now. It is the obstacles I meet that allow me to expand, to stretch my 'lovingness' to include even that.

When we make mistakes and feel we have failed, we quite often get completely side-tracked and use up energy feeling guilty or trying to correct the mistake. If we do get side-tracked in this way we are no longer on our path, unable to go to the next place that we want to be. Many people spend a great deal of time 'lost' in this sort of way.

If we remove the negative emotional attitudes that we have towards our failures and mistakes, we can free a great deal of energy. This we can then use to look constructively at what happened and gather information that can help us change what we do in the future. If we allow ourselves the freedom, we can learn much of great value from where, how and when we went astray.

Fear of failure

If we learned that it was not all right to fail, this attitude can have a profound effect on what we allow ourselves to do in the future. Fear of failure can prevent us from even trying to get our needs met or attempting new things, thus severely limiting us as human beings.

In our education system, where only one person can come 'top' it is very hard for children not to pick up negative attitudes and feelings about 'getting things wrong'. If you were told that you had to take an exam at the end of this course (which you don't!) most of you would feel some level of anxiety about it. The learning process would be changed for you and probably not in a very constructive way.

Children do not need to be taught how to learn, develop and explore the world - they are born with these abilities. The concept of failure however, is one that is learned, and one that affects us all through our lives.

Building Bridges

If there are things that you feel you regularly fail at, it may be a good idea to look at what is going on 'behind the scenes'.

What would happen if you were successful? Do you get something important for yourself out of 'failing' that you might be able to get in a way that is more acceptable to you?

What might stop us listening?

For most of us, real attentive listening is a skill we have to learn and practice. The reality is that we may fumble along at it, jump in and ask questions, give advice instead of remaining quiet and find listening well very difficult. The old habits die hard. Many people have not had much experience of listening or being listened to and so have not had the opportunity to learn the skill. We have all had plenty of experience of not being listened to. At times, even those we are listening to will contribute to how hard we find it.

Building Bridges

Take a little while to think about the things that may make it difficult for you to give full attention and listen.

What is the usual way you react when you are confronted by someone who is upset?

Is this anything like the way your parents or other adults reacted to you when you were upset ?

What do you think you could do to start breaking out of the old habits and start listening instead?

"Please just tell me what to do" is a common plea, and not just from young children.

'When we think we know is when we don't know'.

Chinese proverb

Go easy on yourself

Are you prepared to go easy on yourself and learn these new skills bit by bit without worrying that you are not doing it right?

It is useful to remember that we are all doing the best we know how at any particular moment. The fact that you have begun to learn a new way does not take away from the fact that when you are at home in your normal situation you react in the way you 'know' in that situation.

It is OK to be a good enough listener bit by bit remembering to try things differently and learning from the nice and not so nice examples you experience.

Building Bridges

1 Listening

Commit yourself to really listen - it's best if you do this consistently over for example a period of a day. Really listen when someone speaks to you - stop what you're doing and give them your undivided attention - or ask them to return when you are able to do so. Pay attention to posture, tone of voice and facial expression while you are listening to the words they are speaking. Listen wholeheartedly and check back with them when they have finished to make sure you have understood what was being said.

2 Watching

Choose a situation where you normally interact when it is not strictly necessary to do so - for example: a child at home ...

Deception of familiarity

We tend to think that we know the people we spend a great deal of time with, very well - our colleagues, partners, children, etc. This maybe true, but quite often, when we think we know someone well, we stop updating our information about them, and forget that people are constantly developing and changing.

Take some time to stand back a little and really notice the adults and children you spend a lot of your time with. Look at them as if you were seeing them for the first time.

Appendix 6

REFLECTIVE LISTENING PART 1

What happens when we get upset

We all get upset now and again. Sometimes the upset isn't very strong and doesn't interfere with whatever we are doing at the time. Sometimes the upset is much greater and the strength of the feelings gets in the way of our being able to think straight or get on with everyday tasks.

At these times, our feelings have flooded out our thinking minds and we need quite urgently to unflood ourselves before we can carry on.

Reflective listening

Reflective listening - also sometimes known as "active listening" is about the best way we know for helping people deal with upsets, unflood those feelings, sort out the confusions and work out the solutions to their day to day worries and difficulties. Reflective listening is a mixture of skills that include silence and good attention as well as these three more active ingredients:-

1. **Paraphrasing**

This is a way of helping someone get clearer about what they are thinking and feeling by listening to what they are saying and then repeating to them the gist of the content in a short and simple "paraphrase" using your own words.

2. **Reflecting feelings**

It is often difficult to get clear about thoughts if feelings are getting in the way, so as you listen it is particularly helpful to pick out the feeling words and underlying unstated feelings and reflect these back to the speaker. This helps them become more aware of what is happening inside them and allows them to let go of those feelings and become unflooded.

3. **Reflecting hidden meanings**

In combining paraphrasing and reflecting the feelings it is often possible for the listener to get a sense of what the speaker is meaning even if they can't get it for themselves. Offering your sense of things to them may well help them to make the connections they need to be able to help themselves.

The value of expressing feelings

In the world in which we live, thoughts and deeds are valued much more than feelings. We train children to think clearly often whilst also training them not to express their feelings.

However, bottled up feelings have to go somewhere; they may either explode periodically in dangerous ways, in the home, at work or on the streets; or they may become locked into our bodies and cause anything from minor aches and pains to migraines, ulcers or serious medical conditions.

Helping people learn to express their feelings safely and considerately is one of the most useful things you can do.

As we let our feelings out we can experience a great sense of relief, like a heavy weight removed from our shoulders. Not only will we feel lighter, calmer and happier, other people will experience us that way too.

Having let go of the unexpressed feelings, we will be more ready to face the world around us, the people in our lives and the tasks we have to do.

Sometimes I need to see my reflection in another person in order to remember who I really am.

More on reflective listening

Reflective listening is the skill of mirroring back to a person, in your own words and manner, what that person is saying to you.

Reflective listening allows the speaker to hear what they are saying, see what they are meaning and feel what is happening, and through this process, come to a better understanding of themselves and their situation.

At its simplest level, it is a process of listening with full attention that includes repeating back a shortened version of what the speaker says - known as paraphrasing.

The time when most of us use this skill already is when we are being given directions to get somewhere. We take in the information, then say it back to the giver to check whether we have got it right. We are converting what has been said into our own words to make sure of our own understanding.

With reflective listening you are doing just the same thing but with the emphasis is on helping the other person to get clear about what is going on for them.

Paraphrasing what the other has said also goes a long way towards preventing misunderstandings - we often think or feel that we understand what a person has said but this is just guesswork, unless we check our understanding out with the speaker.

When your words mirror clearly what is being said you will get a "yes" response from the speaker, verbally or non-verbally. When your paraphrase misses the mark the speaker naturally corrects it. In this way, an inaccurate paraphrase will be far more use than a question or reassuring statement.

Paraphrasing deals mainly with the content of the message you are receiving; the words, facts and information. You feed back, in your own words the essence of what the other person is saying to you in a short form. The paraphrase should be simple and to the point and actively reflect only the important points of the other's message. Using too many words can completely distract the speaker from what they are saying. Using your own words when you do this is very important.

"I can never tell you 'what you said', but only 'what I heard'. I will have to rephrase what you said, and check it out with you to make sure that what left your mind and heart arrived in my mind and heart intact and without distortion".

John Powel

Just repeating the exact words like a parrot can stop the conversation completely. Using your own words convey to the speaker that you have really listened and understood and it helps you to know that you understand.

In summary:-

- Reflect the content of message.

- Be short and to the point.

- Reflect only the essentials of the message.

- Use your own words.

Key phrases

When we start to use reflective listening it is all too easy to use the same sets of words all the time. We then end up sounding rather boring and the people we are trying to help may switch off. Below you will find a selection of phrases other people have found useful at different moments in the reflective listening process.

We call these phrases "lead-ins", and they are important because they tell the other person that our paraphrase is what we guess or think they are saying rather than an attempt to lay down the law.

So, for example, where the statement "you're feeling upset" might produce resentment or irritation, the more tentative statement "I have a sense that you're feeling upset" or "I think that ..." invites agreement or disagreement, and allows the communication to move to the next stage.

As you practise this kind of listening, you will develop your own approach that feels natural to you.

Maybe you will find that you can convey an open-ended tentative approach without having to use these sorts of lead-ins at all.

"My daughter came thumping downstairs half-undressed one morning, shouting: 'Where's my red jumper? My striped blouse is in my cupboard, so is my blue sweater, but I've looked everywhere for my red jumper and can't find it!'

Normally I would have told her not to make such a fuss and would have complained about all the washing I had to do. But this time I decided to try something different:

I said: 'You've found some things to wear but not the red jumper you really want'.

She said: 'It's a pain. I expect it's still in the wash. I suppose I'll have to wear something else after all'.

I was amazed.

As you practise this kind of listening, you will develop your own approach that feels natural to you. Maybe you will find that you can convey an open-ended tentative approach without having to use these sorts of lead-ins at all.

Building Bridges

To be able to do this, you will need to find someone who will be prepared to help you develop your listening skills. Get them to talk about an important event or person in their life. When you feel it is relevant, usually after an important statement of feelings or facts, paraphrase what was said and check that you have got the gist. When you have paraphrased, the other person has to tell you if you have understood what they were saying. If you haven't you then spend time refining your paraphrasing until the person says you have "got it".

This exercise can be quite revealing about the many ways we misunderstand what people are saying to us and it can help us see more clearly how we sift information incorrectly.

How reflective listening helps the speaker

When you listen reflectively you are checking with the speaker that you really heard what they meant to say. This stops you from getting their messages wrong, gives the speaker a feeling of safety because they know they have been understood and allows the conversation to flow more freely, which helps them explore their problem.

They can then get to the problem that is really bothering them, which is rarely the same as the one that they start talking about. People in the helping professions are trained to look beneath what is called the "presenting" problem that a person comes to them with. We don't usually start talking about our deepest worries immediately; we "test the water" first or "sound someone out" before we start to reveal ourselves fully to them. Reflective listening, done with care and compassion, helps people through these initial stages. It also stops you, the listener, from trying to solve the minor problem the speaker is talking about first.

If you were to do that, they would have no chance to explore what it is that is really bothering them.

How do I start? *Something happened today, do you want to share it?*
Is there something I can help with?
I'd like to hear about it if it would help.
Do you want to tell me about it?

He's clammed up! *It doesn't look as if it is easy to talk about it.*
If you decide that you would like to talk later, I'll be here.
I'm happy to listen any time you want.

I'm confused *I'd like to help, but I don't know what is going on.*
I'm trying to understand but I'm finding it hard.
I'm sorry, I don't quite understand.
Let me check, is it that ....
I'd like to help but I don't know how.

She's confused *You seem confused to me.*
Then it isn't (original problem) you're worried about (don't like, are afraid of), it is ....
Part of you wants to .... and part wants to (do the opposite).
Am I right in thinking you don't understand (what/ how/why)?

He's stuck, avoiding or going round in circles *It is hard to talk about…..*
Sounds/looks as though you're uncomfortable (sad, hurt) about this.
I feel there's something we haven't got to yet.
I wonder if there is anything else going on?

We're ready for a solution, but how do we get there?
You're looking for some ways to sort this out, can you think of something that might work?
You want to find some way to work this through. What do you think you can do about this?
You want some help with this. Let's see what we can think of together. Got any ideas?
You want to clear this up, yet you don't know/aren't sure how.
I get the idea you want to work this out somehow .... any ideas?

Children, in particular, often make only indirect attempts to get their deeper needs met. They want a drink at bedtime, they want something to eat just after lunch, etc. If we meet these surface needs all the time the child never gets what they were really wanting. You may wonder why they don't just come out with the real problem. Yet think of the number of times you have felt off-colour or fed up and not really known why. Reflective listening to your child's concerns can prevent this from happening.

Reflective listening can help people in two important ways. Firstly, it can make it easier for some people who are not really aware of their feelings, or what is going on inside them emotionally, to get back in touch with their feelings again. Just doing this often adds the missing piece they needed in order to begin to solve their problem.

Secondly, when a person is overwhelmed by feelings, reflective listening lets them know that it is all right to have those emotions and gives them the chance to express them fully. Expressing the emotions has the effect of releasing the pent-up energy and drains off the emotion, after which the person generally feels a great deal better.

Reflective listening helps people feel strong and in control of their lives because it acknowledges what they are experiencing and thus who they are. Too often in our world we are told by others what we are doing, feeling and thinking. Reflective listening gives us a chance to see, hear and feel ourselves for ourselves - it puts us back in touch with who we really are!

Emotions

We have thoughts in our minds and sensations in our bodies and a combination of these two produces what we call emotions or feelings. Usually it is a thought that triggers an emotion although we need not necessarily be aware of the thought.

Repressing our feelings

Repressing our feelings has several undesirable effects. Firstly, not releasing our emotions means that they are stored inside our bodies and cause tension which builds up into aches and pains and can even lead to serious illnesses in later life.

Secondly, it takes energy and hard work to keep emotions buried, energy that is needed in order to live our lives fully NOW. We have all experienced at some time the sluggishness that goes with depression or feeling bad and, conversely, the release of energy and good feeling when we have finally blown up and got something off our chest.

Our partner is late home, and hasn't called to let us know what's going

    on - a fact.

We worry about all the awful things that might have happened –

    thoughts.

Our stomach begins to hurt and we want to vomit - sensations.

The combination of these things = worried sick.

Thirdly, we can build up an enormous amount of fear about the repressed emotion, believing that if we ever let it out it will damage either ourselves or other people.

Finally, emotion can be repressed so well that we are not aware of it all. Part of us becomes dead or numb - a part that we need in order to be fully human.

Any emotion can be repressed: sexual feelings, anger, confidence, loneliness. In some societies, even feelings of love and compassion towards others are often not allowed expression.

To function fully and well we need to be in balance, neither too much in our heads, thinking all the time, nor overwhelmed constantly by our feelings or the repression of them.

The use of rational informed creative thought and emotional intelligence (the constructive use and expression of our emotions) enables us to become self-actualised - centred, aware, and living fully - the condition which American psychologist Abraham Maslow described as the pinnacle of human existence. (See Maslow's pyramid in **Appendix 3 – "Whose Problem"** on page 119)

Joey

Usually young children are able to experience their emotions freely:-

Little Joey couldn't put his train set together, got increasingly frustrated and then angry. He broke the train set and kicked the cat. Then he sat down and cried his eyes out. His mother came and mended the train and stroked the cat and Joey smiled happily and ran off into the garden.

In a very short space of time Joey has gone through quite a wide range of emotions; he has felt them, expressed them and then gone on to the next thing in his life.

All this works quite well until somewhere along the line little Joey learns that it is not okay to be angry or that "big boys don't cry".

Learning this doesn't stop Joey from experiencing his emotions but it does change what he does about them. Instead of expressing them freely and getting them out of his system he begins to push them down inside his body - they have to go somewhere!

He also begins to feel bad and guilty about having the emotion in the first place. If his parents have told him that "big boys don't cry", they obviously know what's right, then there must be something wrong with him if he wants to cry.

What's worst of all is that, if they find out, they might not love him anymore.

And so it starts, the long weary road into guilt, being separated from his feelings, bad thoughts about himself, fear that if he shows what he is really feeling and who he really is, he won't be accepted and loved. It is a very sad process.

Reflecting emotions

We have talked about paraphrasing, the method of reflecting a person's words. Now we are going to look at ways of reflecting feelings, which are often nothing to do with the words that are being spoken.

Because we live in a society that does not readily accept the free expression of emotion, we often try hard to mask our feelings from each other.

"We know too much and feel too little."

Bertrand Russell

We may speak confidently even when really we are fearful or we may carry on a seemingly normal conversation even when we are deeply upset. But these attempts at masking are rarely completely successful because we usually display our emotional state, whether we intend to or not, through all kinds of non-verbal behaviour. So this is where we now have to concentrate our attention.

"Since non-verbals are the major means of communicating emotions, they are central to understanding many of the most important things that others communicate to us".

Gerard Egan

Most of us have a sensitivity to emotions, to a greater or lesser degree. When we were small we sensed, for instance, whether our parents were angry or anxious. We know instinctively when not to approach someone. We notice when there is an "atmosphere" which makes us uncomfortable. Learning to reflect feelings is about developing this emotional sensitivity a bit more.

We do this by focusing our attention on how messages are being sent rather than on their verbal content.

There are four main areas to look at:-

1. Listen for the use of "feeling" words by the speaker.

If the speaker is using words that truly express their feelings, then you feed them back, just as you did with paraphrasing. For example:-

"You enjoyed your night out but you felt lonely when you had to go home alone".

169

However, sometimes people express their feelings in words that, on the surface, mean the opposite of what they are intending to say. You understand their true meaning from the way they speak.

For example:-

"Oh yes, I had a lovely time last night", said in a sarcastic manner, means just the opposite of what it says. So in this case you pick up the underlying feelings and reflect those:-

"You didn't enjoy yourself when you went out".

2. Focus on body language and non-verbal behaviour.

This involves being aware of facial expression, body posture, tone of voice, bodily movements and gestures and also developing a sense of how strongly or otherwise they feel from the level of their energy.

It is these things that will tell you most clearly what a person is feeling and what you pick up from them may be completely at odds with what the speaker is actually saying.

"I really did enjoy going to the school party". If this is said with conviction but also with a definite shake of the head, it would tell us that though part of the child enjoyed it, there was a part that didn't.

The speaker may or may not be aware of a discrepancy between their words and behaviour. When you reflect back the feelings you have become aware of, you put them in touch with the feeling side of themselves. They are likely to feel more comfortable because you have understood and be encouraged to carry on talking. For example:-

"So, most of you had a good time and there is a part of you that didn't".

3. Problem described factually

Many people do not use feeling words at all and describe their problem in a very factual way. In these instances it is often possible to infer feelings from the overall content of what they are saying.

For example:-

"As soon as I went out it started to rain, then the bus was late and, when I finally got there, they didn't have any left, then, to cap it all I had my purse stolen!"

At no point does the speaker mention how they feel but we can pick up the likely feelings from what has been said, even just from reading it on this page. One response might be:-

"Sounds like you had a dreadful time!"

4. Use own feelings and imagination to understand

You can use yourself, your own feelings and your ability to imagine how you would feel in a similar situation. At best, of course, this can only be guesswork, although people do have similar feelings in difficult situations. Reflecting the feelings that you guess someone is experiencing will soon give you an idea of whether you are right or not. If you are not, the speaker will probably say so and tell you why.

Some more guidelines

- Say when you don't understand and ask the other person to make it clear for you.

- Avoid telling people that you know how they feel; you cannot know, only guess.

- Focus on the feelings and choose accurate feeling words.

Being able to find the word that accurately reflects the speaker's experience is very helpful to them. Where feelings are concerned this can be quite difficult. Our society does not value feelings and few people talk openly about their feelings, so it is easy to be at a loss for words to describe them.

Giving feedback

As you start to practise these new skills, you might like to give some thought to how others can help you and you can help other people put these skills to best use. Being given and giving feedback is the most practical way to learn. Use the following guidelines when asking anyone to help you develop your skills.

Feedback guidelines

Be descriptive. Describe your own reactions, how you felt and what you thought about the behaviour in question.

Be specific. Avoid making judgements and generalising. So: "You are always withdrawn and sullen" would change to: "When you sit slightly outside the circle and don't enter the discussion I feel as though you are somewhere else".

Give your feedback immediately after the behaviour has occurred, if you can.

Remember that feedback is most useful when it is asked for, although children may at times benefit from unsolicited feedback when they are just beginning to learn how their behaviour affects others.

Check that your feedback was received properly. If you are unsure, it might be useful to ask the person to repeat what you said.

Use feedback constructively. It should benefit the person receiving it and should be about behaviour they can change.

If appropriate, check the reactions of others who were there - do they have similar feedback to give?

- Feedback means giving back to a person your own perceptions about what that person has just done or said.

- Feedback enables a person to check out whether what they think they are doing and saying comes over as they expect to others.

- Some of our behaviour is outside our own awareness but can be noticed by others. Feedback helps raise our awareness of this unconscious behaviour which in turn enables us to communicate more congruently.

- Accurate feedback helps us understand ourselves and so continue to grow.

Building Bridges

Practise reflective listening as often as possible, starting with small and relatively simple issues. Allow yourself to use this new skill in the home as well as outside it: even just saying sympathetically to a harassed looking shop attendant: "My it looks like you've had a hard day" can help them get through a difficulty patch. Get lots of easy practice before you tackle major emotional problems.

Appendix 7

REFLECTIVE LISTENING PART II

When not to reflective listen

Helping someone with an upset can take time. If you are too busy or have needs or worries of your own to attend to, suggest some other time or other person to do the listening.   If you are involved in the upset or problem you may not be the best person to help sort it out.

Listening to yourself

Most people are aware of having different parts of themselves - or inner voices representing the different ways they feel about things. It is possible to develop a part or voice that will reflective listen to all the other parts when we are feeling upset or in confusion.   We can help ourselves by listening inside our heads or even in front of a mirror.

Communications barriers

Many old patterns and beliefs get in the way of listening to others. As children we learnt to switch off at times, to doubt and judge others, and to spend most of our listening time working out what we were going to say when it is our turn to speak. All these things stemmed from not having been listened to in our turn, and can get in the way now as we try to listen reflectively to others.

Unhelpful responses

With the best will in the world we may set out to help people with a problem and either have no effect or make it worse. Common unhelpful responses include reassuring, taking their minds off it, denying the feelings, sharing our own problems to divert them from theirs, or simply giving "good advice". We all use responses like these at times, having learnt them as children from our parents, teachers and other adults. Feeling guilty or blameful towards ourselves or others is in itself an unhelpful response. We can all learn to react in other more useful ways in future.

More about reflective listening

So far, we have considered reflecting content and reflecting feelings. When we put this all together we have true reflective listening. It isn't easy to become a good listener, so it might be useful here to recap and expand some of our suggestions.

Remember what we have said about not coming across as dogmatic and interpretive. To avoid this, we suggest using simple "lead-in" phrases that offer your reflective response more tentatively.

For example:-

"I sense that... you feel angry because the parcel was late and you can't get your mother's present to her on time".

or

"I expect... you feel upset and hurt because he didn't call you".

This format is just to help you at the beginning: there is no need to stick to the same words each time. You could, for instance, just as easily say: *"I sense you are upset"* rather than *"I sense you feel upset"*.

Words like "since", "about" and "that" can be used instead of "because". Finding your own way of doing it is obviously more effective because it is "real" for you. Try different methods and pick the one you feel most at home with.

The most useful responses are the shortest ones, ones that include all you want to reflect in the smallest number of words. This way the speaker's conversation is not unduly interrupted but they know that you are "with them".

Some examples:-

statement - "He had a go at me in front of the whole office!"

response - "You must have felt awful".

statement - "I can't read his writing, and he wants this typed up for the meeting this afternoon".

response - "How frustrating for you".

statement - "They just seem to keep on piling work onto me - now I have to produce the performance statistic as well!"

response - "You sound as if you're not sure you can cope with it all".

It isn't useful to pretend that you understand what someone is saying or feeling. It is O.K if you don't understand - say so - and ask them to explain some more. Avoid telling people that you know what they are thinking or that you know just how they feel. Many people doubt, quite rightly, that others can know these things, so saying you do can distance you from them. It is far better to demonstrate your understanding with empathetic responses rather than tell them you know.

Vary your responses. These can range from silence, body movements like a nod of the head, and minor encouragements like the repetition of an important word through to reflecting in your own words the content, feeling or meaning of what they are saying. Like learning to drive a car, you will probably start out feeling a bit awkward with your new skills, yet with practice, they become second nature.

Be aware of your tone of voice. Our voices can reflect very clearly how we are feeling without us being aware of it - think about how you talk to someone that you want to get rid of, and then think about what your voice sounds like when you are talking to someone you love and want to get close to. When reflective listening, use the tone of your voice as a tool. Make sure it is appropriate to the situation.

Be patient. You may spend a long time listening to someone and yet they still go away seeming not to have found their solution. This is absolutely nothing to worry about. They may mull over what was said and discover something new and useful for themselves or they may need lots more listening time before they begin to find their way out of whatever it is that is troubling them. For others, just being able to talk freely may be the solution. Being heard and understood can in itself give people the very thing that they were looking for - deep caring contact with another human being.

Reflective listening is a wonderful skill for helping others but if there is no reason to use it, don't. Like everything else, it can be overdone and flogged to death. Using it all the time will drain your energy and drive your family and friends mad. If you get comments like: "She's off again!" or "Why don't you talk properly to me any more", then the chances are you are overdoing it.

More about when not to reflective listen

Probably the most important time to be wary of using it is when you need to take care of yourself and don't have the energy and inclination to concentrate on another's problems. If you continue to try and help others when you haven't met your own needs you will become drained and the quality of the help that you are giving will be low. It is in everyone's interests that you look after yourself!

We suggest you avoid using reflective listening when you feel unaccepting of the other person. If your own negative thoughts and feelings keep intruding, the other person is likely to pick that up and you will not come across as helpful. Be congruent in your thoughts and feelings about wanting to be there for the other person. It isn't useful to pretend to be accepting because you think you "ought" to help; you have the right not to help if you don't want to.

Too close for comfort

Another time when reflective listening will probably not be useful is when you are too involved in the problem. Here your thoughts and feelings get caught up in the problem in the same way as for the speaker. This is most likely to happen with people who are very close to you and who have a problem that involves you, making it difficult for you to set aside your feelings while you help them.

For example:-

You have had a lot of input in a presentation that a colleague had to make. When the colleague returns from the meeting looking upset because the presentation was not well received, you will probably feel as defensive or as let down as your colleague, and would be unable to help your colleague deal with the way they felt.

Using the idea of "who owns the problem?" can be helpful here. If it is you, it is not an appropriate time for you to be trying to listen to them. In this situation, it may be enough to share your feelings, so that you can create some space in you to listen; or you may have to say that you are not feeling able to help right now because you are too upset and arrange a time to help later.

It is possible that you will always be so upset about a particular problem that you will not be able to help later either. In this case, it might be useful for you to find someone else to listen to the person with the problem.

There may be times when you are too rushed or busy to be able to listen attentively to someone else's upsets. Tell them this and then you can avoid undue hurt feelings by making a time to get together later on.

Finally, be wary of using reflective listening when all you are being asked for is information.

More about listening to yourself

You have learned a great deal about how to listen to others effectively. You can use these same skills to listen to yourself when you are upset or have a problem. There are quite a number of skills and techniques that you can use to overcome the fact that there is only one of you! They all require that you keep part of yourself detached from the problem you are having.

1. Reflective listening to yourself

Listen reflectively to your own inner voice to find out what is going on inside you. What are the thoughts and feelings you are having? Allow yourself to air them fully and listen to what you are saying with the same care and respect you would give to another person you were helping.

2. Gestalt therapy technique

In Gestalt therapy, developed by Fritz Perls, there is a technique in which you use cushions or chairs to represent the parts of you that are having problems. For example, if you were having a problem with your body you would have two cushions, one for you and one to represent your body. You would then have a conversation with your body. When you were speaking you would sit on your cushion and when your body was speaking you would sit on the cushion that represents your body. In both places you use the first person when you are talking, that is:-

> You - "I don't understand why you are so painful all the time?"

> Switch to body cushion "I'm fed up, you never look after me
>   properly and you just forget that I exist most of the time".

> You - continue until you feel you want to stop.

This technique requires that you let go as much as you can and trust that things will come up that will let you know more about what is happening inside yourself. You may, in the process, bring to the surface many different parts of yourself, in which case you use a different cushion for each one.

3. Top-dog/Under-dog

Fritz Perls also noticed that most of us have two distinct types of voices in our heads that surface time and time again. One he labelled Top-dog; this voice is loud and bossy and always telling you what you should, must or ought to do. The other he labelled Under-dog and this voice is weak and unable to stand up for itself. These two voices continually war with each other whereas it would be better all round if we could get them to understand each other more and get closer together - just like reconciling two fighting children.

Top-dog needs to learn to be more understanding and accepting, avoiding using labels and blame. Under-dog needs to learn to stand up for itself and be more assertive. Play out both roles as they apply to yourself and use the detached part of yourself to mediate between them.

4. Inner family

Most people recognise that they are made up of differing parts or aspects. It is almost like having an internal family. All these parts have needs (perhaps one part wants challenge and another part wants comfort) and, if these needs aren't met, they will act up just like members of a real family do.

Use your detached part to help identify them and get their needs met. Quite often it is only one or two parts which cause you real problems.

These are the ones that feel you never meet their needs, which are usually to do with needing love, rest or fun.

5. Higher self or guardian

Some people develop a part of themselves who acts as an all-wise, all-knowing being who can be called on at times of trouble to give help and support. We all have an older and wiser part inside ourselves, one that understands us and knows what we need to be doing. We may recognise this being as ourself or the part may be seen as a person completely separate from ourselves. In whatever way this part is imagined it can be a very powerful ally to contact when your reserves are low.

6. Listen with your body

Our bodies continually send us messages which we don't listen to until they get so loud that we become ill. When we get tired a lot or constantly have headaches, for instance, our bodies are telling us that we are putting ourselves under too much strain. Usually it is mental or emotional stress that causes these kinds of symptoms. What is happening in your body is a barometer for what is happening in your mind. Your body needs loving and caring for in just the same way as a young child does. It isn't just a machine that gets you about. Listen to its needs, for they are your own.

More about communication barriers

We all put up barriers of one kind or another which get in the way of good communication with others. These are developed in our childhood as a response to not being listened to and not being allowed to speak freely.

We learned to worry what others might think about us if we said what we really felt and thought!

We learned that people often weren't honest and straight with us, so we had to make our own assumptions about was really going on.

We discovered we had to compete for speaking time, so we learned to rehearse what we wanted to say whilst another was speaking, thereby missing what was being said.

We learned that often people did not mean what they said, so we learned to tune out their voices and tuning out became a habit.

We learned to label and judge what others said. For example: "Don't listen to him, he is stupid!" or "No one in the Government knows what they are talking about".

Genuine contact with other people is made very difficult by these judgements and labels.

What do we do instead of listening?

Poor listening develops into a habit in much the same way as slouching or poor posture. We have many ways of occupying our minds when we are not really listening to what someone is saying to us:-

- we compare ourselves with the speaker, hoping that we will come out favourably.

- we "mind-read": not fully trusting the words they are speaking, we try to work out what we think they are really thinking and feeling.

- we rehearse what we want to say in reply.

- we filter the communication, maybe filtering out the things we don't want to hear or only listening for the things that may affect us. We prejudge the person, write them off and cease to listen.

- what is being said triggers off a daydream of our own which we pursue privately unknown to the speaker.

- we relate everything that is being said to our own personal experience and get involved with reliving that instead of listening.

- Some or all of these things can be going on in a listener's mind while apparently listening to what is being said, although the speaker usually senses that they are not being attended to fully.

Can you identify what it is that you do when you are not interested in listening to what is being said, when you do it and who with?

NB : Avoid beating yourself with a big stick about it, just become more aware of your own personal patterns.

Building Bridges

Who can you talk freely with and why?

Who can't you talk freely with and why not?

Who can't you be bothered talking to or listening to - why not?

How did your parents describe the talk of the following groups of
        people? e.g. "Children talk rubbish!"

men	women	old people	children	police
teachers	foreigners	rock stars	drug addicts	parents
tramps	hippies			

Labels flash before our minds as high speed (as they probably did for you just then) and may make us put up a barrier against another person without our even realising that it has happened.

How many people did you really see, hear and make contact with today? How many of them really made contact with you?

Why no-listening listening?

Much of the behaviour that goes under the guise of listening has another purpose entirely.

For example:-

- Pretending to be interested so that others will like you.

- Half-listening because it is the polite thing to do.

- Pretending to listen because you don't know how not to without offending.

- Listening because you want to be listened to.

People listen fully when they really want to understand someone, to learn something, or to give help and caring to another.

Everyone pretends to listen at times but as long as you have the choice (that is, you are capable of real listening) and are aware that you can choose, it isn't a problem. The more real listening you do, however, the closer you will get to people. Because real listening says "I care about you".

Stock responses

In much the same way that we learned listening blocks as a child, we also developed patterns for "helping" a person who is experiencing stressful and emotional problems. Many of these patterns are the stock responses our parents used when we had a problem that they had difficulty coping with. Like pretending to listen, these patterns go under the guise of being helpful when really they are unhelpful, because they don't allow people space to find their own solutions.

The following are examples of these unhelpful responses: they block the conversation and come between the person and their problem.

- Criticising - making negative comments, "you should" or "you ought" statements, fault finding.

- Name-calling and labelling - putting the other down, labelling them and thereby making them feel less of a person.

- Diagnosing - playing amateur psychiatrist: "I can read you like a book".

- Praising - a positive judgement about another is still a judgement and makes you a higher authority over them.

- Ordering, threatening, moralising, advising and questioning - all ways of providing your solution to another's problem. Only their solution can promote their growth, no matter how helpful yours are.

- Diverting - pushing the other's problem aside as if it were of no consequence, "taking their mind off things".

- Logical argument - focusing on facts when it is usually the feelings that need consideration.

- Reassuring - attempting to stop the other from feeling the negative emotions they are experiencing. This may appear to be comforting but in fact it is stifling.

Using your new understanding of these barriers to communication to point a finger of blame at yourself or another is also a barrier to communication and is a most unhelpful response. Use your increased knowledge to encourage yourself and others.

Building Bridges

Choose the block to listening that is most common to you and, over a period of a few days, notice when you use it and who you use it with. Really become familiar with it without trying to change it yet.

Next choose one person who is important to you whom you would like to stop blocking and reflective listen instead.

Notice what happens to you when you try to resist the block. Go easy on yourself - blocking habits are strong and have had along time to develop and become ingrained. They need gently easing out with love and care, not beating with your big stick.

Practise listening by using the radio. Note words that trigger off negative feelings or your sympathy. These trigger words appeal to prejudice and statements that appear logical but are not. Teach yourself to take in the gist of the discussion and develop a sense of what the feelings underlying the words might be. Become aware of when and why you want to stop listening and do something else.

Practise using your sense of hearing. At various times during the day shut your eyes and concentrate on identifying as many sounds as you can in your environment.

Listen to music and focus your attention on picking out individual instruments.

Childrens' auditory games such as recognising a pre-taped sound, or Blind-Man's-Bluff, where position is determined by sound of movement are also very good for focusing hearing.

Being there

Allowing people the freedom to fully experience what is happening to them can be the greatest gift that you can give them. All people struggle with their internal thoughts, feelings and emotions and it is through doing this that they grow - the struggle may or may not be painful for them but they need the freedom to do it. Too often we feel that we have to do something or say something in order to help another when all they really need is the open caring contact with another human being.

Building Bridges

Listen for when you and others use the stock responses we have mentioned. Try to think what might be a more useful way of helping, in the circumstances.

If you can clearly identify that you use one or more stock responses yourself, ask yourself these questions about each:

- In what situation do you use it?

- Do you use it with a particular type of person?

- What is happening inside you at the time?

- Does it come up in response to a certain emotion?

- Can you identify how you would really like to be responding instead?

- Who taught you the response?

- What happens when you want to use it and you stop yourself?

Another useful exercise is to imagine or remember how you react when stock responses are used on you by other people. Most of us can remember feeling somehow discounted by them in our childhood, but by the time we are adults we are often so used to them that we repress our reactions.

After all, we don't feel that we have to do something to help a person when they feel happy or in love. We just let them get on with it!

Using reflective listening instead of the stock responses is a good way to begin to break the pattern.

The next time someone close to you is hurt or upset, try meeting them where they are without saying anything. Just be there, letting them go through whatever is happening to them. Be aware of your urges to speak, make better or avoid and just keep them to one side. Be there quietly and wait for them finish.

Doing this takes trust: trust in yourself and trust in the fact that you, being 100 per cent present and loving, are all that is needed. You don't need to do anything except open your heart to the child - they will know.

"Don't just do something – stand there"

Haim Ginott

Appendix 8

NEEDS AND WANTS

Defining ourselves

It is not easy to answer the question: "Who am I?" It is always much easier to talk about what I do or what role I play in life. It is very much an expected part of the world we live in that we define ourselves in terms of what we do. So for the vast majority of people, their relationship with their children and their partner and their jobs is more important than their feelings about themselves. It means we define ourselves in terms of other people most of the time.

This is particularly noticeable in women because the social expectation in our Western World is that women should put other people first. When they first get married they are usually expected to consider their husband's job, his comfort and even his happiness as more important than their own. It may be possible to do this and still keep some independent life. However, if they have children together, it is still most likely to be the woman who abandons her job to have a full-time career in the home.

Even if we leave aside the rights and wrongs of this situation, what does it actually mean for most women? Putting the children and husband first - or just the children if they are one of the growing-number of single mothers - frequently means not only giving up work and staying home; it probably also means giving up hobbies, learning to do without time on our own and time with our friends, not going out much, not reading much - in fact, not doing many of the things that we used to do before we had a child.

On the whole, mothers are expected to take everyone else's needs into account all of the time and sacrifice their own.

This is perhaps the biggest difference between mothers and fathers. Most mothers who don't work outside the home give up all their own needs as described, while mothers who do work run the home as well - and still feel guilty about not being there all of the time for their child; whereas fathers who work may well be working very hard to support "the family" but they don't usually feel guilt and the chances are they are also getting more of their personal needs met through their work and leisure-time activities.

The biggest risk of putting others first all the time is that it can drain us to the point where we have nothing left to give. To avoid this risk it is really useful to start thinking about who and how we want to be for ourselves, besides being in a relationship with someone else. What ways are there that we can feel good about ourselves as individuals separate from the roles we play and the job we do?

Valuing our own needs

Many people play a number of roles - employee, mother or father, partner, home-maker, breadwinner, son or daughter. Each role has demands and requirements - there are needs and wants of others which must be met in some way, and which often force the postponement or even disregard of individual needs.

But, your needs are as important as those of your children, your parents, your partner, your employer or anybody else.

In fact you are the first priority most of the time. If your needs are met and you love and care for yourself well you will then have plenty of time, energy and love to give to others. We all have basic needs: to love and be loved, to laugh and play, to have peace and quiet and safety, to be valued, respected and cared for.

Somehow we learned that if we meet our own needs somebody else will lose out or if we meet others' needs then we still lose out.

What most of us didn't learn was that everyone's needs are 100% important and that there are ways to meet everyone's needs without anyone losing out.

In a couple relationship, or a family relationship, there are individuals who have needs and there is the relationship itself that has needs, almost like another person.

For instance John and Wendy and their daughter Jill all have needs as individuals in their own right. They also have needs in relating all together as a family. Within this small family there are three individuals and four relationships:

> John and Wendy
> Wendy and Jill
> John and Jill
> Wendy, John and Jill

Meeting the needs of all these people and relationships is possible if we work from the basic idea that everyone's needs are important. Thinking out how to do it can be a great deal of fun and develops flexibility and caring behaviour in all concerned.

Ways to meet needs

Most of us have learned a variety of ways to get our needs met. We learn from our parents, our teachers, our friends and enemies, fictional heroes and heroines and also villains. Most of this learning took place when we were very young. At that time, we chose the most effective ways we knew to get our needs met. As we grow up, those old ways may not seem as useful any more. Luckily, it is possible to change. A useful first step is to recognise as precisely as possible what it is we want to change.

At the risk of generalising madly, the types of behaviour we use to meet our needs fall broadly into three categories. The examples given below are extreme to make the point clearly. Most of us fall somewhere in between them all.

Three styles of meeting needs

All of life is about meeting our needs. Some people do it consciously and some without really being aware of it. There are a variety of ways we can go about it, and we usually learnt which one to use as small children.

1. Behaving submissively

People who behave in a submissive way don't usually ask for what they need but try to get it by giving in to other people and putting everyone else's needs first. They may not even believe they have needs and spend time apologising for what little they do manage to get from others. In this way they often get looked after by stronger people. However, at the end of the day they will probably be resented and rejected for their very weakness as well as ending up feeling resentful themselves.

2. Behaving aggressively

People who behave in an aggressive way are at the other end of the scale. They are the strong dominating types who demand that their needs be met and their views taken into account. They hold power over other people and believe themselves to be superior. They usually get their way and make it to the top of the pile.

As they have to do so on the backs of other people they tend to make a lot of enemies. The fear that underlies their aggression breeds on itself as they become scared that they may lose their power over other people.

3. Behaving assertively

People who behave in an assertive way are quite different from either of the other two. They know what their needs are and are prepared to express them openly. At the same time they take other people's needs into consideration and actively help everyone to get their needs met. People who behave assertively are more likely to be in touch with their feelings and are better able to respond to other people's, as a result they will not steam-roller over others like those that behave aggressively, or lie down as a doormat like those that behave submissively.

How many ways can you think of to meet everyone's needs in the following situation?

> *Jill has a need to play with water and be with her Dad.*
> *Wendy has a need for physical affection.*
> *John has a need to cool down and relax.*

They all have a need to be together.

Behaving submissively

Also labelled passive, victim, or permissive behaviour. People who behave in a totally submissive way don't express their needs directly, they do it indirectly through mixed messages and body language, or else they don't express them at all. They may smile a lot and apologise, in words and manner, for their very existence. Their voice may be weak and hesitant, they often ramble and use vague phrases and rely on others to guess what they mean.

Quite often they slouch, fidget, have difficulty in making eye contact and never look as if they mean what they say. They don't respect their own needs and rights and allow others to violate their space.

The advantages of behaving submissively

If a person has always behaved submissively this position is comfortable and safe. There is less responsibility in this position. After all, if you always follow others, no one can blame you if things go wrong.

People behaving in a submissive way quite often get protected and looked afte - they unconsciously entice others to do these things for them.

Behaving submissively quite often allows you to control others and can be a very persuasive tactic for getting your own way.

The disadvantages of behaving submissively

People who live this way, never really live their own lives. They are constantly giving in to the wishes and desires of others. They often miss out on deeper relationships.

This is because deep, intimate contact can only take place between people who are being truly themselves, whereas people who behave submissively are busy making themselves into what they believe others want, leaving no real self to love or be loved.

Behaving submissively all the time usually ends up with other people feeling guilty, irritated or pitying.

Excessive sacrifice for others can breed resentment in the very people for whom the sacrifices are made and can lead to rejection, which is the last thing the person wants.

By acting submissively and so repressing their feelings, they may lose touch entirely with their wants and needs; they may become numb and appear to have no feelings whatsoever.

…But repressed needs and emotions have a way of leaking or bursting out of people, so that suddenly they blow up angrily or subtly ruin pleasant occasions and make life difficult for themselves and others. Repressed wishes and emotions that don't leak out can take their toll on the body, making them ill.

Behaving in a submissive way means that they have difficulty taking charge of their lives or making constructive changes for themselves.

Behaving aggressively

People who behave in a totally aggressive way usually have no problems in stating what they want and need but it is quite often done at the expense of others. They have an air of superiority and strength and all their energy is directed outwards. They often use sarcasm and humorous put-downs against others and make lots of judgmental "You..." statements. They can act in ways that are cold and deadly quiet, flippant or loud and shrill. They are comfortable standing with their feet wide apart, their hands on their hips and with a jutting clenched jaw. They often point a finger or make a fist. Their throat, neck and shoulders are often very tense. They are so intent on being right that they never hear what others say.

The advantages of behaving aggressively

People who behave like this usually get their own way. They win in most situations. It is a comfortable place to be if they have behaved this way for a long time. They are usually very effective in securing what they want, e.g. power, position and material possessions. They are very active in shaping their own lives and are also very good at controlling and having power over others.

The disadvantages of behaving aggressively

Many people behave aggressively because they are fearful - they operate from the position of "attack is the best form of defence".

Behaving aggressively earns you enemies who then want to "get back at you", either by counter-aggression or by resisting, lying, defying or sabotaging you. Controlling others takes time and energy and you have to be on guard all the time in case someone puts one over on you.

Behaving aggressively tends to de-humanise, so such people lose touch with feelings of love, compassion and understanding for other human beings. This is one of the reasons that armies are trained so aggressively - if you can feel another man's pain, how can you kill him? Trying to form worthwhile intimate relationships can be difficult for such people; how can you love someone that you dominate and how can they love you?

Aggression alienates people from each other.

Building Bridges

One way to become aware what those two types of behaviour feel like is to act them out. The best way to do this is just for **fun**, exaggerating the roles to make them extreme.

Do it with someone you feel at ease with - a friend, a partner, or a child. Children are very good at this sort of thing and it can be very enlightening and funny to watch them "pretending" to be a bossy teacher or angry parent.

Here are some hints for playing each role: In the totally submissive role, you are very dependant on others; you pull in your body so that you occupy less space in an effort not to be noticed; you look up at others rather than directly at them; and you don't look them straight in the face; your voice is soft and hesitant - you are afraid of being "loud".

Short statements you could make include:-

> *"Whatever you say is all right with me".*
> *"I don't know what I think, you will have to decide for us".*
> *"I can't manage without you".*
> *"I'm sorry if I have put you out, I'll change what I'm doing if you want"."*
> *"I have an opinion but you wouldn't want to hear it".*

Maintain the role for at least five minutes to give yourself a chance to really get into it. Walk around and do simple things like making a cup of tea and serving the person you are with.

How did you feel playing this role? How did your muscles feel? What was your breathing like? Did some of the behaviour feel familiar to you or was it totally alien to you?

If you behaved like that all the time, what might you need to do in order to stop doing it? Bearing in mind the idea that we only ever behave in ways that meet an underlying need, what may the need be in this case?

Looking at these sorts of questions may help you to understand where this sort of behaviour comes from and why it develops in the first place.

Now play out the aggressive role and ask yourself the same question when you have finished.

In the aggressive role, pretend that you are an aggressive boss who is getting at an employee for not being "up to standard". You stand up a lot and lean towards the other person in a slightly threatening stance. You put your hands on your hips or point a finger at your employee whilst you shout at them in a loud aggressive voice. You use lots of sentences with "you ..." in them, for example:-

> "You are always doing things wrong".
> "I am sick and tired of having to do all the work for you".
> "You are about as much use as a wet blanket".
> "You are lazy and stupid and you are not worth employing".

Behaving submissively and behaving aggressively are two sides of the same coin. Both stem from fear and both are behaviours we learned in order to get our needs met. Both behaviours can hurt the mind, the body, other people and therefore the world. When we behave submissively or aggressively, we fear to be ourselves.

The extremes we have described here are thankfully not so common. In reality most of our behaviour lies some way between the two, and may even be an ever-changing mixture of both.

Learning by watching others

Just watching other people, on television, in the street, the supermarket or at work, can give you a great deal more information about these two types of behaviour.

Watch with your heart as well as your mind and understand that most people are behaving the best way they know how, to get their needs met, whatever your own feelings and judgements about what they are doing.

Whether they normally behave submissively or aggressively, people sometimes adopt the opposite behaviour in certain circumstances. For instance the victim blows up and behaves very aggressively when they can't take any more and the persecutor can switch into submissive behaviour when being confronted by someone behaving even more aggressively.

For many people it is the situation which decides which behaviour they choose. For instance the man who behaves in a subservient way at work may rule his wife and children with a rod of iron.

Behaving assertively

We said earlier that there were three general types of behaviour we can use to get our needs met. The third one is behaving assertively which allows you to meet your own needs and express yourself fully and openly yet not violate the rights and feelings of others.

True assertiveness is "a way of being" in the world, at ease with yourself, and aware of both your own and other people's value as human beings. In short, you like yourself and you like other people. Behaving in an assertive way means that you respect yourself and others. If you are faced with someone who is interfering with your needs, you are prepared to confront them respectfully and firmly and at the same time help them if they feel upset at being confronted.

Behaving assertively involves a large degree of compassion not only for yourself but also for other people as well.

The advantages of behaving assertively

People who behave assertively soon gain the respect of others. They get most of their needs met in life and often feel fulfilled in what they do and how they are. Other people are attracted to them as models of how to live and can often be empowered by their example to change the way they live too. If it were common in our society at all levels from the personal to the political, true assertive behaviour would revolutionise the way the whole world operates.

The disadvantages of assertive behaviour

THERE ARE NO DISADVANTAGES TO TRULY ASSERTIVE BEHAVIOUR !

The difference between NEEDS and WANTS

One useful way to develop a practical understanding of assertive behaviour is to differentiate between needs and wants. In thinking about John, Jill and Wendy's needs earlier, you may have thought of several ways that they could all have satisfied them. In nearly all cases it is possible to think of more than one way to meet the need we have. And yet, how often do we get stuck thinking that there is only one answer to our needs?

When we are stuck like that it is because we are considering only our "wants" and not the underlying needs.

"I decided that I really needed to go to college. I had a friend who was also married with a family who had done that and it had made so much difference to her life. My family were all somewhat put out by the suggestion so I discussed the matter with another friend who was a particularly good listener. As I talked it through, I began to realise that my need wasn't to go to college - that was a want. What I needed was to be stimulated, feel that I was more than just a Mum at the kitchen sink, get to meet some new people and have some fun. Coming to that understanding made it possible for me to go home and talk it all through with my family. I may still go to college, but right now I'm finding lots of other ways to get those needs met".

For example:-

Bill has a slight cold and wants to stay off work. He probably feels he that he needs to stay at home. The reality is that there are rumours of redundancies at work due to a decrease in the company's market share.

Bill needs a sense of safety and security, and the thought of redundancy scares him. At home he feels safe, so he uses his cold as an excuse to meet his need for safety and security.

"My four-year-old Michael wanted to play with the living room furniture just as I was about to receive visitors. Normally we would have got into a row about it. - So this time I worked through with him what he needed and soon got clear that he wanted to build a spaceship for which he thought he needed the furniture. I accepted that building a spaceship was important to him and asked him to help me think of another way he could do it. In the end we agreed that he could have an old sheet and use the old chairs from the garden shed. He played outside for hours on his own!"

Getting help to meet your needs

It's not always easy to identify needs as opposed to wants, or to know how to go about meeting them. We may also have needs that right now we cannot hope to get met. Our financial and social situation may well limit us and it may well feel as if there is nothing we can do about it. That may be the case and even taking small steps to change the way we behave can begin to shift things in the world in which we live.

Understanding clearly our needs and slowly learning to take into our own hands the power to get them met is an important first step. Taking such a step is easier if we feel we are doing it with others rather than all alone. It is important that we get emotional support to help us make the changes we want in life.

Give some thought to who can offer you this support in your life. If you have no one, consider obtaining professional support. Thankfully, there is no longer such a stigma attached to seeking the aid of a professional counsellor.

Modern counsellors are professional 'listeners' who, by their listening and support can help us clarify and prioritise our needs, and discover the means in our lives to fill them.

Building Bridges

Think of one thing you want in your life and write it down.

Now ask the question "what will having / doing that do for me?"

Write down the answer under your original want. Now, thinking about the first answer, ask the same question again and write the second answer under the first.

Go on with this exercise until each time you ask the question you get the same answer. At which point you will probably have reached the underlying need behind the want.

Repeat the exercise with another want.

This exercise is fun and useful to do with friends and family.

Appendix 9

SHARING FEELINGS

Getting closer to people

Most people want to get on well with others and feel close to at least some people. You can only feel close to people you know and who know you. For people to be able to really know what you are like, you have to show and tell them. We call this "self disclosure" and it requires being open and honest about yourself.

Acceptance and caring depend on close, caring relationships, but we grow up in a world where there is considerable fear about getting close to other people. Young children have to be taught not to speak to strangers in case they are assaulted. They learn that they must not trust too readily.

Teenage girls may be taught to be suspicious of young men in case they want "only want one thing". Boys are taught not to express their feelings, which alienates them from each other. So we may well become wary about building up relationships with others.

We are not helped by the fact that in our society many basic relationship skills for instance communicating our feelings and meeting our own and others' needs are not taught to us, even though we now live in a world where such things could well be regarded as basic survival skills.

In fact, we are more usually actively discouraged from meeting our own needs and making known our thoughts and feelings. It is a wonder, in a way, that we ever do become close to anyone. There are plenty who don't and who suffer badly from isolation and loneliness. The increase in mental illness and suicide, on the one hand, and computer dating agencies, on the other, points to the fact that we have a serious problem in relating to each other happily.

We all live within our own worlds where we have set our own limitations on who we relate to and how much of ourselves we show to other people. Some people are very open and share a great deal of themselves; others are more reserved and take a lot of getting to know. They have to feel very safe before they "open up" to others.

Others only know us to the extent that we allow them to. We are in charge (even if we don't realise it) of how close we get to others. If we learned, for some reason, to be secretive and withdrawn in our childhood we still have the option, as adults, to change that behaviour if we want to. We can ask ourselves whether we really want to behave that way any longer and whether it is worth it to us to take risks to change it. We may need some help to find out how we came to feel like that.

Self disclosure involves knowing who you are, what you think and believe and would like, what your needs are, what your feelings are and knowing how and when you want to reveal this information to others.

It also involves being self-defined - not waiting to see how others behave before you decide what you yourself are going to say or do.

It means being who you are, not in a dogmatic, stuck way but in a dynamic, fluid way. It means you take decisions about what you say or do according to the particular situation you are in, rather than on the basis of inflexible rules you have set yourself.

To be able to do this you need a secure sense of your self-worth and of your own value in the world - the right of every human being, including you.

Create an Autobiography

You can do it in writing or make a tape recording of "your story" or express it in a series of pictures or cartoons - whichever appeals to you most.

Aim to end up with information about yourself that will enable others to understand you better. It may include:

- *What it was like for you at school.*
- *People you admired a great deal as a child.*
- *The jobs that you have found most interesting.*
- *Places you have visited that were important to you.*
- *The people you have loved and cared for deeply.*
- *The biggest loss of your life.*
- *Some of the best moments in your life.*
- *Your greatest achievement.*
- *Your hobbies and interests.*
- *The funniest thing that ever happened to you.*

But who am I?

If you feel or think that you have lost touch with who you really are, try writing an autobiography, as suggested in the box above .

Doing this will begin to give you a better picture of who you are and what has been important in the development of you as a person.

Much of the information that you first disclose about yourself to another person concerns the FACTS of your life and past history - the sort of things that you have probably just put in your autobiography. But as your relationship with another person deepens, you begin to disclose some of your thoughts and feelings about life.

These might include:-

- Beliefs and opinions you hold that are important to you.
- Events that were extremely emotional for you.
- Your fears and concerns, past and future.
- Your hopes for your life.

- Some of the problems that you have had with past relationships.
- Your general preferences and tastes.

To begin to look at these areas of yourself, ask yourself these questions:-

- What do you believe in?
- What stirs great emotion in you?
- What do you really like to do?
- What do you dislike doing?
- What are you scared of doing?
- What do you dream of being able to do?
- What are your strengths and weaknesses?

So far we have looked at the facts of your life and some of your feelings about life in general. These are the sorts of things that we most often disclose to others to some degree or other. But there is, of course, another form of self disclosure which is simultaneously the most rewarding and the most risky. This is the "here and now" disclosure in which you express the thoughts and feelings that you are having at this very moment. It might mean:-

- Saying what attracts you to the person you are talking to.
- Saying how you are affected by the other person's behaviour right now.
- Telling the other person some of the things that you don't feel comfortable about in them.
- Saying what you would like from being with them.
- Saying how you feel about how the other person responds to what you are saying.

Here-and-now disclosure means being aware of how you are feeling and what you are thinking right now and allowing yourself the freedom to express those things, in a way that respects yourself and the other person.

The risks of self disclosure

If we want other people to accept us they have to know us. However, there is always the risk that they may not like what they come to know. There is even the risk that unscrupulous people will take advantage of our honesty and openness and try to use what they know of us against us. It is necessary to learn to judge just how much to share and how much to keep to ourselves and perhaps be prepared to take a few more risks than we might have done in the past in the hope of getting even closer to people in the future.

HOWEVER OPEN I AM WITH MYSELF, OTHER PEOPLE MAY **NOT** LIKE WHAT I SAY

I CAN CHOOSE HOW MUCH OR HOW LITTLE TO SAY

AND SOMETIMES I CAN TAKE A RISK AND SAY SOMETHING MORE

Saying what you see

Say what you actually see and hear, from your own standpoint, rather than what you assume is

going on for another person. So, instead of saying:-

- "You are not listening to me," you would say:
  "I see you staring off into space and not responding to my questions."

- "You are interrupting" would change to:
  "You are starting to talk before I have finished what I want to say!"

The first statement in each example is quite often taken as an attack, the second is factual information that leaves the listener free to reply however they wish. This structure may seem somewhat unwieldy at first but it does focus your attention on speaking about what you are seeing and hearing.

Feeding this information back to the other person in a straightforward way prevents a lot of the interpretation that can get in the way of clear communication.

Saying what you think

Your ideas, beliefs and opinions are important because you are. If you don't express them you deny your self-worth.

Many of us have been brought up to believe that talking for ourselves in this way is somehow wrong, big-headed or selfish and so we learned to distance ourselves from what we were saying.

For example:-

We don't do that, do we, Daddy?

One can't always be aware of these things.

That looks like a nice film, doesn't it?

It might help if you didn't make so much noise.

Most people don't like that sort of thing.

We talk in generalities to avoid revealing our true selves.

Take a moment now to change the above statements into "speaking for yourself" statements. Expressing yourself using personal pronouns lets others know that you are owning what you say and that you don't necessarily expect others to agree with you.

For example: Instead of saying: "one finds it difficult to control one's anger," say: "I find it hard to control my anger". The person you are talking to may not share the problem!

Ideas and opinions are not irreversible. You may often want to change and develop your ideas, in the light of new information. Making "thinking" statements does not mean that you will be held to them for ever.

> I believe ....
> In my opinion ....
> I think ....
> It seems to me ....

Use the above introductions to make some statements about thoughts, opinions and beliefs that you don't normally air. Imagine yourself saying things of this kind to your boss, your mother, your best friend - anyone who seems appropriate.

Saying what you feel

It is not always obvious to someone else that we are feeling a particular emotion - they can't always see that we are feeling hurt, for instance. And the emotions we do show can sometimes be confusing. For instance, we can cry either because we are happy or because we are sad. Even if what we are feeling is obvious, some people find displays of emotion uncomfortable and may choose to ignore them unless we involve them in some way. For these reasons it is a good idea to say what you are feeling.

Part of the problem of having been encouraged not to share our feelings may be a lack of the right words to describe them.

Read through the list of feeling words in the box on the next page - just some of those that people use.

Notice the ones that are familiar, and think about when and where they are used. Reading the list will automatically begin to increase the number of feeling words you use. Remember that quite often we use the words "I feel" when we really mean "I think". For example:-

"I feel that you are ignoring me" is an opinion, not a feeling. "I feel rejected" is the feeling statement.

If you say the words "I feel that .." at the beginning of your statement then it is likely that you are talking about a thought and not a feeling.

We often substitute opinions and evaluations for feeling statements, and these can be recognised by the fact that we usually put a "you" into these statements instead of an "I".

For example: "You are a bully," instead of "I feel hurt."

One way to be sure that you are speaking for yourself when expressing your emotions is to say "I feel....."

Feeling Words

Pleased	calm	comfortable	satisfied
bored	fearful	silly	daring
confused	lonely	elated	glad
embarrassed	hesitant	surprised	eager
kind	uneasy	angry	tired
aggrieved	proud	contented	cautious
scared	confident	discontented	comfortable
anxious	cross	tense	excited
stubborn	hopeful	energetic	foolish
shocked	trapped	loving	warm
relieved	apathetic	annoyed	flustered
jealous	stupid	troubled	weepy
happy	frustrated	solemn	serious
despairing	miserable	relaxed	wonderful
peaceful			

Saying what you would like

When you tell others clearly what you would or would not like, they know what to expect and can act accordingly. Unfortunately many of us have been taught to keep what we want to ourselves or that it was impolite to

I'D LIKE IT IF YOU'D COOK DINNER TONIGHT

be direct, so we must express our wants in devious or roundabout ways.

We have this beautiful double-bind in our society which is summed up in the two following statements: "If you ask, you don't get" and "I want doesn't get". Between the two it is very difficult to sort out what to do in order to get what you want!

Have a go at making "I would like" statements out of the following:-

214

- "You don't cuddle me like you used to".

- "That sounds like a really interesting play".

- "My friends get to go out with their husbands once a week.".

Openness, honesty and truth

- What does telling the truth mean?
- How do we decide to tell the truth or not?
- Why do we fear telling the truth in some situations and not others?

All these are questions that we ask ourselves at some time or another and finding the answers can at times be very difficult for us.

- Do I tell my best friend that her husband is having an affair?
- Do I tell my boyfriend that I don't like the earrings he bought me?
- Do I tell my little daughter what strangers could do to her?
- Do I tell my wife when I am attracted to somebody else?
- Do I tell my little boy that I don't like his best friend?

Truth is not something unchangeable that stands forever: it changes all the time, as does the degree to which we as individuals feel able to speak our truths.

Perhaps we all have private places inside where no one is allowed to go. We also have less private places where people who are very close to us are allowed, then we have a sort of open space where lots of people are allowed to go. And we have the ability to close ourselves off almost completely when confronted with someone we feel is a threat to us.

So, the amount of truth about ourselves that we show varies with the type of relationship we are in.

We may also have inner truths that we hide even from ourselves, though others may often recognise them. These hidden truths may be painful ones (for instance, that we believe we are unlovable) or they may be positive ones that we can't allow ourselves to accept, like how valuable we are. We cannot cope with the knowledge of them, and won't, until we are ready to.

You cannot force anyone to accept their hidden truths.

Not telling the truth

Not telling the truth is usually called "lying" and lying is generally regarded as not a very good thing to do. We teach our children that lying is wrong and that teaching is backed up in our schools.

There are two problems with this oversimplified view of lying. The first is that, if you want to teach children to believe that lying is wrong, you must not lie in their presence - ever. You cannot allow yourself "white" lies, such as saying on the phone to someone who wants to visit that you are going out. Working out when a lie is not a lie can be quite a complicated question for adults but for children it is very simple - a lie is a lie whether it be large or small.

The second problem is that we lie for a reason. If we just regard lying as wrong and take a dogmatic or moralistic attitude on the matter, we can miss the needs underlying the lies that are told. For instance, we sometimes lie:-

- To avoid what we perceive as being worse consequences if we told a truth.

- To get something we want.
- To avoid pain, our own or other people's.
- To present ourselves in a good light.

Lying takes energy because it means suppressing the truth and energy is needed in order to suppress anything. This is why people often feel great relief and a weight off their shoulders when they tell a truth they have been witholding. Lying also complicates matters.

"When someone tells me a piece of the truth which has been withheld from me and which I needed in order to see my life more clearly, it may bring acute pain, but it can also flood me with a cold, sea-sharp wash of relief. Often such truths come by accident, or from strangers."

Adrienne Rich

Generally, the more safe and secure we feel with ourselves the more open and honest we allow ourselves to be. Being open and honest allows people to trust us and to get closer to us.

"My commitment is to truth as I see it each day ...."

Gandhi

Being open and honest with children is no different than with adults. In fact, if we want our children to be open and honest and have integrity, our complete honesty with them is very important. If they are brought up in an atmosphere that is safe enough to allow honesty they are far more likely to develop these qualities.

We often try to "save" children from various truths that we regard as in some way "awful" or too difficult for them to take. When we do this, we are taking it upon ourselves to judge the child's ability to deal with something that we ourselves are finding difficult.

"If you tell the truth you don't have to remember anything."

Mark Twain

We are allowing an experience that we have labelled negatively to influence our openness with our child. Saying, truthfully, to your children that you are unable to tell them the truth right now and explaining to them why you feel like that is itself a truth.

> *"Telling lies to our children is wrong.*
> *Proving to them that lies are true is wrong.*
> *Telling them that God's in his Heaven and all's well with the world is*
> *   wrong.*
>
> *The young know what you mean.*
> *The young are people.*
> *Tell them the difficulties that can't be counted, and let them see not*
> *   only what will be, but see with clarity these present times.*
>
> *Say obstacles exist they must encounter, sorrow happens, hardship*
> *   happens.*
> *The hell with it. Who never knew the price of happiness will not be*
> *   happy.*
> *Forgive no error you recognise.*
> *It will repeat itself, increase, and afterwards our pupils will not forgive*
> *   in us what we forgave".*
>
> **Yevtushenko**

Be kind to yourself, it is human for you to have things that are difficult to cope with. Being honest with yourself and having compassion for your own weaknesses is the first step towards being more open with others.

Building Bridges

Another way we avoid self disclosure is by asking questions of others instead of making statements for ourselves.

"Why are you late?" (said in an angry voice)

Ways we block self disclosure

Young children quite naturally announce what they think and feel until they are stopped by embarrassed adults. Children learn from being stopped that what they feel and think is wrong; they grow up into adults who daren't express their true selves and who feel they have done something "bad" if they do.

"Do not lie to your children ever, either by omission or by commission. If you choose to hide the truth from them, say so and why, truthfully."

Claude M Steiner

What were you not allowed to speak about? Were/are there taboo subjects in your family? Some of the most common are:-

- Things to do with bodily functions, like serious illness, dying, pleasurable sex,
- going to the toilet, AIDS, homosexuality, menstruation, giving birth, etc.
- Things to do with family history, e.g. "We don't talk about Uncle Willie", or being very disapproving (but never mentioning) that a particular cousin had an illegitimate baby.
- Different religious beliefs.
- Unconventional behaviour.
- Violence.
- The fact that parents are not the authority on everything.
- Emotions such as anger, hatred, jealousy or expressions of love and warmth.
- Our personal thoughts and needs.

Many of the taboo areas take on a magical, fascinating or fearful aspect for children who then, as adults, spend a great deal of time trying to come to terms with things that were not talked about openly when they were younger.

Awareness of the blockages and difficulties we experience as adults due to attitudes that surrounded as when we were children, gives us a responsibility to make sure that any children within our sphere of influence do not suffer under similar attitudes or prohibitions. Allowing children their free expression of thoughts and feelings at the same time as teaching them respect and love for others means that they can retain their "here and now" responses and be more open and friendly.

And we can protect children from being hurt themselves by giving them clear, straightforward information about the dangers they may encounter from other people who are less open and honest than they are. We all risk danger to ourselves every day and making a child unduly fearful of the world will prevent them from ever living in it.

Building Bridges

The following questions are to help you focus on the beliefs you hold about truth. You may find some of them no longer accord with the person you are now and you may wish to change them.

If you were told that you had six months to live, what are the unsaid thoughts and feelings you would want to express and to whom, before you died? Which, if any, relationships would you like to make well, so that you could leave knowing that you were at peace with those people?

- Are you happy and at ease with the amount of openness you show towards those close to you?

- Do you trust those close to you with a true picture of yourself or do you pretend to be other than how you are because of a sense of duty or obligation?

- Do you answer their questions openly and honestly or are there areas which you find difficult to handle?

- Are you honest with those close to you about your thoughts, feelings and needs as a person in your own right?

- If you have problems in this area are you aware of what they are about? Or do you just react without thinking?

- Do you believe that certain things should be kept from your children and those close to you? What and why?

- What is your biggest fear about speaking the truth?

- What would you need in order not to experience that fear?

- What is more important to you than not telling the truth?

- How do you feel when the truth is caringly told to you?

- How do you feel when you are deliberately lied to?

"In my family one of the subjects that was never spoken about was minor physical ailments like indigestion, piles, heartburn and so on. To this day I am not quite sure what indigestion is or what it feels like even though I might get it. This lack of information also meant that I did not understand other people's experiences of these ailments and I found it difficult to empathise with them".

Appendix 10

CHALLENGING

Challenging unacceptable behaviour: the 4 part I-message

When others people behave in ways that interfere with us or we don't like, it is time to own the problem and stand up for our own rights and needs in an assertive way. Being successful in challenging someone who is interfering with your needs requires the development of the skills of self-disclosure. The first step is to make sure that the person interfering with your needs is fully aware of the fact.

It is useful to try and understand the motivation for the unacceptable behaviour. Often the individual is unaware that his/her behaviour is unacceptable, and the behaviour is usually engaged in to meet his/her own needs.

Informing them that their behaviour has an unfavourable impact on those around them may be enough to bring about a change in their behaviour. If not, it will initiate the chance to discuss how to solve the problem. In challenging in the way described below we are in fact stating the problem and asking for help or co-operation in solving it.

In essence this means we are asking for help in having our needs met by the removal of the behaviour that was an obstacle to this objective in the first place.

The aims of challenging

In challenging someone about their behaviour, bear in mind everything that you are actually trying to achieve.

You want to:-

1. **Bring about a change in the behaviour ...** You want somehow to change the situation you find unacceptable, so what you do needs to be effective.

2. **Avoid bad feelings ...** You want to avoid getting into fights and power tussles as you challenge the behaviour.

3. **Maintain everyone's self-esteem ...** Each challenge can be an opportunity for those involved to develop good feelings about themselves, by treating each other respectfully. Labelling behaviour is one way to ensure that feelings are hurt, and that everyone ends up

feeling less good about themselves.

4. **Encourage growth and development** ... Each time we challenge unacceptable behaviour, we create an opportunity for growth and development, by fostering positive communication, encouraging flexibility in ourselves and others, and improving relationships. We are also providing a potential learning experience for all concerned, because when the situation is resolved comfortably, it is possible that the method may be used by others, simply because 'it works'.

Expressing yourself congruently

When others are interfering with us getting our needs met we need to be able to express ourselves in a congruent manner if we want to bring about some change in the situation. The ability to honestly express the level of your feelings is very important in sending I-messages.

To do this, we need to be clear about the answers to the following questions. We shall use Mary's problem as our illustration. Mary is fed up with picking up her children's clothes from all over the house.

What is going on that is interfering with her needs?

We need a factual description of the behaviour, so we have to stick to what you see and hear and avoid interpretations. Mary could describe the children as messy or inconsiderate; in fact what they are doing is leaving their clothes about the house instead of in their rooms.

What effect is their behaviour having on her?

How is it interfering with Mary getting her needs met? Because Mary cannot stand having clothes lying around the house she picks them up whenever she finds them, thus creating more work for herself.

How does she feel about the effect that it is having on her?

Here we need to get in touch with the feelings and how to describe them. The clearer we are about what we are feeling the more congruent our expression will be. Mary wasn't unduly bothered for a while. Now it feels as though half her time is spent picking up clothes and she has reached a point where she feels used by her children and that makes her resentful.

Include a request for help.

Say something like: "I don't like what is happening and need your help," or "I have a problem, will you help me with it ...?" By doing this you are giving the other person a chance to realise that you are not attacking them; you are trusting them to be helpful and co-operative.

Behaving Congruently

How do you confront the person? Armed with this information, how you confront someone is of vital importance. You need to inform the other person of all these things. The more supporting information you can provide, the more likely they are to accept your case and so change the

227

behaviour you find unacceptable. The form of your confronting message will thus include:-

- a description of the behaviour
- the effect of that behaviour;
- how you feel;
- a request for help in solving your problem.

Mary's challenge might go something like this:-

"When you leave your clothing around the house I end up picking it up and I really resent the extra work Please can you help work out what we can change so that it doesn't happen any more!"

There is no set order for the parts of the challenging message. It is important to include all four elements and they can be switched round as feels most comfortable.

Mary's challenge could equally have been:-

"I've got a problem I'd appreciate help with: I feel really resentful when I have to pick up the clothes you leave around the house. It makes more work for me and I feel like I'm a slave!"

More on challenging

When it is our needs that are not being met - when the problem belongs firmly to us rather than to someone else - it is time to be assertive and bring about change.

There will be times when we are suffering because of something we have not said or done.

Another example from Mary:-

Mary was upset because her birthday had passed without any major celebration. Her husband had given her a present, yet she would have liked the chance to go out and celebrate in style. When talking through her unmet needs with a friend she realised she had never told him about wanting a celebration. Her needs were not being met because she hadn't voiced them!

Building Bridges

Remember back to your childhood and times when you were told off by your parents or other adults for doing things they didn't like.

- who owned the problem in the situation?
- how were you told off?
- what did they do and say?
- how did you react and feel?
- did you want to change what you were doing at the time?
- how would you have liked them to react instead?

Even as you do this exercise, it is useful to remind yourself that your parents, teachers and friends reacted towards you in the best ways they knew at that time. Normally people either model their behaviour on the behaviour they witnessed as child, or consciously set out to change it. Either way, the behaviour you were exposed to as a child will have an effect on the way you behave yourself. By looking back, you make yourself aware of the patterns you have adopted, and give yourself alternatives. Making new ways work for you requires energy, so you can do without wasting it on blaming your parents or feeling guilty too.

There will be other times when our needs are being interfered with by something that other people are saying or doing.

Mary was late for evening class at the college two evenings running because her husband was not home on time from work. He knew that she had to go out and yet was giving more weight to his own need to stay late at the office.

Mary needs to challenge her husband's behaviour. On the rare occasions in the past when she had confronted him it was more of a head-on attack than an assertive challenge. She would wait until she was so angry that she could barely control her temper and so it was hardly surprising that she ended up being vicious. The inevitable result was that her husband became very defensive and attacked her in return, to save himself. Bad feelings were all that could possibly result.

In the above example, Mary was not being assertive at all; she was being aggressive. The important difference is that in being assertive you take the other person's feelings and needs into account even as you firmly stick to your guns and insist on your rights to get your needs met.

Mary's new assertive challenge went like this:-

> *"I'm really fed up and I need your help! You have come home half an hour later than agreed two Tuesdays running with the result that I have been late for my class. That course is very important to me and I feel as if you are not taking me or it seriously by being late."*

By challenging him before she loses control of her temper she is valuing herself and protecting her interests, ending up feeling stronger and more worthwhile.

By challenging him in a loving and non-labelling way she is complaining about his behaviour without attacking him - and so not damaging his self-esteem. She is therefore far less likely to experience defensiveness on his part and more likely to get him to change the offending behaviour; and by asking for his help she is giving him the chance to realise that he should take her needs more seriously and consider her in all he does - a process that will encourage him to develop his awareness of himself as a person and as her partner.

In this way, Mary is satisfying all the important points of a useful challenging I-Message.

Examples of challenging

Sam's two sons, aged three and four, used to fight to get to his knee first when he came home from work. Sam himself was usually exhausted and grumpy after a day's hard work and the long journey home, so the last thing he wanted was to be jumped on and squabbled over the minute he walked through the front door.

In the past he had struggled to put up with it because of feelings of guilt at having to spend so much time away from the family, working the long hours his job demanded. Finally, unable to cope with stress at work, and the daily onslaught at the front door, he discussed the problem with his partner, who suggested he give the 4-part-I message. To his pleasant surprise both boys willingly backed off and agreed to give him the short space he wanted to himself on arriving home.

The following day, when he arrived home, they dashed up as usual, the older one in the lead. Then they stopped in their tracks and the older one turned to the younger one and said: "Remember we agreed to wait until Dad is ready, and then you go first for a cuddle".

In challenging the boys in a firm and gentle way he managed successfully to bring about a change in the unacceptable behaviour. He also gave them the opportunity to work out how to get their own needs met without interfering with his unduly. In this way he presented them with an important opportunity to become more caring and responsible.

Building Bridges

Think of some of the things that other people do that you find unacceptable. For each thing, write on a piece of paper:

- **what they do or say** just a simple short sentence that describes what you don't like. Avoid long descriptions - e.g. she jumps on me in bed in the mornings

- **what is the actual effect on you** - e.g. I get a shock and it hurts me

- **how you feel about it** - use words appropriate to the situation and the person you are addressing - simplify if the other person is a child. I feel scared and my body hurts

Then write out a four-part challenging message for each example:-

e.g. *Jenny, I have a problem I'd like you to help me with. It's about the way you wake me up in the mornings. When you jump on me, it hurts and I get a scary shock. What do you think you could do so I don't feel so bad on waking up?*

Another example:-

Joan shared a computer station with Avril, and found Avril's habit of leaving her empty dispenser coffee cups wherever she happened to be quite infuriating.   At first she had disposed of the cups without complaining, but now felt that 'something had to be done'.

The challenge went like this:-

"I've got a problem that I need you to help me with. I know you love your coffee, and accept that it's not always possible to stop what you're doing and take your empty cups to the recycle bin. When I get to the computer station, there is always at least one empty cup, but usually more than that cluttering up the desk. If they get knocked over there's a real danger that the dregs left in the bottom could damage my papers. I don't mind dealing with the odd cup, but I'm starting to find it difficult not to get angry or annoyed with you".

Avril was apologetic, and seemed genuinely surprised that her forgetfulness was a problem for Joan. She promised to be more attentive, and to deal with her coffee cups more efficiently.

Of course, it is not always the case that challenges work at the first try. Sometimes it is necessary to raise the matter more than once, or to find a way to help everyone remember what they undertook to do. It is too easy sometimes to think that people are being deliberately unco-operative when they do things that we find unacceptable, especially things which we have challenged them about before.   There are many reasons for non-compliance with our requests or the contracted behaviour. It may be useful to consider some reasons for apparent 'failure'.

When I-Messages don't work

There will be times when your I-Messages do not bring about any change in the behaviour you don't like. When this happens, it is most useful to check out how you sent the message and in what way it was worded - perhaps with a friend to help work through the different parts.

1) Was it really your problem?

For all sorts of reasons there are times when we are unhappy with what other people are doing even though it doesn't actually interfere with our needs. It may also be that we are taking on a problem that wasn't ours in the first place. (See *'Whose Problem?'* to clarify this issue)

"I used to get really upset when my husband was away on business, and he sat in the pub with colleagues, drinking and socialising till the small hours of the morning. I was concerned about his lack of sleep, especially when he had to spend long hours driving on the motorway the next day. Now I realise that it's his life and his body, and it's his decision whether or not he gets enough sleep. What he does is his problem - my only problem was a need to try and control his behaviour."

If you send an I-Message and cannot come up with a concrete and tangible effect on you, an actual way that what they are doing is interfering with your needs, it is unlikely that it will achieve what you want.

2) **Were you congruent?**

Being congruent means expressing yourself in such a way that all the parts of your message - the words, the body posture, the tone of voice - match up with the feelings inside, you are being as straight with them as you can be.

As well as the risk of toning down your challenge until it has no effect, there is the risk that you can overshoot so far that you will not be taken seriously.

"Having been so shy about confronting them all these years, my first I-Messages were ridiculously tentative – 'would you mind terribly ... only it's a bit of a nuisance' when in fact it was a flaming bore. No wonder no one took me seriously".

3) **Were you are acting aggressively rather than assertively?**

Was it a really sneaky You-Message? Try as hard as you might it may be that right now you haven't managed to make the switch from aggressive confrontation to assertive challenging.

What was your I-Message really like? Did it contain labels and put-downs? Was it of the "when you always behave like an inconsiderate slob, I feel ...." type that lacks an assertive description of the behaviour? Using you-messages (labelling) instead of I-messages (owning the problem, and stating its effect) tends to breed aggression and ill-will rather than co-operation.

4) **Was there conflict of needs and values?**

However hard we try to be congruent, and give I-messages, it may be that the needs of the other person or persons get in the way, and provide an overwhelming stimulus or motivation for them to continue behaving in the way we find unacceptable. Then we both own the problem and will have to find some way to "problem solve" or negotiate to find an answer.

The hypnotic effect of language

"I consider many adults (including myself) are or have been, more or less, in a hypnotic trance, induced in early infancy: we remain in this state until - "when we dead awaken", as Ibsen makes one of his characters say - "we shall find that we have never lived."

R D Laing

We learn how to think and what to believe about ourselves from the messages the important adults in our lives sent us as children (and may still be sending us). If a child has always been labelled "clumsy" or "dumb" he will very likely grow up behaving that way. We all have a real need to be accepted and if that means satisfying other peoples' expectations we will do so.

If our parents and teachers expected us to be brilliant or helpful and labelled us that way, we may very well have grown up resenting having to be bright or helpful.

Awareness of our 'programming' is useful, not only to understand our own behaviour, but also as 'preventative' in the 'programming' of the children in our lives. Our influence is likely to be most profound on our own children, but it can happen that a comment we make or choose not to make can have a profound effect on a child we may see only once, when it reinforces or works to break down programming that is already established. Consider this next section as it applies both to children in your life, and to the child that you once were - the child within, as part of the process of understanding your own programming.

What is said to, and about, children matters because they are likely to believe it. If you tell a child something often enough they can become "programmed" into believing it. This is why as adults we quite often have negative beliefs about ourselves that are very hard to change.

Beliefs like:-

- I am stupid.
- I'm not good enough.
- I will never be any good.
- I am clumsy.
- I will never be successful.
- No-one will ever love me.
- I am just lazy.

Children aren't born with these beliefs - they are programmed into believing them by the adults who bring them up. We do this programming in two ways:-

1. Directly

In what we say to the child and how we behave towards them. For example saying "You are so clumsy" and not trusting them to touch or carry things.

2. Indirectly

By talking about our children both when we know they can hear us and when we think they can't hear us. For example, saying "She is very shy and never talks to anyone" while the child is standing next to you, or "I am really fed up - I don't think I was cut out to be a mother. I wish I had never had John because he is such a nuisance," said to a friend in the kitchen while John plays in the next room.

Children have amazing hearing and, like adults, they are desperate to know what is being said if they think they are the topic of conversation.

Over the years, often repeated messages from parents become self-fulfilling prophesies.

Negative messages tend to be remembered more clearly because they are usually delivered with more energy and power than positive ones. So messages we send when we have reached the end of our tether and get very angry have far more impact on the child than an occasional "I love you", said as the child is rushing into school.

Messages are also registered unconsciously by the child and may be played out in later life without the person ever realising why.

Common ways children are programmed

1. **Put-downs**

Saying negative things about the child when making simple demands: "Leave that alone, you clumsy boy".

2. **Making comparisons**

"You are just as bad as your father".

3. **Setting examples**

"Why can't you work hard like your brother?"

4. **Talking to others about the child's faults when they can hear**

"He is such a nuisance, he is always bothering me".

5. **Taking pride in behaviour that will cause trouble later on**

"She is such a flirt, she is going to be a right little heart-breaker when she grows up

6. **Using guilt**

"Look what you are doing to your mother".

Reasons for doing this

- Adults tend to treat children in the same way they were treated.

- The belief that children can be shamed into better behaviour - and this must be done by telling them how bad they are.

- Tired and depressed parents, whose needs aren't getting met, lashing out at someone smaller and weaker.

Building Bridges

What does your inner voice say to you about who you are and what you can do? Catch those thoughts whenever they pass through your mind and write them down. Thoughts like: "I'm always so slow" or "I have to get on with it; whether I like it or not."

- Are these thoughts really true?

- Is it really true that you can't do this or that thing or that you must do this other thing?

- Where did these beliefs come from and why are you still being hypnotised by them? Would you like to wake up from your trance and begin to see, hear and feel the real world again?

- How are you hypnotised by others: your parents, family, friends, children? What do they say you are, what do they say you can do or cannot do? Are their words true? Are you really like that?

Appendix 11

BEING FIRM AND GENTLE

Appendix 11 – Being Firm and Gentle

Styles of parenting

When we were little we probably encountered three types of people:-

- Those who were authoritarian and had a lot of power and authority over us and whom we may have feared;

- Those who were very weak, who let us walk all over them and whom we may have discounted or ignored;

- Those who were straight with us, who treated us with respect and whom we probably liked a great deal.

Unfortunately for us, there are not so many of the third type, so we don't get much chance when we are growing up to model ourselves on that sort of behaviour.

We live in an authoritarian society and this shows most clearly in the way we treat children today. As any parent knows, children are not well received by the general public. They are "noisy", "dirty" and "a nuisance". We only have to take a normally curious five-year-old into a restaurant or on to a train to find that out for ourselves.

"I used to teach in a secondary school that had a large population of West Indian children. At the discos I was amazed to see 16-year-old black boys bringing their infant brothers and sisters with them, and enjoying it! They laughed, played and danced with them and treated them with as much care and affection as they did their friends.

At adult functions whole families would come, including grand-parents and babies. There was a sense of togetherness about their families that I had not experienced before. In their society children were an integral part of what was happening and they weren't banished to bed if a party or a celebration was going on".

- a white teacher

The old Victorian idea that children should be seen and not heard is still with us, however enlightened we might think we have become. We may be less authoritarian about our children at home nowadays but, in Britain, we are still authoritarian in public. There are so many places that children can't go and so many things that they are not allowed to do, as any parent is very well aware.

In other European countries, such as Spain or Italy, children of all ages are to be seen with their parents in restaurants in the evening. No one seems to mind when the very young ones run up and down and play. They are just part of the family group. It is clearly possible to be far more accepting of children in public than normally happens in Britain.

Even at home, we may be more authoritarian than we imagine. Or else we may claim that we are the exact reverse and consider ourselves permissive parents. Reverse is the right word because authoritarianism and permissiveness are just different sides of the same coin. Someone once said that a permissive parent was a failed authoritarian one and there may be some truth to this.

Let's look at what this means a bit more closely.

Building bridges

Think back to your childhood and choose one person from each group we've mentioned: someone who bossed you around; someone who let you do everything you wanted; and a person who was straight with you and treated you with respect.

Describe to someone else, or on paper, each person and their behaviour.

Then describe how you felt and what you thought when you were with each one.

What were the advantages and disadvantages of each of these people's behaviour?

Which one are you most like?

The authoritarian approach

This person knows what is best for you and they tell you in no uncertain terms what to feel, think, believe and do. They are the authority on everything and if you don't do what they say you are in big trouble. They will curtail your freedom and might even resort to verbal and physical violence to get you to do what they want.

They are powerful and strong personalities and can be frightening. Even if they don't physically abuse you, you will probably be afraid of them. They look angry a lot. They speak in a loud, powerful voice and have a tendency to loom over you.

They always seem to get their own way and win every argument - they are the boss.

Such people can, at first sight, appear to have everything going for them. They get their own needs met and they are often quite successful in the world. They have to do a lot of fighting for what they want but they don't seem to mind that too much. It is the people whom they boss and hurt and tread on who have the difficulties.

There are three types of responses to authoritarian behaviour: *fight, flight or submission.*

The *fighters* are the children who appear to go along with the authoritarian adult but secretly hate them and plan to get their revenge. Or they attempt to stand up to them and get badly bruised, mentally as well as physically. They may grow up hardened and determined that no one will ever try to walk all over them again.

The children who opt for *flight* are those who decide to keep out of the way as much as possible, which usually means withdrawing into themselves. Unfortunately, if they do withdraw into themselves, they may end up unable to respond even to other people who aren't authoritarian and so may never get their own needs met.

Yet others may *submit* under the onslaught and make a decision early on in their life that their needs are of no value. They learn to give in at the first sign of pressure from someone else and have no sense of self-worth.

Behaving in an authoritarian way can severely damage the self-worth of another individual, especially when they are young and unable to employ adult skills to help themselves. The authoritarian approach means that you get your own way but also it means that others are afraid of you and may not like you.

Behaving in an authoritarian way means that you have to be on guard all the time; you are never allowed to show human weakness.

Behaving in an authoritarian way means not being truly yourself and being cut off from warm loving relationships.

The permissive approach

Behaving permissively is the other side of the story. With this behaviour you are not allowed to get your own needs met and you allow others to walk all over you.

You may appear open, loving and kind, you may appear to be doing all the right things, but all of it is done at the expense of yourself. You give and give but it is never enough. The people around you always seem to want more and you can never satisfy them. You are taken for granted all of the time and always seem to be left to clean up the mess. Your generosity is never recognised or returned and you can quite often end up resenting your children, and partner if you have one.

People respond to those who behave behave permissively by walking all over them, and often end up disliking them. Children react to this permissiveness by pushing and pushing in an effort to find some limits. They sense that the adult is doing and saying things that they don't really want to and they push for the adult to become congruent and real.

Many children cannot cope with the amount of power that the parent behaving permissively gives to them and they begin ordering the adult around and demanding that all their needs be met instantly without taking anyone else into account.

Behaving permissively means that others pity you or take advantage of you. Behaving permissively means that you never get to live your own life. Behaving permissively produces the very thing that you are striving to avoid - children who behave aggressively and who disregard the needs of others.

The authoritarian and permissive approaches are not actually so different. They are both examples of the use of power. In the first case, the parent yields it and, in the second, the child. Authoritarian and permissive behaviour are just at opposite ends of the same power line.

A new way

If we want to relate to other people more usefully and respectfully, it is worth while trying to get off the line of power altogether. We need to find ways to meet everyone's needs and that means working in a constructive way to come up with mutually acceptable solutions. We need always to be aware of both our own needs and rights and those of others.

This means we value ourselves and others and we are straightforward and honest in communicating our thoughts and feelings when our needs are being interfered with. We listen when others tell us we are interfering with theirs. We place value on our own skills, wisdom and experience and use them to help others when necessary.

Behaving assertively

Challenging unacceptable behaviour with I-Messages that satisfy the basic aims of changing unacceptable behaviour, maintaining self esteem all round and facilitating the growth of all parties is the ideal way of behaving.

If you have developed a habit of letting others get away with behaviour that interferes with your needs, it is time to start behaving assertively.

At the same time, if you tend to react aggressively or in an overbearing way even when you don't own the problem, it is time you started behaving assertively as well.

The benefits to you and everyone around you will be a greatly increased sense of self-worth on all sides, better feelings all round, and all of you meeting more and more of your needs more of the time. People who behave assertively are liked and respected by others. They take responsibility for their own needs and help others to do the same. People who behave assertively contribute to the well-being of the world just by behaving the way they do.

When I-Messages don't work

There will be times when your I-Messages do not bring about any change in the behaviour you don't like. When this happens, it is most useful to check out how you sent the message and in what way it was worded - perhaps with a friend to help work through the different parts.

"I used to get really upset with the state of my son's bedroom and go on and on at him. Now I realise that what actually happens inside his door is not really of any concern to me. He is the one who has to live with the mess. I set a good example in the rest of the house and that is as much as I can do - I am no longer sure I have the right to get angry with him when he fails to clear it up. It's his problem not mine".

Three-year-old John was struggling to complete a huge stickle brick construction when his mother said it was time for them to collect Susan from school. Needless to say, he didn't want to leave, yet working through his need to stay and his mother's need to go and collect Susan would have left Susan waiting alone outside the school gate.

---

1. Was it really your problem?

For all sorts of reasons there are times when we are unhappy with what other people are doing even though it doesn't actually interfere with our needs. If you send an I-Message and cannot come up with a concrete and tangible effect on you, an actual way that what they are doing is interfering with your needs, it is unlikely that it will achieve what you want.

2. Were you congruent?

As well as the risk of toning down your challenge until it has no effect, there is the risk that you can overshoot so far that they cannot take you seriously. Being congruent means expressing yourself in such a way that all the parts of your message - the words, the body posture, the tone of voice -match up with the feelings inside. It means you are being as straight as you can be.

3. You are acting aggressively rather than assertively

Try as hard as you might it may be that right now you haven't managed to make the switch from aggressive confrontation to assertive challenging.

What was your I-Message really like? Did it contain labels and put-downs? Was it of the "when you always behave like an inconsiderate slob, I feel ...." type that lacks an assertive description of the behaviour?

> *"Having been shy about confronting people for many years, my first I-Messages were ridiculously tentative – 'would you mind terribly ... only it's a bit of a nuisance' when in fact it was a flaming bore. No wonder no one took me seriously".*

4. The need to behave as they are is stronger than the need help you with your problem.

At the end of the day, however careful and congruent your I-Message, it may just be that the other person feels that their needs come first right now and they don't care about your problem.

It may be that they have a problem too and that is why they are behaving in the unacceptable way. At this point, you have the difficult task of deciding whether you are going to put your needs to one side temporarily while sorting their problem, or find some other way of meeting your needs without their co-operation.

If both parties have a problem that cannot be solved independently, you are a situation of conflict. The authoritarian approach would be to force

---

NEGOTIATION

Negotiating solutions to conflicts and issues is a complex and difficult procedure. By following through these stages, a mutually acceptable solution can be found:-

- Listen to and acknowledge the feelings on both sides
- Sort out the needs from the wants of both sides
- Brainstorm possible mutually acceptable solutions to the needs
- Evaluate and choose a mutually acceptable solution
- Agree the practical steps to implement the solution
- Come back later to check out the usefulness of the solutions

---

the other party to do it your way, the permissive approach would be to let them win. The assertive approach is to treat each other with respect and sit down to talk about it and find a mutually acceptable solution.

This is the process of negotiation. It is simply a combination of self-disclosure - stating your needs, and reflective listening - hearing the other's needs, repeated until you are all clear as to what the real underlying needs are. Then and only then can you brainstorm possible ways to meet all the needs.

Saving energy with the "Soft No"

There are times when the situation does not lend itself to negotiation, and an unpopular view or decision has to be implemented. This situation arises quite frequently within families, and also in work situations where a management decision has to be carried through.

On these occasions it is useful for us to be firm about what we want and what is to happen in a particular situation. Being firm doesn't always have the desired effect - we may end up losing our cool and saying and doing things we later regret.

It is much more effective if we can find a way to be firm and gentle at the same time.

Being able to use the "soft-no" comes from feeling calm, centred and happy with who you are and what you are doing. It really feels comfortable for you to be saying no. Your body stays soft and relaxed and your voice is clear and firm. You continue to use the words you first used and you don't get into discussion or argument about what you are saying.

You don't apologise, with words or by your manner, for what you are doing. People, especially children, sense the weakness that often underlies an apology.

If you begin to tense your body or feel angry you need to be able to let go of those feelings and come back to being calm and relaxed. That is, you control your feelings before they have taken you over. Unless you are a brilliant actor, the "soft-no" won't work if you don't feel peaceful and sure of yourself. It has to be congruent.

Many effective teachers learn this skill and use it with large groups of children. Professionals who deal with very disturbed children use it too, often managing to remain calm and peaceful for two or three hours while they gently restrain a kicking, biting, swearing child until he or she has calmed down enough to talk to. The soft-no attitude is a skill well worth acquiring, and the way to start is to learn how to keep your body relaxed.

Building bridges

Set aside a bit of time to think through some of the situations where you get into battles with other people. Make a list of the regularly occurring scenes and then go through them one by one.

Remembering what you have just read in these notes, what other ways can you now think of to handle each of these scenes?

You may find it useful to find someone to talk through each of the situations with.

Remember that as you can begin to change the ways you react, those around you will begin slowly to change the ways they react as well.

Sticking to agreements

June was fed up with her teenage childrens' habit of leaving lights on. When she had been out for an evening, she would often come home to find every light in the house still on, even though all the children were in bed.

June had mastered the art of negotiating with her children, so they held a negotiating session and June got agreement that her children would make sure lights were off before going to bed. But the problem repeated itself. So June called a second session to make sure everyone was truly in agreement with the solution. They were. Yet only a week later she came home again to find the house ablaze.

On this occasion she went and woke all the children up - even though it was after 11 p.m - and calmly and firmly told them to get out of bed and turn off the lights.

She met some strong resistance (each child put the blame on someone else), yet she stuck to her demand, expressing it more quietly rather than more loudly, until they were all assembled downstairs to switch off the lights. It was the last time the lights were left blazing in the house!

Appendix 12

HISTORY REGARDING MUSES

The muses were nine sisters born of the mother Mnemosyne (goddess of memory) by the father Zeus. These famous and talented daughters were later worshipped in their own right.

They were worshipped chiefly in the district of Pieria, near Mount Olympus, a rich, well-watered country, whose springs were said to inspire those who drank of them. Hence the Muses were probably first thought of as nymphs of the springs.

Of these famous and talented daughters it was only in later times that different functions were assigned to separate Muses, and distinction made in the manner representing them. They are Calliope, Clio, Erato, Euterpe, Melpomene, Polyhymnia, Terpsichore, Thalia (comedy pastoral poetry), and Urania or Aphrodite (astronomy).

Their qualities are described below:-

Calliope is the muse of heroic song and epic poetry, is the most distinguished of the nine, and sometimes appears alone to represent all her sisters. She is represented either seated, with a tablet and pen, or standing, crowned, with a roll of writing in her hand, or again, with a trumpet wreathed with laurel twigs, through which she proclaims the deeds of heroes.

Clio is the muse of history. She holds a half-opened roll of parchment and a pen, while a chest containing other rolls is placed beside her.

Erato is the lovely one, the muse of love poetry. Her symbol is a lyre. She sings songs of love and marriage and is the muse of love poetry. She is crowned with myrtle and roses and plays the lyre with many strings, often carrying a dart, the weapon of Eros.

Euterpe is the muse of lyric poetry and music, the giver of delight, as goddess of music whose symbol is the double flute that she is shown playing.

Melpomene, the muse of tragedy and elegiac poetry is a tall, grave figure in the flowing garment worn by tragic actors. Her left foot is raised on a rock, and she holds a tragic mask in her hand. Sometimes she holds a club, sword, or some other attribute of a famous hero.

Polyhymnia is the muse of singing, mime and sacred dance and eloquence. She is goddess of religious poetry. She is called the inventor

253

of Myths and hence is represented in a thoughtful attitude. Sometimes she leans on a pillar and bends slightly forward in an attitude of quiet attention. She is partly or completely veiled, representing the hidden truth which legends present in symbolic form.

Terpsichore, the joyful muse of the dance, (dance and of choral song), has the lyre, and tambourine with little bells. Her light robe is girt up, and she is represented in dancing pose.

Thalia, the muse of comedy and pastoral poetry, appears in the dress of a Bacchante, holding in one hand a shepherd's crook, and in the other a comic mask as her symbols.

Urania, the heavenly one, is the muse of astronomy. A globe of the heavens, sometimes partly veiled, stands beside her; in one hand she holds compasses, and with the other she points to the sky. She wears a crown of stars.

Appendix 13

THE CASE OF JANIE

Appendix 13 – The Case of Janie

I remember the case of Janie very well. She came to me in a fragile state riddled with food allergies and constantly tired. Her arms, legs and trunk including breasts were (she said) like a patchwork quilt of white scars where she had slashed herself with a Stanley knife for years on end (a fact which I could verify to some extent when I saw her several years later on a summer's day with new confidence and wearing short sleeves).

She was married to a company director and had three sons. The family was quite wealthy. She was blonde as well as beautiful, slim and very elegant to boot.

When we worked with our first Mnemodynamic incident, she saw on her TV screen herself as a 7 year old. Regularly, Grandfather would put her to bed. Before that he would bath her and then perform oral sex with her.

Generally speaking caress to one's genitalia gives pleasurable feelings, and indeed this was the case, so the feelings she related were a list containing *'trapped, forced, excited, guilty, responsible, disgusting, dirty, trapped, helpless and powerless'* amongst others. During this part of the Mnemodynamic session I anchored her survival to start with, plus the later choice she had in choosing Michael as a husband and sexual partner saying:-

> *"Please let her know about Michael and the boys ahead of her. She won't always be trapped like this, she WILL be able to make her own choices of sexual partner later on".*

She did that. Then I said:-

> *"Regarding what grandfather did, he should have known better because he was the grown up and she was the child. He had stalked her, groomed her and was preying on her. He should have been locked up and the key thrown away".*

We continued through the session well enough and she left the little girl feeling *"happy and playful".* She took the little girl with her to look after her. What I said was rather strong and you may well have done it differently but I thought that the responsibility and guilt for the act was not that of the little girl (a guilt for which she would punish herself for the rest of her life) but was that of the grandfather. Immediately after the session as she opened her eyes she was quiet for a few seconds before saying

"They shouldn't have locked him up and thrown the key away".

As gently as I could, maintained that he, as the grown, up was wrong and should have known better, that she, as the child aged seven couldn't rationalise this and that this was why she had felt both guilty and responsible, a stance which to my mind was unreasonable for her to carry. We parted amicably enough though she left without making a further appointment.

It was three or four months before she came back and got to the end of her therapy. The allergies and tiredness stopped. She later also divorced Michael who she realised had been helping her keep feelings of being small and weak for years to make himself feel useful.

She became a psychotherapist in her own right, has now re-married and is very happy.

Appendix 14

QUOTES FROM FREUD

Appendix 14 – Quotes From Freud

This is the part of the process that Freud says will make the client better. The full article is reproduced in the next appendix:

" …… *when we had succeeded in bringing the exciting event to clear recollection and had also succeeded in arousing with it the accompanying affect, …. and had expressed his feeling in regard to it in words, the various hysterical symptoms disappeared at once, never to return. Recollection without affect is nearly always quite ineffective; the original psychical process must be repeated as vividly as possible, brought into statum nascondi and then 'talked out'. In the case of excitation phenomena … the symptoms appear again during this repetition in full intensity and then disappear for ever…."*

Appendix 15

TRANSCRIPT OF FREUD'S PAPER

ON THE PSYCHICAL MECHANISM OF HYSTERICAL PHENOMENA

(In collaboration with Dr. Joseph Breuer, 1892)

I

(First published in the Neurologisckes Zentralblatt, 1893, Nos 1 and 2

(Translated by John Rickman)).

Stimulated by the chance observation, we have for a number of years been investigating the most varied types and symptoms of hysteria with reference to the exciting cause, the event that evoked the phenomenon in question for the first time, often many years before. In the great majority of cases it is impossible to discover the starting point by straightforward interrogation of the patient, be it ever so thorough; partly because it is often a matter of experiences which the patient finds it disagreeable to discuss, but chiefly because he really does not remember and has no idea of the causal connection between the exciting occurrence and the pathological phenomenon. As a rule it is necessary to hypnotise the patient and under hypnosis to arouse recollections relating to the time when the symptom first appeared; one can then succeed in revealing this connection in the clearest and most convincing manner.

In a great number of cases this method of examination has yielded results which appear to be valuable theoretically as well as practically. From the theoretical point of view the results are valuable because, for the pathology of hysteria, the accidental factor is decisive to a far greater extent than is known or acknowledged. In regard to traumatic hysteria it is obviously the accident which has evoked the syndrome; and when we learn from the utterances of patients in hysterical attacks that they invariably hallucinate in every attack a repetition of the original occurrence which evoked the first, the causal collection then also becomes perfectly clear here. The question is more obscure in the case of other phenomena.

Our experience has shown us, however, that the most varied symptoms, usually regarded as spontaneous and , so to speak, idiopathic products of hysteria, have just as strict a connection with the exciting trauma as those mentioned above in which the relation of the two sets of facts to one another is transparent. To exciting causes of this kind we have been able to trace anaesthesias as well as neuralgias of the most varied kind, often of many years duration, contractures and paralyses, hysterical attacks and

265

epileptoid convulsions which all observers had taken for genuine epilepsy, *petit-mal*, symptoms of the nature of tics, chronic vomiting and anorexia carried to the point of refusal of food, the most varied disturbances of vision, constantly recurring visual hallucinations - and the like. The disproportion between the many years duration of an hysterical symptom and the single occurrence which evoked it is similar to that which we are accustomed to see regularly in traumatic neurosis; it was quite frequently in childhood that the events occurred producing a more or less grave symptom which persisted from that time onwards.

The connection is often so clear that it is quite evident how the exciting event has happened to produce just this and no other manifestation; the phenomenon is determined in a perfectly clear manner by the cause; to take the most ordinary example, a painful affect, which was originally excited while eating but was suppressed, produces nausea and vomiting, and this continues for months as hysterical vomiting. A girl watching in harrowing anxiety at the bedside of a sick person falls into twilight state and has a terrifying hallucination while her right arm, which is hanging over the back of the chair, 'goes to sleep'; from this develops a paresis of that arm with contracture and anaesthesia. She wants to pray but can find no words; finally she succeeds in repeating an English prayer which she learnt in childhood. Then later a severe and highly complicated hysteria develops in which she can speak, write and understand only English, while for a year and a half her mother-tongue remains unintelligible to her. – A child who is very ill at last falls asleep, and its mother tries her utmost to keep quiet and not to wake it; but just in consequence of this resolution (hysterical counter-will) she makes a clucking noise with her tongue. On another occasion when she wishes to keep absolutely quiet this happens again, and so a tic in the form, of tongue-clicking develops which for a number of years accompanies every excitement. A highly intelligent man assists whilst his brother's ankylosed hip is straightened under an anaesthetic. At the instant when the joint gives way with a crack he feels a violent pain in his own hip-joint which lasts for almost a year; and so on.

In other cases the connection is not so simple; there exists only what may be called a symbolic relation between the cause and the pathological manifestation, such as normal people also fashion in dreams; for example, a neuralgia links itself on to some mental distress, or vomiting accompanies a feeling of moral disgust. We have had under observation patients who habitually made extensive use of such symbolism. In yet other cases a determination of this kind is not at the first glance clearly intelligible; to these belong precisely the typical hysterical symptoms – hemi-anaesthesia, contraction of the field of vision, epileptiform convulsions and the like. The exposition of our theories concerning this group must be reserved for a more detailed consideration of the subject.

Such observations seem to us to prove the pathogenic analogy between ordinary hysteria and traumatic neurosis and to justify an extension of the concept of traumatic hysteria. In traumatic neurosis the active cause of illness is not the trifling bodily injury but the effect of fright – the psychic trauma. Similarly, our investigations of many, if not of the majority, of hysterical symptoms have revealed causes which must be described as psychic traumas. Any experience which rouses the distressing affects of fright, apprehension, shame, or psychical pain can have this effect and it obviously depends on the sensitiveness of the person concerned (as well as on the further condition which we will refer to later) whether the experience acquires the importance of a trauma. We not infrequently find in ordinary hysteria several partial traumas instead of one grand trauma – a group of causes- which can only achieve traumatic effectiveness by accumulation and which belong together only in so far as they form parts of a whole painful experience. In still other cases circumstances in themselves apparently indifferent have attained an otherwise unexpected importance as traumas, either on account of their conjunction with really effective experiences or because they occurred at a moment of special susceptibility. This importance they then retain henceforward.

But the causal connection between the exciting psychical trauma and the hysterical symptom is not of such a kind that the trauma (like an *agent provocateur)* sets going a symptom which then becomes independent and persists on its own account. On the contrary, we are of the opinion that the psychical trauma or the memory of it, acts as a kind of foreign body constituting an effective agent in the present even long after it first penetrated, and we see the proof of this in a highly remarkable phenomenon which also lends an important practical interest to these results of our observations.

The discovery that we made, at first to our own great surprise, was that when we had succeeded in bringing the exciting event to clear recollection, and had also succeeded in arousing with it the accompanying effect, and when the patient had related the occurrence in a detailed manner as possible and had expressed his feelings in regard to it in words, the various hysterical symptoms disappeared at once, never to return. Recollection without effect is nearly always quite ineffective; the original psychical process must be repeated as vividly as possible, brought into *statum nascendi* and then 'talked out'. In the case of excitation phenomena – contractures, neuralgias and hallucinations – the symptoms appear again during this repetition in full intensity and then disappear for ever. Defects in functioning, paralyses and anaesthesias disappear in the same way, the transitory exacerbation not being of course perceptible in those cases. [1]

One may be inclined to suspect that the explanation lies in unintentional suggestion; the patient expects to be rid of his suffering as a result of the treatment, and this expectation might be the effective factor, not the 'talking out'. But this is not the fact; the first observation of this kind was a highly complicated case of hysteria having symptoms with distinct causes which were separately dispersed, and was analysed on these lines in the year 1881, that is, in the 'pre-suggestion' era. It was made possible by spontaneous auto-hypnosis on the part of the patient, and it occasioned the observer the greatest surprise.

Inverting the phrase *'cessante causa cessat effectus'* we may well conclude from these observations that the exciting experience continues in some way to be effective even years after, not indirectly by means of a chain of causes linking up with one another, but directly as the actual exciting cause - just as, for instance, the recollection of mental distress in full consciousness at some later period may stimulate tears; we thus conclude that *hysterical patients suffer principally from reminiscences.* [2]

---

[1] *Delboeuf and Binet have clearly recognised the possibility of such a therapy as the following quotations show. Delboeuf: "**Le Magnetisme animal**", Paris, 1889: 'Since then it has been possible to understand how the magnetist helps in bringing about recovery. He restores the patient to the condition in which the illness established itself and then with his words he attacks the illness, now in **statu nascendi** - Binet: "Les Alterations de la personnalite", 1892, p.243:…. 'Perhaps we shall see that by bringing back the patient by a mental device to the moment when the symptom appeared for the first time we make him more susceptible to 'suggestive therapy'. – In P. Janet's interesting book " L'Automatisme psychologique", Paris, 1889, there is a description of a cure obtained in an hysterical girl by the employment of a method analogous to ours*

[2] *In the text, it is not possible to separate what is new in the content of this provisional communication from what is also to be found in other authors. E.g. Mobius and Strumpell, who have put forward similar views on hysteria. The nearest approach to our theoretical and therapeutic deductions is found in a few recently published remarks of Benedikt's which we propose to consider elsewhere.*

II

It may at first appear strange that experiences long since past should operate with such intensity, and that the memory of them should not succumb to the fate which we see overtaking all our memories; perhaps these facts may become rather more comprehensible in the light of the following considerations.

The fading of a memory or of its affect depends on several factors. First and foremost it depends on whether an energetic reaction (discharge of feeling) supervened on the affective experience or not. By *reaction* we here mean the whole range of voluntary and involuntary reflexes, by which according to experience the affects are habitually worked off – from weeping up to an actual act of revenge. If this reaction occurs with sufficient intensity a great part of the affect disappears; common speech bears witness to these facts of every-day observation in the expressions 'to cry oneself out', 'to storm oneself out (*sich austoben)'.* If the reaction is suppressed the affect remains attached to the memory. An insult which is returned, if only in words, is remembered differently from one which had to be endured in silence. Common speech also recognizes this difference in the psychical and bodily consequences, and most characteristically designates silently endured suffering as a *Krankung,* [3], wound, injury, mortification. The reaction of an injured person to the trauma has a really complete 'cathartic' effect only if it takes the form of a fully adequate reaction, such as an act of revenge.

But man finds a surrogate for such an act in speech, by the help of which the affect may be almost as effectually 'abreacted'. In other cases talking is itself sufficient as a reflex, for example, complaining or relieving the burden of a secret (the confessional!). If a reaction of this kind by word or deed, or in the mildest cases by tears, does not ensue, the memory of the occurrence retains for a time its affective tone.

'Abreaction' is, however, not the only kind of solution at the disposal of the normal psychical mechanism in a healthy person who has met with a psychical trauma. Even if the memory is not abreacted it becomes merged in the great complex of associations, and is then ranged alongside of other experiences which perhaps contradict it; thus it undergoes correction by means of other ideas.

After an accident, for example, the remembrance of the danger and the

---

[3] *(There is no satisfactory translation of this highly expressive German word, which is obviously allied to* Krank = *ill. – Ed).*

subsequent (weakened) re production of the terror is accompanied by the memory of the sequel, of the rescue and the consciousness of present security. The memory of an injury to the feelings is corrected by an objective evaluation of the facts, consideration of one's actual worth and the like, and thus the normal man succeeds by means of associations in dissipating the accompanying affect.

In addition to this there is also that general effacing of impressions, that fading of recollection called 'forgetting', which tends more than anything else to absorb ideas which has lost their affective tone.

Our observations have shown that those memories which give rise to hysterical phenomena are retained with wonderful freshness and with full affective tone for a long period. But we must mention as a further striking fact, to be turned to account later, that these recollections are not at the disposal of the patient in the way that his more commonplace memories are. On the contrary, when the patient is in his usual psychical condition these experiences are completely absent from his memory or are present to it only in the most summary manner. Only when patients are questioned under hypnosis do these memories recur with the undiminished vividness of recent events.

Thus for six months one of our patients under hypnosis reproduced with hallucinatory vividness everything which had excited her on the corresponding day of the previous year (during an acute hysteria); her mother's diary, of which she knew nothing, attested the perfect accuracy of the reproduction. Another patient lived through with hallucinatory clearness - partly in hypnosis, partly in spontaneous attacks - all the experiences of an hysterical psychosis which she had suffered from ten years before, and in regard to which amnesia had been almost complete until the moment of the re-emergence. Several aetiologically important recollections dating back fifteen to twenty-five years were of astonishing integrity, and intensity of feeling; on reproduction their effect had the full force of new experiences.

As a reason for this we can only conjecture that these recollections have met with an exceptional fate in reference to all the ordinary processes of effacement discussed above, for we find that they relate to traumas which have not been sufficiently abreacted; closer investigation of the reasons which have prevented the operation of the latter then shows us at least two groups of conditions under which reaction to the trauma does not ensue.

In the first group we reckon those cases in which the patient has not reacted to the psychical trauma because its nature excluded the possibility of any such reaction, as in the case of the apparently irretrievable loss of a loved person, or when social conditions made a reaction impossible, or when the trauma concerned something which the patient wished to forget and therefore deliberately repressed[4] and excluded from his conscious thoughts. Under hypnosis we discover painful ideas of precisely this character underlying the hysterical phenomena (e.g. in the hysterical deliria of saints and nuns, of abstinent women and well-brought-up children).

The second group of conditions is not determined by the content of recollection, but by the mental condition of the patient at the moment when the given experience occurred. That is to say, among the exciting factors of hysterical symptoms we also discover under hypnosis ideas which though not in themselves significant owe their preservation to the circumstance that they happen to coincide with a seriously disabling affect, for example, terror, or with a directly abnormal mental condition, such as the half-hypnotic twilight state of day-dreaming, auto-hypnosis, and the like. In these cases it is the nature of these conditions which made a reaction to the experience impossible. Naturally both determinants may and often do occur together. This happens when a trauma effective enough in itself occurs during a state of seriously disabling affect or of altered consciousness: but it seems that in many persons an abnormal state of this kind is produced as the result of a psychic trauma which then in its turn makes a reaction impossible.

Both groups of determining conditions have this in common: that the psychical traumas which are not resolved by reaction will also fail of solution by means of associative absorption.

In the first group the patient's intention to do so causes him to forget the painful experiences and consequently to exclude them from association as far as possible. In the second group the associative absorption does not succeed because sufficient associative connection does not exist between the normal state of consciousness and the pathological state in which these ideas originally arose. We shall have immediate occasion to go more closely into these conditions.

Thus it may be said that the ideas which have become pathogenic are

[4] *(This is the first occasion on which this term was used. Later it became the author's technical term for the* unconscious *process by which thoughts are excluded from consciousness – Ed)*

preserved with such freshness and affective force because the normal process of absorption by abreaction and by reproduction in a state of unrestrained association is denied them.

III

In describing the conditions which according to our experience are decisive for the development of hysterical phenomena from physical traumas, we mentioned the abnormal states of consciousness in which such pathological ideas arise; and we laid stress on the fact that the recollection of the effective psychical trauma is not to be found in the normal memory of the patient, but in his memory under hypnosis. Indeed, the more we occupied ourselves with the phenomena the more certain did our conviction become that that splitting of consciousness, which is so striking in the well-known classical cases of *double conscience*, exists in a rudimentary fashion in every hysteria and that the tendency to this disassociation – and therewith to the production of abnormal states of consciousness, which may be included under the term *'hypnoid'* – is a fundamental manifestation of this neurosis. This view is in agreement with those of Binet and the two Janets; we have not had the opportunity, however, to confirm their highly remarkable discoveries in reference to anaesthetic patients

We should like therefore to supplement the often-quoted phrase 'hypnosis is an artificial hysteria' with another – namely, 'the existence of hypnoid states forms the foundation and condition of hysteria'. There is one thing in common to all these hypnoid states and to hypnosis, in spite of all their differences – namely, that the ideas which emerge in them are marked by great intensity of feeling but are cut off from associative connection with the rest of the content of consciousness. These hypnoid states are capable of association among themselves and the ideas belonging to them may in this way attain different degrees of psychical organization. Incidentally, however, the nature of these states and the degree of their inaccessibility to the rest of conscious processes would very probably vary in a fashion very similar to that of hypnosis, which ranges from light sleepiness to somnambulism, from complete recollection to amnesia.

If such hypnoid states exist before the manifest illness, they provide a foothold upon which the affect establishes itself with its pathogenic recollection and its subsequent somatic manifestations. This situation corresponds to dispositional hysteria. But our observations show that a severe trauma (such as that in a traumatic neurosis) or a troublesome suppression (for instance, of sexual affect) can effect a splitting of groups of ideas in people previously free from it, and this would constitute the mechanism of psychically acquired hysteria. Between the extremes of these two forms we must recognize a series within which the readiness to dissociation in the persons concerned and the volume of affect roused by the trauma varies inversely.

We have nothing new to say concerning the origin of dispositional hypnoid states. They often develop, we believe, from the 'day dreams' so frequently met with also in healthy people, great opportunity for which is provided, for instance, in the feminine occupation of needlework. The question why the 'pathological associations' formed in such states are so strong and why they influence somatic processes so much more strongly than ideas habitually do is part of the problem of the operation of hypnotic suggestion in general. Our experiences teach us nothing new on this point; they do, however, illuminate the contradiction between the statement 'hysteria is a psychosis' and the fact that one finds among hysterics people with the clearest and most critical intellects, of great strength of character and will power. These characteristics in such people are valid for their waking thoughts; in the hypoid state they become alienated from their conscious personalities as we all are in dreams. But whereas our dream-psychoses do not influence our waking existence the products of hypnoid states intrude as hysterical phenomena into waking life.

IV

Almost the same conclusions that we have just formed concerning hysterical symptoms of long duration may be repeated concerning hysterical attacks. As is well known, we possess a schematic description of the *'grande attaque'*, worked out by Charcot, according to which four phases may be recognized in a complete attack: (1) the epileptoid, (2) that of violent movements, (3) that of *'attitudes passionnelles'* (the hallucinatory phase), and (4) that of the concluding delirium. According to Charcot, all the various forms of hysterical attack (which as a matter of fact are more frequently observed than the full *grande attaque*) are derived from a shortening, lengthening, omission or isolation of these separate phases.

Our attempt at explanation has to do with the third phase, the *attitudes passionnelles*. When this is well marked it will reveal itself as an hallucinatory reproduction of a memory important for the outbreak of the

273

hysteria, i.e. the memory of the one grand trauma in what is called traumatic hysteria, or of a series of inter-related partial traumas which lie at the root of ordinary hysteria. The remaining alternative is that the attack will reproduce those experiences which were raised to importance by happening to occur at a time of special sensitivity to traumas.

But there are also attacks which seems to consist of nothing but motor symptoms and in which the *phase passionnelle* is lacking. If we can succeed in establishing a *rapport* with the patient during such general clonic attacks, during tonic catalepsy, or during an *attaque de sommeil,* or better still, if we succeed in summoning up an attack while the patient is under hypnosis, we find that these attacks too are based on the memory of a psychic trauma or series of traumas which usually finds expression in an hallucinatory phase. For instance, a little girl has suffered for years from attacks of general convulsions which might have been epilepsy and had in fact been taken for it. To establish a differential diagnosis she was hypnotised and was promptly seized by an attack. When asked, 'what do you see now?' she answered: 'The dog, the dog is coming!'. Further enquiry revealed that the first attack of the kind had appeared after she had been chased by a mad dog. Therapeutic success later confirmed the diagnosis of a psychogenic malady. - A clerk who had become hysterical in consequence of being assaulted by his superior suffered from attacks during which he fell to the ground in a frenzy of rage, but without uttering a word or betraying any signs of an hallucination. An attempt to produce the attack under hypnosis proved successful, and the patient revealed that he was again living through the situation in which his superior had openly insulted him in the street and thrashed him with a stick. A few days afterwards he returned complaining that the same attack had occurred again, and this time he revealed under hypnosis that he had been living through the situation which provoked the actual outbreak of the disease, i.e. the trial in court where he failed to obtain compensation for the injury.

The memories which come to the fore in hysterical attacks, or can be wakened during them, correspond also in all other respects with the exciting occurrences which we have found at the root of hysterical symptoms of long duration. Like these, they relate to psychic traumas which have remained unresolved by abreaction or by associative mental operations; and like these, they – or at least their essential constituents – are absent from the store of memories of which normal consciousness is made up; they belong to the ideational content of hypnoid states of consciousness with their narrow fields of association. Finally, they also admit of the therapeutic test. Our observations have often demonstrated that a memory of this kind which had hitherto provoked such attacks lost

274

this power as soon as it was brought during hypnosis to a reaction or to associative readjustment.

The motor phenomena of hysterical attacks are to be explained partly as a general mode of reaction to the affect which accompanies the memory, and may be compared, for example, with the beating movements of all the limbs which even an infant makes use of for the purpose; and partly as signifying direct emotional expressions of this memory; although they also elude this explanation to some extent as do the hysterical stigmata in chronic symptoms.

There is yet another aspect of the hysterical attack which reveals itself in the light of the theory we have just indicated: that in hysteria there are present ideational groups (arising in hypnoid states) which, cut off from associative relations with the remainder but associable *inter se,* establish a more or less highly organized nucleus of a second consciousness, *a condition seconde.* An hysterical symptom of long duration then corresponds to an intrusion of this *condition seconde* into the somatic innervations usually controlled by normal consciousness; an hysterical attack, however gives evidence of a higher oranisation of the *condition seconde* and, when of recent origin, signifies the moment at which this hypnoid consciousness takes possession of the subjects whole personality (i.e. an acute hysteria); but recurring attacks which contain a memory signify a recurrence of this moment. Charcot has already suggested that the hysterical attack is probably the nucleus of a *condition seconde.* During the attack, control of the entire somatic innervation has passed to the hypnoid consciousness. Experience shows that in these cases normal consciousness is not always completely superseded; it may even perceive the motor phenomena of the attack while the psychic processes of the latter escape its notice.

The typical course of a severe hysteria is, as is well known, that first an ideational content is formed in hypnoid states, which then, when sufficiently developed, takes possession during a period of 'acute hysteria' of the somatic innervation and personality of the patient, creates chronic symptoms and attacks, and then recedes until mere vestiges of it are left. If therefore the normal personality can regain control, what remains of the hypnoid ideational contents then returns in hysterical attacks and again temporarily produces in the patient similar states, which are again susceptible themselves and predisposing to the influence of traumas. A sort of equilibrium between the psychical groups united in the same personality is then frequently established; attacks and normal life exist side by side without affecting one another. The attacks then arise spontaneously, as memories commonly do, but they may also be provoked, just as any memory may be aroused according to the laws of association. Provocation of an attack occurs either by stimulation of an hysterogenic zone or by a new experience resembling the pathogenic experience. We hope to be able to show that no essential difference exists between the two conditions, apparently so distinct; that in both cases a hyperaesthetic memory has been stirred. In other cases this equilibrium is very unstable, the attack appears as an expression of the vestiges of hypnoid consciousness when ever the normal personality is exhausted and powerless. It is not impossible that in such cases the attack may be divested of its original significance and may return as a motor reaction without content.

It remains a task for further enquiry to discover what are the conditions determining whether in any given patient an hysteria will take the form of attacks, or chronic symptoms, or a combination of both.

V

It is now clear how the method of psychotherapy which we have just described leads to recovery. By providing an opportunity for the pent-up affect to discharge itself in words the therapy deprives of its effective power the idea which was not originally abreacted; by conducting it into normal consciousness (in light hypnosis) it brings it into associative readjustment or else dispels it by means of the physicians' suggestion, as happens in cases of somnambulism combined with amnesia.

We regard the therapeutic effect achieved by employing this procedure as important. We naturally cannot cure that element in hysteria which is dispositional; we can do nothing against the return of hypnoid states. Even during the productive state of an acute hysteria our procedure cannot prevent the phenomena which have just been removed with such difficulty being forthwith replaced by new ones. But when the acute stage has passed off and its vestiges remain in the form of chronic hysterical symptoms and attacks our method will frequently remove them in turn, and the results are permanent because radical. It therefore appears to us that in this respect it far surpasses the effect of removal by direct suggestion which is now practised by psychotherapeutists.

Although, by thus disclosing the psychical mechanism of hysterical phenomena, we have now made a further step along the path which Charcot first opened up so successfully with his explanations and experimental imitations of hystero-traumatic paralyses, we nevertheless do not conceal from ourselves that it is only the mechanism of the hysterical symptom that has been brought within our grasp and not the inner causes of hysteria. We have but touched upon the aetiology of hysteria and have really only been able to throw light on the causes of its acquired forms – the significance of the accidental factor for this neurosis.

Appendix 16

Winnicott: background information

Appendix 16 – Winnicott Background Information

Winnicott was born in Plymouth, Devon to Sir John Frederick Winnicott, a merchant who was knighted in 1924 after serving twice as mayor of Plymouth, and his wife, Elizabeth Martha (Woods) Winnicott.

The family was prosperous and ostensibly happy, but behind the veneer, Winnicott saw himself as oppressed by his mother, who tended toward depression, as well as by his two sisters and his nanny. His father's influence was that of an enterprising freethinker who encouraged his son's creativity. Winnicott described himself as a disturbed adolescent, reacting against his own self-restraining "goodness" acquired from trying to assuage the dark moods of his mother. These seeds of self-awareness became the basis of his interest in working with troubled young people.

He first thought of studying medicine while at The Leys School, a boarding school in Cambridge, when he fractured his clavicle and recorded in his diary that he wished he could treat himself. He began pre-med studies at Jesus College, Cambridge in 1914 but, with the onset of World War I, his studies were interrupted when he was made a medical trainee at the temporary hospital in Cambridge. In 1917, he joined the Royal Navy as a medical officer on HMS Lucifer.

Later that year, he began medical studies at St Bartholomew's Hospital Medical College in London. During this time, he learned from his mentor the art of listening carefully when taking medical histories from patients, a skill that he would later identify as foundational to his practice as a psychoanalyst.

He completed his medical studies in 1920, and in 1923, the same year as his first marriage (to Alice Taylor), he obtained a post as physician at the Paddington Green Children's Hospital in London, where he was to work as a paediatrician and child psychoanalyst for 40 years.

Winnicott rose to prominence just as the followers of Anna Freud were battling those of Melanie Klein for the right to be called Sigmund Freud's true intellectual heirs. Out of the Controversial discussions during World War Two, a compromise was established with three more-or-less amicable groups of the psychoanalytic movement: the Freudians, the Kleinians, and the "Middle Group" of the British Psychoanalytical Society (later called the "Independent Group"), to which Winnicott belonged, along with Ronald Fairbairn, Michael Balint, Masud Khan, John Bowlby, and Margaret Little.

Winnicott's career involved many of the great figures in psychoanalysis and psychology, not just Klein and Anna Freud, but also Bloomsbury figures such as James Strachey, R. D. Laing, and Masud Khan, a wealthy Pakistani émigré who was a highly controversial psychoanalyst.

During the Second World War, Winnicott served as consultant psychiatrist to the evacuee programme.

He divorced his first wife in 1951 and, in the same year, married Elsie Clare Nimmo Britton, a psychiatric social worker and psychoanalyst.

Winnicott's treatment of psychically disturbed children and their mothers gave him the experience on which he built his most influential concepts, such as the "holding environment" so crucial to psychotherapy, and the "transitional object," known to every parent as the "security blanket." He had a major impact on object relations theory, particularly in his 1951 essay "Transitional Objects and Transitional Phenomena," which focused on familiar, inanimate objects that children use to stave off anxiety during times of stress.

His theoretical writings emphasized empathy, imagination, and, in the words of philosopher Martha Nussbaum, who has been a proponent of his work, "the highly particular transactions that constitute love between two imperfect people." A prime example of this is his ideal of the "good-enough mother," the imperfectly attentive mother who does a better job than the "perfect" one who risks stifling her child's development as a separate being.

Winnicott died in 1971 following the last of a series of heart attacks and was cremated in London.

Appendix 17

Notes from a Mnemodynamic Practitioner

Appendix 17 – Notes from a Mnemodynamic Practitioner

It's been several years since I taught graduate students towards The United Kingdom Council for Psychotherapy (UKCP) registration. One of my phrases from the first couple of training days was "The single most important thing you bring to a psychotherapeutic session is yourself!"

It is very interesting to me that Richard Croston has taken Mnemodynamic therapy and made it his own. See what you think …

Mnemodynamic Therapy: Richard Croston

Mnemodynamic therapy is a technique for reducing the emotional response attached to a particular event. In the most extreme cases there may have been a specific trauma experienced by the client and they have flashbacks to that time and experience inappropriate emotional responses in other situations to stimuli which may appear not to be connected to the original trauma.

Like a number of other techniques including EMDR and the Fast Phobia Cure (rewind technique) it attempts to desensitise the client. These techniques can all be approached in a "cookbook-type" of approach in which the therapist learning the technique it told the exact words to say and then they are expected to follow the manual to the letter. For Mnemodynamic therapy this is a good idea to start with until you are fluent with the words and the process before putting more of yourself into the technique as an alternative.

My alternative approach is to try to tease out the principles of the approach and the way in which it changes the experiences for the client. This latter approach depends more on the sophistication of the therapist and their ability to hold a situation which has high emotional content and which can produce major emotional responses from the client. Some teaching tends to suggest that the benefits will not occur unless the technique is followed to the letter but my experiences of these techniques is that just is not the case. Some parts of the technique can be missed out and still a positive response is achieved. In order to use a belt and braces approach I tend to adopt the following procedure. Like Samuel Pepys you can use the techniques three times in a session. He said that the benefit of the diary was that "You can experience an event three times, once when it happens in the flesh, once when you write it down and recall it, and once when you read it back".

1. I usually explain a complex procedure to a client before I do it and make the suggestion that it will be valuable and help them to get over a trauma and let some of the emotions go.

2. I carry out the procedure.

3. I get the client to reflect on the way they have experienced the procedure.

I explain that a normal process would be that desensitisation of a traumatic event occurs as we talk to people about it. Each time we repeat the sequence of the event we experience slightly less emotional response. This happens naturally and has the effect of turning the event into history which is non-emotional and we end up talking about it as if it had happened to someone else. In situations of extreme trauma this process does not work and each time the event is recalled it makes the event more real and the emotions stronger. It is a bit like a scratched record. The thoughts and feelings are repeated and at each repetition the groove gets deeper and harder to shift.

What follows is the gist of a session that I had with a client Peter aged 51. He had worked in the same organisation for the last 20 years and reached a senior position. He had experienced a major trauma when he had been asked to attend a disciplinary meeting with his boss and the head of HR. His union representative was unable to attend because they were ill. He was not told the exact nature of the meeting before he got to the room. He was told immediately that the outcome of the meeting was a forgone conclusion. He was told that he had to sign a record of the meeting admitting an inappropriate relationship with a work-colleague. If he did not sign the record he would not be able to return to his job. He was told that the report would stay on his file for the next 18 months so that if there were any further problems it would be used as evidence against him. This would mean that he would not be able to apply for another job as he would not get a good reference. (I have changed the name, age of the client and disguised the context.)

Pre the altered state session, I suggest to the client:-

"This is a <u>powerful technique</u> which helps the natural process of turning an experience into history which is unemotional. (It is important to talk about the trauma situation so that the client is able to move on. Although there is a natural resistance this has to be overcome.)

"You can remember these difficult experiences because you are in a place here where you can feel safe and secure with me."

"I want you to tell me about the sequence of the event from the time before it occurred to the time after the event when you were calm and safe again away from the situation. I will write down a sequence of the key parts of the event."

"You don't need to be in a trance type state to carry out this technique and in many ways it is best just to close your eyes. Can you close your eyes now?"

"I want you to give me words that describe the feelings that you had at the key point of the experience. I will write them all down. Tell me when you have given me all the feelings. Remember that you are safe and secure here with me and that you have survived the experience."

The words for the feelings given by this client were:

Bullied
Harassed
Abused
Politicised
Humiliated
Angry
Cold, no warmth
Detached

Note: The problem for me was that I did not think that all the words used were exactly feelings. This did not matter because the words were the best words that the client could find to describe his experience. By using these words I automatically would link into the mindset of the client.

I suggested that he could take each feeling and get rid of it bit by bit.

Bullied - Imagine this as a pie. Cut it into slices and picture yourself throwing away each slice. *When you feel that you have let all this feeling go let me know.*

Harassed - Imagine this feeling written on a piece of paper. Screw it up and throw it away in a waste paper basket and perhaps you can set fire to it. *When you feel that you have let all this feeling go let me know.*

Abused - Take this feeling and see it written on a piece of paper and imagine it being put through a shredder and then throw it away. When you feel that you have let all this feeling go let me know.

Politicised - Imagine that this word is written on a piece of paper. Picture yourself digging a hole and bury it. You know that the paper will rot with time. *When you feel that you have let all this feeling go let me know.*

Humiliated - Picture a cake that represents this feeling of humiliation. Take the cake and break it up into tiny pieces. Scatter the cake for the birds and watch them eat up all the tiny bits and watch them fly away. *When you feel that you have let all this feeling go let me know.*

Angry - Picture it written on paper and drop it into a waste paper bit. *When you feel that you have let all this feeling go let me know.*

Cold, no warmth / Detached - Take these feelings and remember them in the room that you were in. Picture yourself leaving the room and being met by your family and good friends. Let them tell you that they really value you. They can give you a hug each and they tell you that none of the things you have experienced were your fault. They remind you that you have survived this difficult experience just as you have had other difficult experienced and survived them. Hear them saying that they will be there for you in the future and will help you in any way they can. *When you feel that you have let all this feeling go let me know.*

During our training Fran Renwick demonstrated the technique.

Early childhood experience

I re-experienced a trauma that I had when aged about 3 years. An aunt who had looked after me and lived with the family decided it was time to leave the family and live in her own house. The loss was very strong. At the time there was no obvious explanation and there was no opportunity to discuss the loss.

Recent trauma

Appendix 17 – Notes from a Mnemodynamic Practitioner

Another student looked at a situation in which he had nearly drowned only a couple of years earlier.

Both of us experienced a really significant emotional response to the recollection. It was very easy to picture the situations vividly simply by being asked to close our eyes and go back to a significant problem event that we wanted to resolve in a different way. The way in which we let the emotions go was different but the effect seemed to work in just the same way. It would be possible to get clients to go back to a problem time without actually telling the therapist exactly what the situation was. You need to define a sequence in the client's mind and establish survival before doing the work on the emotions.

A reflection on whether the particular event chosen is important

A useful reflection is that perhaps the event chosen is not critical to the process. If we experience some critical event we immediately use our past experiences and past emotional labels to reference it. We have a list of emotions that we know well and we look to see how the event has triggered these emotions. The diagram below shows how this seems to work. By letting go of the emotions recalled at any key event we are naturally letting go of that well of emotion that we carry around with us.

Event 1		Event 2		Event 3		Event 4	
Facts Listed	Referenced Emotions	Facts Listed	Referenced Emotions	Facts Listed	Referenced Emotions	Facts Listed	Referenced Emotions
a	fear	f	fear	k	fear	p	fear
b	alone	g	alone	l	alone	q	alone
c	angry	h	angry	m	angry	r	angry
d	vulnerable	i	vulnerable	n	vulnerable	s	vulnerable
e	sad	j	sad	o	sad	t	sad

By **Richard Croston** MSc., PGDHP,
Mnemodynamic Practitioner, **UKCP registered HypnoPsychotherapist**

Appendix 18

THE OUTLINE 'SCRIPT' FOR MNEMODYNAMIC THERAPY

Mnemodynamic Therapy – a model by Sue Washington

1. Find out some POSITIVE details in the life of your client if you don't already know them - family, career, personal strengths, achievements and so on.

   Begin the process:- The UN-BRACKETED, UN BOLDED words from now are your 'script'. Stick as near as you can to these words for the first 100 clients then let it go and put yourself in!

2. **5 Minute Contract and connection with the past:-** SO often when we have a problem like this, it is there because of something that happened to us in the past. We have a way of finding that out pretty quickly. Would you be prepared to go along with me just for five minutes, so that you see how I work, and we can see if what you're feeling in the here and now is to do with past things? **Get agreement.**

3. **Consent and distancing:-** If I were to ask you to close your eyes & picture a TV screen out here with a picture of you on it, could you do that? (To ascertain this is your only prerequisite. If 'yes' then). Close your eyes to shut me out, and put a picture of you, (..............) out here on a TV screen, and say 'yes' when you've done that. (Yes) Thank you. **If the answer is 'NO' then use another technique!**

4. **Finding the event or period of life:-** Imagine there's a videotape machine/DVD player by the TV and a remote control in your hand. Re-wind the cassette recorder/DVD. Take the picture back & back & back & back & back. I want you to look for a time when a younger than you (..................) was in some situation or other of difficulty and when you've found the picture, stop the machine and say 'yes' to let me know you've done that. (Yes) Thank you.

5. **Age of event of difficulty**. How old is (................) out here on the screen?

6. **Describe scenario**. What is happening for her/him here? (He/she will normally describe the scene – not to do so is exceptional. If she can't then work content free).

7. **Reflective listening to list the feelings:-** What is she feeling? (Prompt in a reflective-listening way by putting yourself mentally in the scenario and think how you would feel. Be brief and to the point, but explore corners. You will improve with practice. List the feelings on

your sheet.   Build on the reported feelings to find strength of the feeling; client says "angry". Furious? Enraged? Murderous?)

8. **Anchoring:-** (Anchor 'now' resources)....

    Acknowledge that this was a difficult time/situation but (s)he DID survive or you wouldn't be here now! And tell me when you've done that .... (Yes). Thank you. (After this point in the script, what we have just done is called 'acknowledge' and is shown as 'ack'.)

    (You could include problem ownership here)
    (You could include sending back the adult cognition here). I guess if she knew back there about (the positive things you ascertained earlier) she'd feel better about where she's at. Is that so? (Wait for a reply which sense says is going to be affirmative because of how you have asked the question). Let her know this (fact / these things/ about the life she now has). I know you'll find a way.

9. **Re-feeling:- Do this with the words the client gives you and in the order they give.** He/she's younger / little / smaller, over there, and you're big / grown-up here, and besides which, I'm supporting you. Help him/her by lifting / taking that (............) and feel it for her, here, where you're safe with me, and let me know when you've done that. (ack.). (Repeat for each feeling. In the unlikely event the client "can't," leave, and return at the end. If there is still difficulty, cut into sections as with an apple-pie. To have to do so will be exceptional).

10. **In the next column of reframes/actions** (First, here, always get your client to):

    (i)   **validate,** Validate younger (..........). tell her what (s)he's feeling is perfectly reasonable under the circumstances, perfectly valid. (Acknowledge)

    (ii)   **normalise,** Let her know that there's nothing odd about her, anyone else would feel that way under those circumstances too! (Acknowledge)

    (then do your best to)

    ASSOCIATE the client with his/her younger self from now.

PRIORITISE what you work with here. Let someone OUT from being trapped, and to treat them for SHOCK, before you start to be cognitive about problem ownership for example.

(iii)Take (…name) by the hand and bring him to now. Let me know when you have him/her

(iv) There is often 'shock' in the list of feelings: Go to (… name..) in the picture and treat her for shock as you would anyone else. Give her a cup of hot sweet tea even if she is not very keen on it, and wrap her up in something **warm.** (ack)

(v) Your younger person may have had 'sadness', 'upset'. (THINK what YOU need when you are sad or upset) Listen to him / her – proper, good quality 'deep' listening, the best you've ever done, whilst you 'hold' the situation for him/her whilst he/she works it out for him/herself ….(ack)

(vi) reframe with their younger self –

a) (if there has been "confusion", "bewilderment" use cognition, for example). Use the words – "I can imagine you've spent a long time getting your head around this event ever since it happened. Help her by sending back that cognition you have now as a grown up, back to her in the picture. Tell me when you've done it. (ack)

b) (For "lonely" or "alone" or "unsupported" or "unloved" or "unlovable" or "rejected"). Go to her now as a (mum, aunt, granny) and acknowledge what she did for you, to help you be all you are now. Thank her for it and say to her "I know you feel (alone) but you're not. I'm from time future. You and I are one, and I will always be here. I love you and will never, ever leave you". Let her know that until she knows it through to the middle her bones. Tell me when you have done it.

c) **(You may choose to use problem ownership here. It IS OK for you, the therapist, to have an opinion, and to come down on the side of RIGHT).** That man should not have done this to her/him. He was a grown-up and she/he was a child and he should have known better.

d) (For issues to do with abuse, it is important to help the youngster with their feelings of responsibility by helping feedback **your** common sense and **their** grown-up cognition).

e) acknowledge, here, Say to her, "Thank you for going through all that for me, because without doing that for me I wouldn't be me now, and I'm really rather glad I am!" Tell me when you've done it. (Ack.)

11. **Re-Resourcing**:- I know that you have had a problem (with {whatever it is .. be specific}), but I can certainly see your (capabilities, strength etc.). Send back to that younger (........) a jolly good dose of that strength, togetherness, resourcefulness, that you have now, back to him / her - enough to help not only with THAT situation that (s)he is in, but with any other difficulty which might arise in the future, and tell me when you've done that.....

12 **Checking out**:- What sense do you get of her now?

13 (Depending on the answer, repair as necessary. If there are left over feelings, deal with them quickly by reflectively listening & doing 7 – 12 again. If then you get words like "happier" ask the client/patient what she needs to do to make "happier" into "happy". Do your best to get your client's younger part to a state with out an "ier" on the end. Leave with as much resolution as you can, then double check:). Is she equipped enough to continue in that situation? (If the answer is yes, then you have options. You can do 14/15 or 16).

14 Good. Press the video button once again, & take the picture back to the grown-up person you started with. Let the picture fade - Let the screen go - Open your eyes.

15 (If the answer at 14 is "no", Do 6 – 13 again, or if that approach to you as the operator seems inappropriate, then you have options. One I often use is to let the grown up take the child to a park, beach, playground...). Let her play and play until her heart is content and her body tired. Let her sit upon your knee and put her head on your chest and rest or sleep, perfectly safe. Here you have a choice. S/he can go back into the picture in the video if you'd like, or my preferred option, to have you keep him. What would you like to do?

16 **(Either)** Let her melt into you, totally, utterly completely safe, where you can watch over her (check that your client has the younger person

safely inside her... Toni Lee Isaac uses "make her very small and hold her in your heart").

(Or) Let her go back in to the picture (straight on to 18/19).
GOOD. I'm glad you have him safe. You may find yourself doing playful whacky things between now and when we meet again – having a lollipop, or jumping in a puddle. IF that happens, I want you to let it, and indulge that part of yourself.

17 And whatever it is on the video out here, fast forward to where you started with you, grown-up (............). Let the picture go, let the screen go and then

18 Open your eyes.

19 (Check out your client in the fully normal state. You will need to listen to your client for a while and continue validating, reframing and normalising).

Bibliography

Birley, P. (2005) Thesis **"A Hermeneutic Phenomenological review of the hypnosis literature - Psudo Memory and Hypermnesia"** unpublished doctoral thesis.

Binet (1982) "**Les Alterations de la Personalite**" in "**On the Psychical Mechanism of Hysterical Phenomena: Preliminary Communication**" from Sigmund Freud, 'Collected Papers', Vol 1., (1924), Hogarth Press, London (first published in the *Neurologisches Zentralblatt,* 1893, nos 1&2.

Blythe, P. (1971) **"Hypnotism its Power and Practice"** Arthur Barker Ltd., London.

Breuer, Dr.J, (1982) in "**On the Psychical Mechanism of Hysterical Phenomena: Preliminary Communication**" from Sigmund Freud, 'Collected Papers', Vol 1. (1924), Hogarth Press, London (first published in the *Neurologisches Zentralblatt,* 1893, nos 1&2. [Translated by John Rickmann]

Collins English Dictionary (1994) Harper Collins, Glasgow.

Corkhille-Briggs, D. (1975) **"Your Child's Self-Esteem"** Dolphin Books, Florida, USA.

Cutner Green, A. (2010) "**The Child Within – A Journey Towards Peace Of Mind**" from "**Moving Memories: Mnemodynamc Therapy**" unpublished manuscript.

Darnton, R., (1968). "**Mesmerism and the end of the Enightenment in France**" President and Fellows of Harvard College, USA.

Delboef (1889) "**Le Magnetisme Animal**" in "**On the Psychical Mechanism of Hysterical Phenomena: Preliminary Communication**" from Sigmund Freud, 'Collected Papers', Vol 1. (1924), Hogarth Press, London (first published in the *Neurologiches Zentralblatt,* 1893, nos 1&2.

Deutsch, F. (1939). "**The Choice of Organ in Organ Neuroses**" Int. J. Psycho-Anal., 20:252-262.

Du Maurier, G. (1894) **"Trilby"** Oxford World Classics (1998)

Ellis, A. (1962) **"Reason and Emotion in Psychotherapy"** Citadel, New York, USA.

Ellis, A. (2004) **"All Things Considered: CBT's Controversial Founder"** National Public Radio (NPR), 3rd June 2004 accessed 23:3:2010.

Freud S. and Breuer J. (1892) **"On the Psychical Mechanism of Hysterical Phenomena: Preliminary Communication"** from Sigmund Freud, 'Collected Papers', Vol 1. (1924), Hogarth Press, London (first published in the *Neurologisches Zentralblatt,* 1893, nos 1&2. [Translated by John Rickmann]

Freud S (1923) **"The ego and the id**" in J. Strachey (ed.)(1961) *Standard Edition, vol. 19,* (pp 1-66)

Freud, S. (1926) **"The Question of Lay Analysis**". In Freud, A. (1991 Ed.) "**The Essentials of Psycho-analysis**". Penguin Books: London.

Freud, S. (1933): **"New Introductory lectures on Psychoanalysis"** in J. Strachey (ed.) (1964) *Standard Edition, vol. 22,* (pp 73-4).

Freud, S. (1940); **"An outline of psycho-analysis"** in J. Strachey ed.)(1964) *Standard Edition, vol. 23,* (pp 145-6).

Ginott, Dr H. (1965) **"Between Parent and Child: The Bestselling Classic That Revolutionised Child-Parent Communication"** Three Rivers Press, New York, USA.

Hartland Dr J. (1966) **"Medical and Dental Hypnosis"** Bailliere Tindall.

Hay, L. L., (1988) **"You can heal your Life"** Hay House UK.

Janet, P. (1889) **"L'Automatisme Psychologique"** (Paris) in "**On the Psychical Mechanism of Hysterical Phenomena: Preliminary Communication"** from Sigmund Freud, 'Collected Papers', Vol 1. (1924), Hogarth Press, London (first published in the *Neurologisches Zentralblatt,* 1893, nos 1&2.

Kaplan, R.E.(1975), **"Maintaining interpersonal relationships: A bipolar Theory"** Interpersonal Development 6, 106-119.

Lankton, S. (1980) **"Practical Magic"**

Bibliography

Lewis, Byron A., (1982) **"Magic Demystified"** Metamorphous Press, Oregon, USA.

Piaget, J, Inhelder, B, (1972) **"The psychology of the Child"**. Persus (Basic Books) New York.

Pierce, Dr I. (1986) Lecture in Runnings Park, Gloucestershire.

Rodman, F. R., (2003). **"Winnicott: Life and work"**. Perseus.

Roazen, P., (2001) **"The Historiography of Psychoanalysis"** Transaction.

Roth, I. (ed)(1990) **"Introduction to Psychology"** Open University, Milton Keynes, UK

Shapiro, Edward R. (March 1998). **"Images in Psychiatry: Donald W. Winnicott, 1896–1971".** *American Journal of Psychiatry* **(American Psychiatric Association) 155** (3): 421. http://ajp.psychiatryonline.org/cgi/content/full/155/3/421. Retrieved 19.3.2010.

Sokolov, I, & Pearson, J., (1989) **"Parent-Link"** The Parent Network, London

Thomas, K. **"Psychodynamics: The Freudian Approach"** in Roth, I. (ed)(1990) **"Introduction to Psychology"** Open University, Milton Keynes, UK

Tolstoy, L, N. (1886) **"What then must we Do?"** (tr. Maude, A) The World's Classics, reprint.

Washington S. Hypnotherapy from **"Medical Marriage"** (1997) ed. Featherstone Dr. C., and Forsyth, L., Findhorn Press, Findhorn, Scotland.

Washington, S. (2008) **"Peace of Mind: Pathways to Successful Living"** Mnemodynamics Unlimited

Washington S. (2011) **"Moving Memories: Mnemodynamc Therapy"** unpublished manuscript

Waxman D. (1981) **"Hartland's Medical and Dental Hypnosis"** Bailliere

Tindall.

Winnicott, Sir J. F., **"Encyclopaedia of Plymouth History"**, accessed through www.wickipedia.co.uk , April 29, 2010.

Zafón, C. R., (2004) **"The Shadow of the Wind"** Weidenfeld & Nicholson (Phoenix)

Index

accepting behaviour 121,124
accepting feelings 90-91
acknowledgement viii, 40
aggressively 198
alone 37
altered state 23, 45
anchoring 25, 26
anger 15
auditory 42-3
asking questions 149
assertive 201,245
association 10, 33
assumptions xxxii
assumptions of the model 19
attitudes xxx
authoritarian 242

Behaviourist 19
behaving aggressively 198
behaving assertively 201
behaving submissively 196
behaviour and needs 123
being there 133, 189
belongingness needs 74, 123
bewilderment 37
Blythe P J H. 3, 16, 26
bottoming 47, 50
Breuer Dr.J 265
Broadbent Prof. D. 8
bullying 29

CBT 12
cases 83-86
Centre Training School 46
cesspits 11
challenging 223-234
checking out 41, 46
child abuse 27
child as a guide 140
child within 100
client disclosure 61-2
client perception 51
closer to people 207
closing down 45
Cognitive therapy 12
Cognitive connection 29
Cohen Dr L. 8
communication 139
communication barriers 178
confusion 36-37

conscious 10
consciousness 11
consent 22
constant striabmus 56-58
content free 61
copyright iv
Corkhille-Briggs D. 94
creative 32
cultural 50-51
cup 2

denial 14
defences 118
defining ourselves 193
definition xxx
diagrammatic representation 81-86
different people 107
different experiences 107
difficult 47
dirty 35
disclosure 61-62
dissociation 32, 33
distance 22
distancing 22
Dracula 16
drained 38
drive 10
Du Maurier G. 16
"Dynamic Model" diagram 7

easy on yourself 154
Egan G. 169
ego 11
Ellis Dr A. 12
encouragement 114
endorsements x-xvi
emotional flooding 151
esteem needs 74, 123

fear of failure 153
feelings 61, 87-103
feeling good 89
file 15
five-minute contract 22
finished 45
firm 239-249

Index

flooding/flooded 32
Full Cup theory 4, 70
frozen in time 1
Freud S. 9, 11, 12,13, 18, 25
Freud and conflict 18
Freud (the mind according to) 9

Gandhi 217
gentle 239-249
Gestalt therapy 182
Ginott H. 190
giving feedback 171
good enough 67-71
Grahame G. 29
Groddek Dr. G. 17
Groves D. 1
guilty 39

headache 3, 4
helper 131
Holistic Medicine 20
honesty 215
how problems arise 4
Humanistic 16
Hypnos 16
hypnotic effect of language 234
hypnotic time distortion 62-4
hysterical 263

I-message 225, 232
I can't 31
Id 10
ingredients for helping 135
insecure 39
intention 28,38
intimidation 29
introduction to listening 143
irritable bowel 3, 58-9
insecurity 39
instability 30
Isaac T-L.

Janie 255

kinaethetic 42-3

labels 103-118
labels and expressing feelings 93
Laing R.D. 234
language 22
Lankton S. 43
leading 25
learning from experience 152
learning from others 200
learning from successes 146
learning from mistakes 146
learning stair 72
libido 59-60
licensing agreement viii
lifting off 83
listening 21, 36, 133, 143-189
locked off 2
lonely 37
loss 59-60

manipulated 39
manipulation of emotions 91
Maslow 123, 119-130
mental instability 30
'Mind' according to Freud 9
mind domination 17
model of the mind 1
Mnemodynamic: attitudes behind xxx
Mnemodynamic therapy (name) xxxi
Mnemosyne 253
Mr. Nice Guy Bob 140
multiple incidents 47
mummy 5
Muses 251

narrative 61-2
needs behind behaviour 72-75, 121
needs and wants 191, 202
NLP 19
no 248
normalising 28, 33
Nussbaum M.
nurturing guide 70

old head 30
open ended questions 145
opening 57

Index

openness 215
options in closing 45
organ of choice 17

pain 5
parts of the mind 10
percentage 49, 57
perception 51
perfect 64
Perls Fritz 182-3
permissive 244
Persian carpet 2
physical symptoms 54-5
physiological needs 74, 123
Powel J. 162
problem ownership 35, 75-9,120,129
positive details 21
Powell J 162
praise v encouragement 114
preconscious 10
predicate words 42
preface xxvii
psyche 10

Quigley Dr H.
Quigley J. 48

REBT 12
re-feeling 30
reflecting emotions 168
reflectively listen 24, 159,161
rejected 37
Renwick Dr F.
representational systems 41
repressing 166
responsible 39
re-resourcing 40
Rich A 217
Roth I. 9
Russel B. 169

sad 36
sadness 15
safety needs 74, 123
say what you want 106
saying what you feel 212

saying what you think 211
saying what you would like 214
scenario 24
self- actualisation needs 13
self disclosure 210
self esteem 94
self esteem development 95, 108
session (the first) 21
sessions (therapeutic) 21
setting the scene 22
Shakespeare W. 12
Sgt. Pepper 62
sharing feelings 205-218
shock 37
silence not enough 145
Sirhan S. 17
smoking 53-4
space 22
specific conditions 53–60
statum nascendi 48
Steiner Claude M. 219
stock responses 178
stuck 148
striabmus 56
superego 12
submissively 196
Svengali 16
symptom 3

take away positive 32
Theoretical underpinning XXXII
Therapeutic methods XXXII
Therapeutic sessions 21
Thomas K. 9
Tolstoy L. 129
top-dog 183
trapped 34
Trilby 16
trusting 148
truth 215-218
turned eye 56-58
Twain M. 217

unacceptable behaviour 121,124
unhelpful responses 178
unlovable 37

Index

unloved 37
under-dog 183
unspecified 43
unsupported 37
upset 36,159

validation 33
valuing our own needs 194
variations 61-65
Victorian 6
visual 42-3
visualise (can't) 64-5

we are not our behaviour 121
Webster 48
welcome IX
why this symptom? 3
whose problem 119-129
Winnicott D 67, 279

Yevutshenko 218
younger shoulders 30

Lightning Source UK Ltd.
Milton Keynes UK
05 June 2010

155098UK00001B/5/P